Betty Crocker

the big book of breakfast & brunch

Houghton Mifflin Harcourt

Boston • New York • 2014

GENERAL MILLS

Food Content and Relationship Marketing
Director: Geoff Johnson

Food Content Marketing Manager:
Heather Reid Liebo

Senior Editor: Grace Wells

Kitchen Manager: Ann Stuart

Recipe Development and Testing: Betty
Crocker Kitchens

Photography: General Mills Photography
Studios and Image Library

HOUGHTON MIFFLIN HARCOURT

Publisher: Natalie Chapman

Editorial Director: Cindy Kitchel

Executive Editor: Anne Ficklen

Editorial Assistant: Molly Aronica

Managing Editor: Marina Padakis Lowry

Production Editor: Jacqueline Beach

Art Director and Book Design: Tai Blanche

Composition: David Futato

Production Coordinator: Kimberly Kiefer

For information about permission to reproduce selections from this book, write to
Permissions, Houghton Mifflin Harcourt Publishing Company, 215 Park Avenue South,
New York, New York 10003.

www.hmhco.com

Library of Congress Cataloging-in-Publication Data:
Crocker, Betty.
 Betty Crocker : the big book of breakfast and brunch.
   pages cm
 Includes index.
 ISBN 978-0-544-24770-3 (paperback); 978-0-544-24772-7 (ebk)
1. Breakfasts. 2. Brunches. I. Title. II. Title: Big book of breakfast and brunch.
 TX733.C762 2014
 641.5'2—dc23

2013036040

Manufactured in the United States of America

DOC 10 9 8 7 6 5 4 3 2 1

Cover photo: Top (left to right): Apricot-Stuffed French Toast; Green Goodness
Smoothie; Breakfast Tacos; Dulce de Leche Cheerios® Parfaits

Bottom (left to right): Strawberry Cheesecake Pancakes; Tropical Fruit 'n Ginger
Oatmeal

The Betty Crocker Kitchens seal guarantees
success in your kitchen. Every recipe has been
tested in America's Most Trusted Kitchens™
to meet our high standards of reliability, easy
preparation and great taste.

FIND MORE GREAT IDEAS AT
BettyCrocker.com

Dear Friends,

Morning—it's the best part of the day and whether you are planning a quick breakfast or a leisurely brunch, you'll discover what you need in this comprehensive book filled with great ideas. A morning meal provides energy and helps to keep you going throughout the day so plan to wake sleepyheads with the enticing promise of a hearty, wholesome breakfast every day.

We designed *The Big Book of Breakfast & Brunch* to include a true variety of morning foods. Look for quick blender ideas like Tropical Power Smoothies and Fiber One® Strawberry Smoothies—these recipes are just perfect for hurried mornings and can be ready in a jiffy! And for those days when you have a little extra time, we think you will enjoy cooking up the Breakfast Egg Scramble with Brie or even Banana Buckwheat Pancakes. Plus, for cereal lovers, there are many new ideas and even an Easy Cereal Toppers feature.

This book also has great brunch ideas for those days when you have guests or just some extra time to spend enjoying the morning. Serve the Cheesy Sausage and Egg Bake paired with Triple Berry Coffee Cake or Citrus Mango Muffins and you'll receive rave reviews. Be sure to check out the special feature on Brewing the Best Coffee and Tea—a brunch or breakfast is just not complete without one or the other!

So get ready to rise and shine any morning with this fabulous book of delicious breakfast and brunch ideas—eat hearty!

Sincerely,

Betty Crocker

contents

start happy any day!

Make morning awesome with great food to set the stage right for the rest of the day. Breakfast is about more than nutrition—it's a happy thing that you can do for yourself and those in your home. So bite by bite, make breakfast the best meal of the day.

While ready-to-go options like cereal, oatmeal and yogurt are wholesome timesavers, it never hurts to branch out. With the ideas and recipes in this book, you might not even need to set the alarm very much earlier. Who has time for breakfast? You do—so make the morning meal a priority from now on and just enjoy.

Start-Happy Breakfast Tips

Don't let the morning rush keep you from eating a wholesome, delicious breakfast. Here are some hints on how to make the day start out right.

Make a list before you grocery shop. Half of the breakfast battle is remembering to stock your kitchen with quick and easy breakfast options and ingredients for recipes that you like.

Take a few minutes to gain a few minutes. Everyone tends to be short on time in the morning, so take a few minutes to pull together breakfast the night before. Think about what you would like to eat and leave it handy on the counter or ready to go in the refrigerator.

Drink your breakfast—and not just coffee! Try one of the delicious smoothies—there are many yummy options, like Raspberry-Oatmeal Smoothies, page 16. It's just one of many great choices, whether you're eating in or running out the door.

Bake ahead for delicious options. Make a batch of muffins or a quick bread loaf and wrap individual portions to grab when you're in a hurry. Oatmeal–Whole Wheat–Blueberry Muffins, page 298, and Easy Walnut Bread, page 304, are both good choices.

Think convenience or finger foods. A bowl of cereal is a great healthful option any morning, but when you're really rushed, granola bars or yogurt fit the occasion. Better yet, try dressed-up granola bars, like Blueberry-Ricotta Granola Bars, page 67, or Strawberry-Chocolate Granola bars, page 62.

Let the sun shine in on your morning! When you sit down for breakfast, open the curtains and enjoy some sunlight. It will make you feel alert and will brighten the morning. Add some relaxing music while you eat, and you're on the way to a beautiful day!

Start Happy on a Leisurely Morning

When the week is over and everyone's in less of a rush, brunch offers a welcome change of pace. Family and friends can get together early in the day — but not too early! — to relax, have a great meal, and then continue the day with some nice memories of the visit. Brunch fare is often hearty but easy to make ahead of time, and it's easy to serve either in a casual buffet style or in a more formal setting.

Plan ahead for a variety of foods that include one or two main dishes, fresh fruit and/or vegetable salads and a choice of sweet and/or savory breads. You can keep the beverages simple with coffee, tea and juices. Or for fun, why not serve some festive mimosas for a change?

Start-Happy Brunch Tips

Hosting a brunch can be easy and fun if you just do a bit of planning. Here are some tips that might give you a head start on making the occasion leisurely for both you and your guests.

Write your menu down so that you can check items off as you get things ready.

Choose foods that can be served at room temperature whenever possible. The main dish for a brunch is often the only food that truly needs to be served warm.

Wash and cut all produce ahead of time, except fruits that will discolor (like apples, bananas and pears). Store in separate bags or containers. This can be done the day before the event.

Cook any sausage or other ingredients that must be precooked for inclusion in a brunch casserole. Store in separate containers.

For large amounts, uncooked egg mixtures can be mixed up, covered and refrigerated. Whisk or stir before using.

Make juices or bases for beverage mixtures; cover and refrigerate. Don't stir in last-minute additions, such as carbonated beverages or alcohol, until ready to serve.

Prepare the coffeemaker so that it's ready to start in the morning.

Set the table with your centerpiece, and gather serving dishes and utensils.

CHAPTER 1

grab-and-go
smoothies
&
more

blueberry-grape smoothie poppers

prep time: 15 Minutes ✳ **start to finish:** 4 Hours 15 Minutes ✳ 24 Servings

2 envelopes unflavored gelatin

½ cup cold Concord grape juice

½ cup fresh blueberries

2 containers (6 oz each) French vanilla low-fat yogurt

¾ cup Concord grape juice, heated to boiling

1 Lightly spray 9x5-inch loaf pan with cooking spray, then blot with paper towel; set aside.

2 In large bowl, sprinkle gelatin on ½ cup cold grape juice to soften; let stand 1 minute. Meanwhile, in blender, place blueberries and yogurt. Cover; blend on high speed until smooth.

3 Add hot grape juice to gelatin mixture; stir about 2 minutes or until gelatin is dissolved. Stir in yogurt mixture. Pour into loaf pan. Cover; refrigerate until firm, about 4 hours.

4 Cut into cubes and serve, or cover and refrigerate up to 2 days before serving.

1 Serving: Calories 25; Total Fat 0g (Saturated Fat 0g, Trans Fat 0g); Cholesterol 0mg; Sodium 10mg; Total Carbohydrate 5g (Dietary Fiber 0g); Protein 1g **% Daily Value:** Vitamin A 0%; Vitamin C 0%; Calcium 0%; Iron 0% **Exchanges:** ½ Starch **Carbohydrate Choices:** ½

Start Happy Tips

Make these colorful smoothie poppers up to 2 days ahead, and surprise the little ones with a fun breakfast.

Blueberries are a low-fat food and a good source of fiber and vitamin C.

Blueberry-Grape Smoothie Poppers, Lime Green Smoothie Poppers, Carrot-Mango Smoothie Poppers

lime green smoothie poppers

prep time: 15 Minutes ❋ **start to finish:** 4 Hours 15 Minutes ❋ 24 Servings

- 2 envelopes unflavored gelatin
- ½ cup cold apple juice
- ½ cup packed fresh baby spinach
- 2 containers (6 oz each) Key lime low-fat yogurt
- ¾ cup apple juice, heated to boiling

1 Lightly spray 9x5-inch loaf pan with cooking spray, then blot with paper towel; set aside.

2 In large bowl, sprinkle gelatin on ½ cup cold apple juice to soften; let stand 1 minute. Meanwhile, in blender, place spinach and yogurt. Cover; blend on high speed until smooth.

3 Add hot apple juice to gelatin mixture; stir about 2 minutes or until gelatin is dissolved. Stir in yogurt mixture. Pour into loaf pan. Cover; refrigerate until firm, about 4 hours.

4 Cut into cubes and serve, or cover and refrigerate up to 2 days before serving.

1 Serving: Calories 15; Total Fat 0g (Saturated Fat 0g, Trans Fat 0g); Cholesterol 0mg; Sodium 10mg; Total Carbohydrate 3g (Dietary Fiber 0g); Protein 1g **% Daily Value:** Vitamin A 2%; Vitamin C 0%; Calcium 0%; Iron 0% **Exchanges:** Free **Carbohydrate Choices:** 0

Start Happy Tips

Made with Key lime yogurt, apple juice and fresh spinach, these green smoothie poppers are a great way to start your day!

Use small cookie cutters to cut the poppers into fun shapes.

carrot-mango smoothie poppers

prep time: 15 Minutes ✳ **start to finish:** 4 Hours 15 Minutes ✳ 24 Servings

- 2 envelopes unflavored gelatin
- ¼ cup cold carrot juice
- ½ cup chopped mango
- 2 containers (6 oz each) French vanilla or mango low-fat yogurt
- ¾ cup apple juice, heated to boiling

1 Lightly spray 9x5-inch loaf pan with cooking spray, then blot with paper towel; set aside.

2 In large bowl, sprinkle gelatin on cold carrot juice to soften; let stand 1 minute. Meanwhile, in blender, place mango and yogurt. Cover; blend on high speed until smooth.

3 Add hot apple juice to gelatin mixture; stir about 2 minutes or until gelatin is dissolved. Stir in yogurt mixture. Pour into loaf pan. Cover; refrigerate until firm, about 4 hours.

4 Cut into cubes and serve, or cover and refrigerate up to 2 days before serving.

1 Serving: Calories 25; Total Fat 0g (Saturated Fat 0g, Trans Fat 0g); Cholesterol 0mg; Sodium 10mg; Total Carbohydrate 4g (Dietary Fiber 0g); Protein 1g **% Daily Value:** Vitamin A 10%; Vitamin C 2%; Calcium 0%; Iron 0% **Exchanges:** ½ Starch **Carbohydrate Choices:** 0

Start Happy Tips

Look for carrot juice in the refrigerated case of the produce section.

It's crazy how delicious these carrot and mango smoothie poppers taste! They're a fun, less-mess way to eat fruit-and-yogurt smoothies.

raspberry-oatmeal smoothies

prep time: 5 Minutes　✳　**start to finish:** 5 Minutes　✳　2 Servings

¼ cup old-fashioned oats

1 banana

1 cup frozen red raspberries

1 container (6 oz) French vanilla low-fat yogurt

½ cup cold water

¼ cup coconut milk (not cream of coconut)

¼ teaspoon vanilla

1 Place all ingredients in blender. Cover; blend on high speed until smooth.

2 Pour into 2 glasses. Serve immediately.

1 Serving: Calories 320; Total Fat 8g (Saturated Fat 6g, Trans Fat 0g); Cholesterol 5mg; Sodium 50mg; Total Carbohydrate 53g (Dietary Fiber 11g); Protein 6g **% Daily Value:** Vitamin A 10%; Vitamin C 60%; Calcium 15%; Iron 10% **Exchanges:** ½ Starch, 1 Fruit, 1½ Other Carbohydrate, ½ Skim Milk, 1½ Fat **Carbohydrate Choices:** 3½

Start Happy Tip

Try frozen mango or peaches in place of the raspberries.

raspberry-banana-yogurt smoothies

prep time: 5 Minutes ❋ **start to finish:** 5 Minutes ❋ 2 Servings (1½ cups each)

1 container (6 oz) French vanilla low-fat yogurt

1½ cups soymilk

1 cup unsweetened frozen or fresh raspberries

1 medium banana, sliced (1 cup)

1 Place all ingredients in blender. Cover; blend on high speed about 30 seconds or until smooth.

2 Pour into 2 glasses. Serve immediately.

1 Serving: Calories 290; Total Fat 4g (Saturated Fat 1g, Trans Fat 0g); Cholesterol 5mg; Sodium 160mg; Total Carbohydrate 54g (Dietary Fiber 10g); Protein 9g **% Daily Value:** Vitamin A 15%; Vitamin C 70%; Calcium 35%; Iron 8% **Exchanges:** 1 Fruit, 2 Other Carbohydrate, 1 Low-Fat Milk **Carbohydrate Choices:** 3½

Start Happy Tips

Pretty in pink! Garnish these creamy smoothies with a couple of raspberries on top.

If serving with straws, purchase large-diameter straws to accommodate the thicker texture of these smoothies.

tropical papaya smoothies

prep time: 10 Minutes ❋ **start to finish:** 10 Minutes ❋ 2 Servings (1½ cups each)

½ medium papaya, peeled, seeded and chopped (¾ cup)

½ cup frozen unsweetened whole strawberries

½ cup fat-free (skim) milk

½ cup plain fat-free yogurt

1 tablespoon honey

3 large ice cubes

Sliced papaya or sliced fresh strawberries, if desired

Fresh mint leaves or sprigs, if desired

1 In blender, place chopped papaya, frozen strawberries, milk, yogurt and honey. Cover; blend on high speed until smooth.

2 With blender running, add ice cubes, one at a time, blending until ice is crushed and mixture is smooth.

3 Pour into 2 glasses. Garnish with sliced papaya or fresh strawberries and mint. Serve immediately.

1 Serving: Calories 150; Total Fat 0g (Saturated Fat 0g, Trans Fat 0g); Cholesterol 0mg; Sodium 80mg; Total Carbohydrate 30g (Dietary Fiber 2g); Protein 6g **% Daily Value:** Vitamin A 20%; Vitamin C 120%; Calcium 20%; Iron 4% **Exchanges:** ½ Starch, 1 Fruit, ½ Skim Milk **Carbohydrate Choices:** 2

luscious lemon drop smoothies

prep time: 10 Minutes ❄ **start to finish:** 10 Minutes ❄ 2 Servings (1 cup each)

1 bag (12 oz) frozen broccoli cuts

1 medium banana, cut up

1 cup frozen peach slices

¾ cup pineapple-orange juice

½ cup lemon sherbet

1 Cook broccoli as directed on bag. Rinse with cold water until cooled. Drain.

2 In blender, place ¼ cup of the cooked broccoli and the remaining ingredients. (Cover and refrigerate remaining broccoli for another use.) Cover; blend on high speed about 30 seconds or until smooth.

3 Pour into 2 glasses. Serve immediately.

1 Serving: Calories 200; Total Fat 1g (Saturated Fat 0.5g, Trans Fat 0g); Cholesterol 0mg; Sodium 25mg; Total Carbohydrate 45g (Dietary Fiber 4g); Protein 2g **% Daily Value:** Vitamin A 20%; Vitamin C 260%; Calcium 4%; Iron 6% **Exchanges:** ½ Starch, 1 Fruit, 1½ Other Carbohydrate **Carbohydrate Choices:** 3

Start Happy Tips

For food safety reasons, frozen vegetables must be cooked.

If you can't find pineapple-orange juice, you can substitute pineapple juice.

tropical power smoothies

prep time: 10 Minutes   ❋   **start to finish:** 10 Minutes   ❋   2 Servings (1 cup each)

1 bag (12 oz) frozen broccoli cuts
½ cup frozen blueberries
½ ripe avocado, pitted, peeled
⅔ cup water
½ cup coconut milk (not cream of coconut)
2 teaspoons sugar

1 Cook broccoli as directed on bag. Rinse with cold water until cooled. Drain.

2 In blender, place ¼ cup of the cooked broccoli and the remaining ingredients. (Cover and refrigerate remaining broccoli for another use.) Cover; blend on high speed about 30 seconds or until smooth.

3 Pour into 2 glasses. Serve immediately.

1 Serving: Calories 240; Total Fat 17g (Saturated Fat 11g, Trans Fat 0g); Cholesterol 0mg; Sodium 15mg; Total Carbohydrate 19g (Dietary Fiber 5g); Protein 2g **% Daily Value:** Vitamin A 6%; Vitamin C 25%; Calcium 2%; Iron 6% **Exchanges:** ½ Starch, ½ Fruit, ½ Other Carbohydrate, 3½ Fat **Carbohydrate Choices:** 1

Start Happy Tips

For food safety reasons, frozen vegetables must be cooked.

You can use reduced-fat coconut milk, but the smoothies may be slightly less thick. Leftover coconut milk can be frozen in small quantities for future uses.

green goodness smoothies

prep time: 5 Minutes ❋ **start to finish:** 5 Minutes ❋ **4 Servings (1 cup each)**

1 cup pear nectar

2 cups loosely packed chopped fresh spinach

½ cup chopped seeded peeled cucumber

½ cup plain fat-free yogurt

2 tablespoons honey

2 cups ice cubes

1 Place all ingredients in blender. Cover; blend on high speed about 1 minute or until smooth.

2 Pour into 4 glasses. Serve immediately.

1 Serving: Calories 100; Total Fat 0.5g (Saturated Fat 0g, Trans Fat 0g); Cholesterol 0mg; Sodium 40mg; Total Carbohydrate 22g (Dietary Fiber 1g); Protein 2g **% Daily Value:** Vitamin A 30%; Vitamin C 25%; Calcium 8%; Iron 4% **Exchanges:** ½ Starch, 1 Other Carbohydrate, ½ Vegetable **Carbohydrate Choices:** 1½

Start Happy Tip

Get a nutritional boost of omega-3's and additional fiber by adding a tablespoon of flaxseed with the other ingredients. Be sure to blend long enough to grind up the flaxseed to reap the nutritional benefits.

super spinach smoothies

prep time: 5 Minutes ✳ **start to finish:** 5 Minutes ✳ 2 Servings (1 cup each)

1 cup fat-free (skim) milk

1 pouch (7.6 oz) frozen triple berry nourishing yogurt smoothie

½ cup torn fresh spinach

1 In blender, place milk, contents of smoothie pouch and spinach. Cover; blend on high speed 1 minute to 1 minute 30 seconds, stopping blender to scrape down sides as necessary, until smooth.

2 Pour into 2 glasses. Serve immediately.

1 Serving: Calories 120; Total Fat 1g (Saturated Fat 0g, Trans Fat 0g); Cholesterol 5mg; Sodium 75mg; Total Carbohydrate 20g (Dietary Fiber 2g); Protein 6g **% Daily Value:** Vitamin A 25%; Vitamin C 35%; Calcium 20%; Iron 4% **Exchanges:** ½ Fruit, ½ Other Carbohydrate, ½ Skim Milk **Carbohydrate Choices:** 1

Start Happy Tip
To make this recipe super easy, purchase spinach that is already washed.

triple-treat antioxidant smoothies

prep time: 10 Minutes ✳ **start to finish:** 10 Minutes ✳ 2 Servings (1 cup each)

1 bag (12 oz) frozen broccoli cuts

½ cup frozen strawberries

½ cup frozen red raspberries

½ cup pomegranate juice

⅓ cup vanilla low-fat yogurt

1 teaspoon sugar

1 Cook broccoli as directed on bag. Rinse with cold water until cooled. Drain.

2 In blender, place ¼ cup of the cooked broccoli and the remaining ingredients. (Cover and refrigerate remaining broccoli for another use.) Cover; blend on high speed about 30 seconds or until smooth.

3 Pour into 2 glasses. Serve immediately.

1 Serving: Calories 150; Total Fat 1g (Saturated Fat 0g, Trans Fat 0g); Cholesterol 0mg; Sodium 35mg; Total Carbohydrate 32g (Dietary Fiber 6g); Protein 3g **% Daily Value:** Vitamin A 10%; Vitamin C 80%; Calcium 15%; Iron 6% **Exchanges:** 1 Starch, 1 Fruit **Carbohydrate Choices:** 2

Start Happy Tips

For food safety reasons, frozen vegetables must be cooked.

Pomegranate juice can be found in single-serve bottles in delis or beverage machines, or in larger economy-size containers in the juice aisle of the grocery store.

cocoa–peanut butter–banana smoothies

prep time: 10 Minutes ❋ **start to finish:** 10 Minutes ❋ 4 Servings (1 cup each)

1½ cups creamy vanilla low-fat yogurt (from 2-lb container)

1 cup chocolate milk

¼ cup creamy peanut butter

2 small bananas, sliced

3 to 5 ice cubes

1 cup Cocoa Puffs® cereal, coarsely crushed*

1 In blender, place all ingredients except cereal. Cover; blend on high speed about 30 seconds or until smooth.

2 Pour into 4 glasses. Sprinkle with cereal. Serve immediately.

*To crush cereal, place in plastic bag or between sheets of waxed paper; crush with rolling pin.

1 Serving: Calories 310; Total Fat 11g (Saturated Fat 3g, Trans Fat 0g); Cholesterol 10mg; Sodium 190mg; Total Carbohydrate 44g (Dietary Fiber 3g); Protein 10g **% Daily Value:** Vitamin A 15%; Vitamin C 8%; Calcium 20%; Iron 8% **Exchanges:** 1 Fruit, 1 Other Carbohydrate, 1 Low-Fat Milk, 1½ Fat **Carbohydrate Choices:** 3

Start Happy Tip

Keep a stash of disposable cups with lids so you can have breakfast on the go or just head outside.

creamy mango smoothies

prep time: 10 Minutes   ❋   **start to finish:** 10 Minutes   ❋   6 Servings (1 cup each)

2 mangoes, seed removed, peeled and chopped (2 cups)

2 cups mango sorbet

2 containers (6 oz each) French vanilla low-fat yogurt

1½ cups fat-free (skim) milk or soymilk

1 Place all ingredients in blender. Cover; blend on high speed until smooth.

2 Pour into 6 glasses. Serve immediately.

1 Serving: Calories 200; Total Fat 1g (Saturated Fat 0.5g, Trans Fat 0g); Cholesterol 0mg; Sodium 70mg; Total Carbohydrate 42g (Dietary Fiber 1g); Protein 5g **% Daily Value:** Vitamin A 15%; Vitamin C 35%; Calcium 20%; Iron 0% **Exchanges:** 2½ Other Carbohydrate, ½ Skim Milk **Carbohydrate Choices:** 3

Start Happy Tips

Mango adds vitamins A and C, and the yogurt and milk add calcium and vitamin D.

For the best flavor and color, choose ripe mangoes. Look for skins that are yellow with blushes of red.

If fresh mangoes are not available, look for jars of mango in the produce department. Be sure to drain well before using them in the smoothies.

Easy Yogurt Smoothies

Smooth, creamy combinations of yogurt mixed with fruit and other tasty ingredients are not just good to eat—they're fun to make too. Plus, most of the ingredients for smoothies can easily be kept on hand for a quick breakfast any morning and can be ready for the commute when you are. Start with your favorite flavor of any yogurt—Greek, low-fat or fat-free varieties are all good. For 2 smoothies that are about 1 cup each, start with a 6-ounce container of yogurt. Blend with 1 to 1½ cups fresh or frozen fruit, such as strawberries, raspberries or peaches, and ¼ to ½ cup milk or juice. Add the liquid slowly until the smoothie is the thickness that you like. Add a fruit garnish or a sprinkle of granola, and it's breakfast! Here are some smoothie combinations that you might like to try.

1 Mixed Berry Smoothies: Greek mixed berry yogurt with fresh raspberries and a small banana. Sprinkle with granola after blending.

2 Pineapple-Orange Smoothies: Creamy vanilla yogurt with fresh pineapple and orange juice.

3 Strawberry-Peach Smoothies: Strawberry yogurt with peaches and lemonade.

4 Blueberry and Avocado Smoothies: Greek blueberry yogurt, avocado, blueberries and cranberry-blueberry juice or soymilk.

5 Key Lime Smoothies: Key lime pie yogurt, banana, limeade and milk.

6 Caramel-Chocolate Smoothies: Crème caramel yogurt, banana and soymilk with a drizzle of chocolate syrup stirred in.

granola-berry-banana smoothies

prep time: 5 Minutes ❄ **start to finish:** 5 Minutes ❄ 2 Servings

2 containers (6 oz each) strawberry or red raspberry low-fat or fat-free yogurt

½ cup milk

½ cup fresh strawberry halves or raspberries

1 banana, sliced

4 oats 'n honey crunchy granola bars (2 pouches from 8.9-oz box)

1 In blender, place yogurt, milk, strawberry halves and banana slices. Break up 3 granola bars; add to blender. Cover; blend on high speed 10 seconds.

2 Scrape down sides of blender. Cover; blend about 20 seconds longer or until smooth.

3 Pour into 2 glasses. Crumble remaining granola bar; sprinkle in each glass. Serve immediately.

1 Serving: Calories 450; Total Fat 9g (Saturated Fat 2.5g, Trans Fat 0g); Cholesterol 15mg; Sodium 270mg; Total Carbohydrate 81g (Dietary Fiber 4g); Protein 12g **% Daily Value:** Vitamin A 20%; Vitamin C 45%; Calcium 30%; Iron 8% **Exchanges:** 4 Starch, ½ Fruit, 1 Other Carbohydrate, 1 Fat **Carbohydrate Choices:** 5½

Start Happy Tips

Top each smoothie with fresh strawberries or raspberries.

Fresh pineapple can be substituted for the strawberries or raspberries for a different flavor combination.

fiber one strawberry smoothies

prep time: 5 Minutes ❋ **start to finish:** 5 Minutes ❋ 2 Servings (1 cup each)

1 container
(6 oz) strawberry low-fat
yogurt

1 cup fresh strawberry
halves or frozen
unsweetened whole
strawberries

¾ cup fat-free (skim) milk

2 tablespoons Fiber One
original bran cereal

1 Place all ingredients in blender. Cover; blend on high speed 10 seconds.

2 Scrape down sides of blender. Cover; blend about 20 seconds longer or until smooth.

3 Pour into 2 glasses. Serve immediately.

1 Serving: Calories 160; Total Fat 1g (Saturated Fat 0.5g, Trans Fat 0g); Cholesterol 5mg; Sodium 90mg; Total Carbohydrate 30g (Dietary Fiber 3g); Protein 6g **% Daily Value:** Vitamin A 15%; Vitamin C 80%; Calcium 25%; Iron 6% **Exchanges:** ½ Starch, ½ Fruit, ½ Other Carbohydrate, ½ Skim Milk **Carbohydrate Choices:** 2

Start Happy Tip

For a smoother consistency, crush the Fiber One cereal before adding it to the ingredients in the blender.

honey nut–peach smoothies

prep time: 5 Minutes ✳ **start to finish:** 5 Minutes ✳ 4 Servings (1 cup each)

2 containers (6 oz each) creamy harvest peach or creamy very vanilla low-fat yogurt

1½ cups Honey Nut Cheerios® cereal

1 can (15 oz) sliced peaches in juice, drained

1 cup milk

1 banana, sliced

⅛ teaspoon ground cinnamon, if desired

1 Place all ingredients in blender. Cover; blend on high speed 10 seconds.

2 Scrape down sides of blender. Cover; blend about 20 seconds longer or until smooth.

3 Pour into 4 glasses. Serve immediately.

1 Serving: Calories 220; Total Fat 2.5g (Saturated Fat 1g, Trans Fat 0g); Cholesterol 5mg; Sodium 160mg; Total Carbohydrate 42g (Dietary Fiber 2g); Protein 6g **% Daily Value:** Vitamin A 20%; Vitamin C 15%; Calcium 20%; Iron 15% **Exchanges:** ½ Starch, 1 Fruit, 1 Other Carbohydrate, ½ Skim Milk, ½ Fat **Carbohydrate Choices:** 3

Start Happy Tips

For frostier smoothies, substitute 1⅓ cups frozen sliced peaches, slightly thawed, for the canned peaches.

Cheerios® cereal can be substituted if you want this smoothie to be a little less sweet.

peachy chai smoothies

prep time: 10 Minutes ❉ **start to finish:** 10 Minutes ❉ 3 Servings (1 cup each)

2 fresh peaches, peeled, sliced

2 containers (6 oz each) vanilla thick-and-creamy low-fat yogurt

⅓ cup chai tea latte mix (from 10-oz package)

½ cup milk

Ground nutmeg, if desired

1 In blender, place all ingredients except nutmeg. Cover; blend on high speed about 1 minute or until smooth and creamy.

2 Pour into 3 glasses. Sprinkle each with dash of nutmeg. Serve immediately.

1 Serving: Calories 230; Total Fat 3.5g (Saturated Fat 1g, Trans Fat 0g); Cholesterol 10mg; Sodium 190mg; Total Carbohydrate 43g (Dietary Fiber 2g); Protein 9g **% Daily Value:** Vitamin A 6%; Vitamin C 8%; Calcium 25%; Iron 0% **Exchanges:** 1½ Starch, 1 Fruit, ½ Skim Milk **Carbohydrate Choices:** 3

Start Happy Tip

For the sweetest smoothies with lots of peach flavor, use peaches that are very ripe.

lucky charms®–raspberry smoothies

prep time: 5 Minutes ❋ **start to finish:** 5 Minutes ❋ 2 Servings

1 container (6 oz) raspberry or strawberry low-fat yogurt

¾ cup Lucky Charms cereal

½ cup fresh or frozen raspberries

1 cup fat-free (skim) milk

½ banana, sliced

1 Place all ingredients in blender. Cover; blend on high speed 10 seconds.

2 Scrape down sides of blender. Cover; blend about 20 seconds longer or until smooth.

3 Pour into 2 glasses. Serve immediately.

1 Serving: Calories 160; Total Fat 2g (Saturated Fat 1g, Trans Fat 0g); Cholesterol 5mg; Sodium 130mg; Total Carbohydrate 30g (Dietary Fiber 3g); Protein 6g **% Daily Value:** Vitamin A 15%; Vitamin C 20%; Calcium 20%; Iron 10% **Exchanges:** ½ Fruit, ½ Other Carbohydrate, 1 Skim Milk **Carbohydrate Choices:** 2

Start Happy Tip

The riper the banana, the sweeter the smoothies. Starches change to sugar as bananas ripen.

yogurt bubble tea

prep time: 15 Minutes ❄ **start to finish:** 30 Minutes ❄ 1 Serving

Tapioca "Bubbles"

¼ cup pearl tapioca

Water and sugar called for on tapioca package

Tea Mixture

1 container (6 oz) low-fat or fat-free yogurt

½ cup fruit juice

1 cup crushed ice

½ cup brewed green tea, cooled to room temperature

1 Cook tapioca pearls as directed on package.

2 In blender, place tea mixture ingredients. Cover; blend on high speed until smooth.

3 Using slotted spoon, place tapioca pearls in tall glass. Top with tea mixture. Serve with extra-wide straw so tapioca pearls can be sipped through.

1 Serving: Calories 430; Total Fat 1.5g (Saturated Fat 1g, Trans Fat 0g); Cholesterol 10mg; Sodium 110mg; Total Carbohydrate 98g (Dietary Fiber 0g); Protein 6g **% Daily Value:** Vitamin A 15%; Vitamin C 35%; Calcium 25%; Iron 0% **Exchanges:** 2 Starch, ½ Fruit, 4 Other Carbohydrate **Carbohydrate Choices:** 6½

Yogurt Piña Colada Bubble Tea: Use piña colada fat-free yogurt along with pineapple juice. Garnish with slice of pineapple and twist of orange.

Start Happy Tips

Traditionally, bubble tea uses large tapioca pearls. Use whatever you can find—the recipe is delicious with any size tapioca.

If no package directions are given for the tapioca pearls, make them as follows: In 2-quart saucepan, heat 2 cups water to boiling. Add tapioca; cook about 15 minutes or until pearls are tender but still chewy. Meanwhile, in 1-quart saucepan, heat ½ cup water and ½ cup sugar over low heat, stirring until sugar is dissolved. Set aside to cool, then add to cooked tapioca pearls, allowing them to absorb the sweetness.

cinnamon toast crunch®
cold brew coffee

prep time: 10 Minutes ❋ **start to finish:** 25 Hours ❋ **5 Servings**

¾ cup coffee beans

3 cups cold water

3 cups Cinnamon Toast Crunch cereal

3 cups whole milk

Ice

Whipped cream, if desired

2 tablespoons caramel sauce or topping

Additional cereal, if desired, crushed

1 Grind coffee into medium-fine grounds. Place coffee in large glass container. Stir in cold water. Cover; refrigerate 24 hours.

2 Strain coffee through fine mesh strainer. Strain again through coffee filter; discard grounds.

3 Heat oven to 300°F. Line 15x10x1-inch pan with foil. Spread 3 cups cereal in pan. Bake 10 minutes. Stir well. Bake 5 minutes longer or until toasted. Cool 10 minutes.

4 Add toasted cereal to large bowl. Add milk; stir. Refrigerate 30 minutes.

5 Strain milk mixture through strainer; discard solids. In 2-quart glass pitcher, stir together cold coffee and milk mixture.

6 Pour into 5 glasses filled with ice. Top with whipped cream, caramel sauce and crushed cereal.

1 Serving: Calories 230; Total Fat 7g (Saturated Fat 3g, Trans Fat 0g); Cholesterol 15mg; Sodium 280mg; Total Carbohydrate 36g (Dietary Fiber 2g); Protein 6g **% Daily Value:** Vitamin A 15%; Vitamin C 4%; Calcium 25%; Iron 20% **Exchanges:** 1 Starch, 1 Other Carbohydrate, ½ Milk, ½ Fat **Carbohydrate Choices:** 2½

Start Happy Tips

Use medium or dark roast coffee beans to make the cold brew coffee.

Toasting the cereal intensifies the flavor, resulting in a more flavorful cereal milk.

spiced dessert coffee

prep time: 5 Minutes ❋ **start to finish:** 15 Minutes ❋ 8 Servings (¾ cup each)

6 cups water

¾ cup strong ground coffee (such as French roast)

1½ teaspoons ground cinnamon

8 whole cloves

¼ cup packed brown sugar

½ cup whipped cream topping (from aerosol can), if desired

1 Pour water into 10-cup coffeemaker. In filter basket, mix remaining ingredients except whipped cream. Brew coffee.

2 Pour coffee into 8 mugs. Top with whipped cream.

1 Serving: Calories 30; Total Fat 0g (Saturated Fat 0g, Trans Fat 0g); Cholesterol 0mg; Sodium 5mg; Total Carbohydrate 7g (Dietary Fiber 0g); Protein 0g **% Daily Value:** Vitamin A 0%; Vitamin C 0%; Calcium 0%; Iron 0% **Exchanges:** ½ Other Carbohydrate **Carbohydrate Choices:** ½

Start Happy Tips

Serve coffee in glass mugs with cinnamon sticks for stirrers.

Grate a sprinkling of fresh nutmeg on top of the whipped cream garnish.

creamy chocolate-almond coffee

prep time: 10 Minutes ✳ **start to finish:** 10 Minutes ✳ 4 Servings

½ cup whipping cream

2 teaspoons powdered sugar

⅛ teaspoon almond extract

4 scoops (about ¼ cup each) chocolate ice cream

4 cups strong hot coffee

Chocolate shavings or toasted sliced almonds*, if desired

1 In chilled small bowl, beat whipping cream, powdered sugar and almond extract with electric mixer on high speed until stiff peaks form.

2 Place 1 scoop ice cream in each of 4 cups or mugs. Pour coffee over ice cream. Top with whipped cream. Garnish with chocolate shavings. Serve immediately.

*To toast almonds, sprinkle in ungreased heavy skillet. Cook over medium heat 5 to 7 minutes, stirring frequently until almonds begin to brown, then stirring constantly until almonds are light brown.

1 Serving: Calories 190; Total Fat 15g (Saturated Fat 9g, Trans Fat 0g); Cholesterol 50mg; Sodium 40mg; Total Carbohydrate 13g (Dietary Fiber 1g); Protein 2g **% Daily Value:** Vitamin A 10%; Vitamin C 0%; Calcium 6%; Iron 0% **Exchanges:** ½ Starch, ½ Other Carbohydrate, 3 Fat **Carbohydrate Choices:** 1

Start Happy Tip

Serve this indulgent coffee with chocolate-covered spoons. Look for them at gourmet stores. Or make your own by dipping silver or plastic spoons into melted candy coating, and refrigerate until firm.

mexican coffee

prep time: 15 Minutes ❈ **start to finish:** 25 Minutes ❈ 10 Servings (about 1 cup each)

12 cups water

½ cup packed brown sugar

4 tablespoons ground cinnamon

4 whole cloves

1 cup regular-grind coffee (dry)

½ cup chocolate-flavor syrup

1 teaspoon vanilla

Whipped cream, if desired

1 In Dutch oven, heat water, brown sugar, cinnamon and cloves to boiling, stirring to dissolve sugar. Stir in coffee. Reduce heat to medium-low; cover and simmer 5 minutes.

2 Stir in chocolate syrup and vanilla. Remove from heat; let stand 5 minutes for coffee grounds to settle. Strain coffee into coffee server or 10 individual cups; discard grounds mixture. Serve with whipped cream.

1 Serving: Calories 120; Total Fat 0g (Saturated Fat 0g, Trans Fat 0g); Cholesterol 0mg; Sodium 30mg; Total Carbohydrate 27g (Dietary Fiber 3g); Protein 1g **% Daily Value:** Vitamin A 0%; Vitamin C 0%; Calcium 6%; Iron 6% **Exchanges:** ½ Starch, 1½ Other Carbohydrate **Carbohydrate Choices:** 2

Start Happy Tips

Authentic Mexican chocolate is known for its hint of cinnamon.

If you'd like, pick up a shaker with coffee toppings, such as cocoa and cinnamon, from a coffee or gourmet food shop. Pass the shaker when serving mugs of the hot coffee so folks can sprinkle a topping or two over their whipped cream!

iced vanilla soy latte

prep time: 10 Minutes ✳ **start to finish:** 10 Minutes ✳ 2 Servings

½ cup ground espresso or
French roast coffee

1½ cups water

2 cups vanilla soymilk

2 teaspoons caramel
or chocolate fat-free
topping

Ice cubes, as desired

Sugar, if desired

1 Using drip coffeemaker, brew coffee with water as directed by coffeemaker manufacturer.

2 In medium bowl, stir together coffee and soymilk.

3 Drizzle topping over insides of 2 large glasses. Fill glasses with ice cubes. Pour soymilk mixture over ice. Sweeten to taste with sugar.

1 Serving: Calories 120; Total Fat 3g (Saturated Fat 0.5g, Trans Fat 0g); Cholesterol 0mg; Sodium 210mg; Total Carbohydrate 16g (Dietary Fiber 0g); Protein 7g **% Daily Value:** Vitamin A 10%; Vitamin C 0%; Calcium 30%; Iron 4% **Exchanges:** 1 Low-Fat Milk **Carbohydrate Choices:** 1

Start Happy Tips

Calcium, from dairy foods like milk and from fortified soymilk, can help build bones. Look for low-fat varieties of milk or soymilk options when you can.

Drizzle the topping in interesting designs on the insides of the glasses before filling them.

iced caramel cappuccino

prep time: 5 Minutes ✳ **start to finish:** 5 Minutes ✳ **4 Servings (¾ cup each)**

1½ cups water
2 tablespoons instant espresso coffee powder or granules
½ cup caramel topping
2 tablespoons sugar
1 cup milk
½ cup whipped cream topping (from aerosol can)

1 In 4-cup microwavable measuring cup, microwave water uncovered on High 2 to 3 minutes or until very hot and almost boiling. Stir in coffee powder until dissolved. Stir in ¼ cup of the caramel topping, the sugar and milk.

2 To serve, fill 4 (12-oz) glasses two-thirds with ice. Divide coffee mixture among glasses. Top with whipped cream; drizzle with remaining ¼ cup caramel topping.

1 Serving: Calories 190; Total Fat 3g (Saturated Fat 2g, Trans Fat 0g); Cholesterol 10mg; Sodium 180mg; Total Carbohydrate 38g (Dietary Fiber 0g); Protein 3g **% Daily Value:** Vitamin A 4%; Vitamin C 0%; Calcium 10%; Iron 0% **Exchanges:** ½ Starch, 2 Other Carbohydrate, ½ Fat **Carbohydrate Choices:** 2½

Start Happy Tips

For stronger coffee flavor, refrigerate the coffee and caramel mixture until cold before adding the milk and ice.

For sweeter coffee, squeeze a bit of caramel topping into the bottom of each glass before filling with ice.

Brewing the Best Coffee and Tea

Breakfast and brunch are not the same without freshly brewed coffee or tea. Brewing the best coffee and tea is not hard, but it requires just a bit of diligence. Follow these tips to ensure the best results.

FOR COFFEE:

Use a coffee grinder to grind your own beans for each pot, or choose the correct grind for your coffeemaker. For an automatic drip coffeemaker, use a medium grind; for an espresso maker, use a fine grind; and for a French press, use a coarse grind.

Use cold tap, filtered or bottled water for the best flavor. Serve coffee within 15 minutes of brewing. The longer coffee stays in contact with heat, the more harsh and bitter it becomes. Here are a few ideas for adding flavor to brewed coffee.

1 **Stir in cream, milk or soymilk — add sugar if desired**

2 **Sprinkle with chocolate shavings or stir in dark, unsweetened cocoa**

3 **Add a cinnamon stick for stirring**

4 **Top with whipped cream and a sprinkle of cinnamon or nutmeg**

FOR TEA:

Fill a kettle with cold water. For black or oolong tea, bring the water to a boil. For green or white tea, bring the water to a temperature between 170°F and 190°F. Warm a teapot by filling it with very hot water — let it stand for a couple of minutes, then drain. Add the tea to the warm teapot. Use about 1 teaspoon loose tea leaves or 1 tea bag for each ¾ cup water. Pour boiling (or hot) water over the tea and let it steep for 3 to 5 minutes. Add a bit of flavor with one of the following ideas.

1 **Stir in honey and garnish with a lemon slice**

2 **Garnish with an orange slice**

3 **Stir in milk or cream and sugar**

4 **Add a cinnamon stick for stirring**

chai tea

prep time: 10 Minutes ❋ **start to finish:** 10 Minutes ❋ 4 Servings (1 cup each)

2 cups water

4 bags black tea

2 cups milk

2 tablespoons honey

½ teaspoon ground ginger

½ teaspoon ground cinnamon

¼ teaspoon ground nutmeg

1 Heat water to boiling. Add tea bags; reduce heat to low. Simmer 2 minutes. Remove tea bags.

2 Stir in remaining ingredients. Heat to boiling. Stir with whisk to foam milk. Pour into 4 cups.

1 Serving: Calories 100; Total Fat 2.5g (Saturated Fat 1.5g, Trans Fat 0g); Cholesterol 10mg; Sodium 65mg; Total Carbohydrate 15g (Dietary Fiber 0g); Protein 4g **% Daily Value:** Vitamin A 4%; Vitamin C 0%; Calcium 15%; Iron 0% **Exchanges:** ½ Other Carbohydrate, ½ Low-Fat Milk **Carbohydrate Choices:** 1

Chai Tea Smoothies: Refrigerate mixture until cold. Pour chai tea into blender container; add 1 cup crushed ice. Cover; blend on high speed until smooth.

Start Happy Tips

Prepare the tea up to 24 hours ahead; cover and refrigerate. Reheat just before serving.

Have it your way! Add more honey if you like a little more sweetness.

blueberry bootlegger

prep time: 5 Minutes ❄ **start to finish:** 5 Minutes ❄ 2 Servings (1 cup each)

¾ cup milk

¼ cup light rum

1 tablespoon lime juice

1 pouch (7.6 oz) frozen blueberry-pomegranate nourishing yogurt smoothie

1 In blender, place milk, rum, lime juice and contents of smoothie pouch. Cover; blend on high speed 1 minute to 1 minute 30 seconds, stopping blender to scrape down sides as necessary, until smooth.

2 Pour into 2 glasses. Serve immediately.

1 Serving: Calories 200; Total Fat 3.5g (Saturated Fat 1g, Trans Fat 0g); Cholesterol 5mg; Sodium 75mg; Total Carbohydrate 21g (Dietary Fiber 2g); Protein 5g **% Daily Value:** Vitamin A 4%; Vitamin C 6%; Calcium 60%; Iron 6% **Carbohydrate Choices:** 1½

Start Happy Tips

For a drink without alcohol, omit the rum and increase the milk to 1 cup.

Chill the glasses in the freezer at least 15 minutes for extra-frosty smoothies!

mimosa

prep time: 5 Minutes ❄ **start to finish:** 5 Minutes ❄ 1 Serving

3 oz (6 tablespoons) orange juice, chilled

3 oz (6 tablespoons) champagne, chilled

Fresh orange wedge, if desired

1 In tall glass, pour orange juice and champagne.

2 Garnish with orange wedge.

1 Serving: Calories 110; Total Fat 0g (Saturated Fat 0g, Trans Fat 0g); Cholesterol 0mg; Sodium 5mg; Total Carbohydrate 12g (Dietary Fiber 0g); Protein 0g **% Daily Value:** Vitamin A 0%; Vitamin C 50%; Calcium 0%; Iron 0% **Carbohydrate Choices:** 1

Start Happy Tips

Create your own variation of a mimosa by using a different fruit juice in place of the orange juice.

You'll want to whip up this cocktail just before serving so guests can enjoy the bubbles.

tex-mex bloody marys

prep time: 10 Minutes ✳ **start to finish:** 10 Minutes ✳ 4 Servings

1 medium lime

1 bottle (32 oz) Bloody Mary mix

4 teaspoons taco seasoning mix (from 1-oz package)

Ice cubes

½ medium cucumber, peeled (if desired), cut lengthwise into 4 spears

1 Cut lime lengthwise in half. Cut 1 half into 5 wedges; set aside. From uncut half, squeeze 2 tablespoons juice; place in pitcher. Add Bloody Mary mix and 2 teaspoons of the taco seasoning mix; mix well. Set aside.

2 Place remaining 2 teaspoons taco seasoning mix on small plate. Moisten rims of 4 (16-oz) glasses with 1 of the lime wedges. Dip rim of each glass into taco seasoning mix to coat edge.

3 Fill each glass one-third full with ice cubes; pour Bloody Mary mixture over ice. Garnish each with lime wedge and cucumber spear.

1 Serving: Calories 150; Total Fat 0g (Saturated Fat 0g, Trans Fat 0g); Cholesterol 0mg; Sodium 2090mg; Total Carbohydrate 36g (Dietary Fiber 3g); Protein 2g **% Daily Value:** Vitamin A 4%; Vitamin C 10%; Calcium 4%; Iron 4% **Exchanges:** ½ Starch, 2 Other Carbohydrate **Carbohydrate Choices:** 2½

Start Happy Tip
If you like, stir 1 to 2 ounces vodka into each Bloody Mary for a little extra fun!

freshly brewed tea

prep time: 15 Minutes ✳ **start to finish:** 15 Minutes ✳ 8 Servings (¾ cup each)

Boiling water

Loose tea or tea bag

1 Whether using loose tea or tea bags, preparation method is the same. Start with clean teapot made of glass, china or earthenware. Add rapidly boiling water; allow to stand a few minutes to "hot the pot." Pour out water just before brewing tea.

2 Heat cold water to full rolling boil. (Use water from cold-water tap; water from hot-water tap may contain mineral deposits from water pipes that can affect flavor of tea.)

3 Add tea to warm teapot, allowing 1 teaspoon loose tea or 1 tea bag for each cup of tea. Pour boiling water over tea (¾ cup for each cup of tea); let stand 3 to 5 minutes to bring out full flavor.

4 Stir tea once to ensure uniform strength. Do not judge strength of tea by its color; you must taste it. Strain tea, or remove tea bags. Serve with sugar and milk or lemon, if desired.

1 Serving: Calories 0; Total Fat 0g (Saturated Fat 0g, Trans Fat 0g); Cholesterol 0mg; Sodium 5mg; Total Carbohydrate 0g (Dietary Fiber 0g); Protein 0g **% Daily Value:** Vitamin A 0%; Vitamin C 0%; Calcium 0%; Iron 0% **Exchanges:** Free **Carbohydrate Choices:** 0

Start Happy Tips

Tea is one of the world's favorite beverages, second in popularity only to water.

For eight servings with refills, we suggest brewing two pots of tea at a time.

strawberry-honey bruschetta

prep time: 15 Minutes ⁑ **start to finish:** 30 Minutes ⁑ 16 Slices

1 loaf (8 oz) baguette French bread

1 container (6 oz) plain fat-free Greek yogurt

2 tablespoons packed brown sugar

¼ teaspoon ground cinnamon

16 fresh strawberries, sliced

¼ cup honey

1 Heat oven to 375°F. Cut bread into ½-inch slices; arrange on cookie sheet. Bake about 10 minutes or until golden.

2 Meanwhile, stir together yogurt, brown sugar and cinnamon.

3 Turn oven control to broil. Spread yogurt mixture on one side of each toasted baguette slice.

4 Broil bread slices 4 inches from heat about 1 minute or until mixture is hot. Arrange strawberry slices on yogurt mixture. Lightly drizzle each with honey. Serve immediately.

1 Slice: Calories 70; Total Fat 0.5g (Saturated Fat 0g, Trans Fat 0g); Cholesterol 0mg; Sodium 100mg; Total Carbohydrate 15g (Dietary Fiber 1g); Protein 3g **% Daily Value:** Vitamin A 0%; Vitamin C 10%; Calcium 2%; Iron 4% **Exchanges:** ½ Starch, ½ Other Carbohydrate **Carbohydrate Choices:** 1

strawberry-chocolate granola bars

prep time: 5 Minutes ✳ **start to finish:** 5 Minutes ✳ 1 Serving

4   teaspoons strawberry fat-free Greek yogurt (from 6-oz container)

2   oats 'n honey crunchy granola bars (1 pouch from 8.9-oz box)

2   small fresh strawberries, sliced

1   teaspoon shaved dark chocolate

1   teaspoon sliced almonds, toasted*

1 Spread 2 teaspoons yogurt on each granola bar.

2 Top evenly with sliced strawberries. Sprinkle with chocolate and almonds.

*To toast almonds, sprinkle in ungreased heavy skillet. Cook over medium heat 5 to 7 minutes, stirring frequently until almonds begin to brown, then stirring constantly until almonds are light brown.

1 Serving: Calories 280; Total Fat 9g (Saturated Fat 2g, Trans Fat 0g); Cholesterol 0mg; Sodium 190mg; Total Carbohydrate 41g (Dietary Fiber 3g); Protein 8g **% Daily Value:** Vitamin A 4%; Vitamin C 15%; Calcium 10%; Iron 10% **Exchanges:** 2½ Starch, 1½ Fat **Carbohydrate Choices:** 3

Start Happy Tips

White or milk chocolate can be used in place of the shaved dark chocolate.

On the go? Use the wrapper to carry the topped granola bars with you and enjoy almost anywhere.

berries and cream granola bars

prep time: 5 Minutes ✳ **start to finish:** 5 Minutes ✳ 1 Serving

2 oats 'n honey crunchy granola bars (1 pouch from 8.9-oz box)

4 teaspoons softened cream cheese

2 tablespoons sliced fresh strawberries or mixed berries (blueberries, raspberries, sliced strawberries)

1 Spread granola bars with cream cheese.

2 Top with berries.

1 Serving: Calories 240; Total Fat 12g (Saturated Fat 4g, Trans Fat 0g); Cholesterol 20mg; Sodium 220mg; Total Carbohydrate 34g (Dietary Fiber 2g); Protein 4g **% Daily Value:** Vitamin A 4%; Vitamin C 20%; Calcium 0%; Iron 8% **Exchanges:** 2 Starch, 2 Fat **Carbohydrate Choices:** 2

pumpkin-apple granola bars

prep time: 5 Minutes ✳ **start to finish:** 5 Minutes ✳ 1 Serving

1 container (8 oz) honey nut cream cheese

¼ cup canned pumpkin (not pumpkin pie mix)

2 cinnamon or oats 'n honey crunchy granola bars (1 pouch from 8.9-oz box)

2 tablespoons chopped apple

½ teaspoon real maple syrup

Dash ground cinnamon

1 In small bowl, stir cream cheese and pumpkin until smooth.

2 Spread 2 teaspoons pumpkin cream cheese on each granola bar. Top evenly with chopped apple. Drizzle with maple syrup. Sprinkle with cinnamon.

3 Cover; refrigerate any remaining pumpkin cream cheese.

1 Serving: Calories 220; Total Fat 7g (Saturated Fat 1g, Trans Fat 0g); Cholesterol 0mg; Sodium 190mg; Total Carbohydrate 35g (Dietary Fiber 2g); Protein 4g **% Daily Value:** Vitamin A 15%; Vitamin C 0%; Calcium 0%; Iron 4% **Exchanges:** 1 Starch, 1½ Other Carbohydrate, 1½ Fat **Carbohydrate Choices:** 2

Start Happy Tip

Pumpkin cream cheese is a delicious spread. Try it on bagels, toast or graham crackers.

blueberry-ricotta granola bars

prep time: 5 Minutes ❋ **start to finish:** 5 Minutes ❋ 1 Serving

4 teaspoons whole milk ricotta cheese

2 oats 'n honey crunchy granola bars (1 pouch from 8.9-oz box)

2 tablespoons fresh blueberries

½ teaspoon honey

¼ teaspoon grated lemon peel

1 Spread 2 teaspoons ricotta cheese on each granola bar.

2 Top evenly with blueberries. Drizzle with honey; top with lemon peel.

1 Serving: Calories 250; Total Fat 9g (Saturated Fat 2g, Trans Fat 0g); Cholesterol 10mg; Sodium 180mg; Total Carbohydrate 35g (Dietary Fiber 2g); Protein 6g **% Daily Value:** Vitamin A 2%; Vitamin C 4%; Calcium 4%; Iron 6% **Exchanges:** 2 Starch, ½ Other Carbohydrate, 1½ Fat **Carbohydrate Choices:** 2

Start Happy Tip

Ricotta is a fresh, unaged cheese that is just a bit grainy but smoother than cottage cheese. It is very moist with a slightly sweet flavor.

peanut butter and banana granola bars

prep time: 5 Minutes ❋ **start to finish:** 5 Minutes ❋ 1 Serving

2 oats 'n honey crunchy granola bars (1 pouch from 8.9-oz box)

4 teaspoons peanut butter

12 slices banana (about 1 medium banana)

1 Spread granola bars with peanut butter.

2 Top with banana slices.

1 Serving: Calories 400; Total Fat 18g (Saturated Fat 3g, Trans Fat 0g); Cholesterol 0mg; Sodium 260mg; Total Carbohydrate 50g (Dietary Fiber 4g); Protein 10g **% Daily Value:** Vitamin A 0%; Vitamin C 12%; Calcium 0%; Iron 8% **Exchanges:** 3 Starch, 3 Fat **Carbohydrate Choices:** 3

CHAPTER 2

just for cereal lovers

blueberry-lemon cheerios

prep time: 5 Minutes ❄ **start to finish:** 5 Minutes ❄ 1 Serving

1 container (6 oz) blueberry fat-free Greek yogurt

¾ cup Cheerios or Honey Nut Cheerios cereal

½ cup fresh blueberries

½ teaspoon grated lemon peel

1 teaspoon honey

1 Spoon yogurt into bowl. Top with cereal, blueberries and lemon peel.

2 Drizzle honey over top. Serve immediately.

1 Serving: Calories 310; Total Fat 1.5g (Saturated Fat 0g, Trans Fat 0g); Cholesterol 10mg; Sodium 220mg; Total Carbohydrate 58g (Dietary Fiber 4g); Protein 15g **% Daily Value:** Vitamin A 25%; Vitamin C 20%; Calcium 45%; Iron 35% **Exchanges:** 2 Starch, ½ Fruit, ½ Other Carbohydrate, 1 Skim Milk **Carbohydrate Choices:** 4

Start Happy Tip

To store blueberries for a few days, loosely cover and refrigerate. Rinse well just before serving.

mango–salted caramel cheerios

prep time: 5 Minutes ✳ **start to finish:** 5 Minutes ✳ 1 Serving

1 container (6 oz) French
  vanilla low-fat yogurt

¾ cup Cheerios or Honey
  Nut Cheerios cereal

½ cup chopped mango

1 tablespoon chopped
  toasted almonds*

2 teaspoons caramel sauce
  or topping

  Dash fine sea salt

1 Spoon yogurt into bowl. Top with cereal, mango and almonds.

2 Drizzle caramel over top. Sprinkle with salt. Serve immediately.

*To toast almonds, sprinkle in ungreased skillet. Cook over medium heat 5 to 7 minutes, stirring frequently until almonds begin to brown, then stirring constantly until almonds are light brown.

1 Serving: Calories 390; Total Fat 7g (Saturated Fat 1.5g, Trans Fat 0g); Cholesterol 10mg; Sodium 400mg; Total Carbohydrate 71g (Dietary Fiber 4g); Protein 10g **% Daily Value:** Vitamin A 40%; Vitamin C 60%; Calcium 30%; Iron 35% **Exchanges:** ½ Starch, ½ Fruit, 3 Other Carbohydrate, 1 Skim Milk, 1 Fat **Carbohydrate Choices:** 5

Start Happy Tips

To ripen a mango, place it in a paper bag at room temperature. Ripe mangoes can be placed in a plastic bag and refrigerated for up to 3 days.

To cut a mango, start by using a sharp knife to cut the fruit vertically in half along each side of the seed. Twist the two halves apart, and cut away any remaining flesh. Then score the mango flesh in each half in a crisscross pattern, being careful not to cut through the skin. Flip each half inside out, and remove the square pieces from the skin.

peanut butter–pretzel cheerios

prep time: 5 Minutes ❊ **start to finish:** 5 Minutes ❊ **1 Serving**

1 container (6 oz) French vanilla low-fat yogurt

½ cup Cheerios or Honey Nut Cheerios cereal

½ firm medium banana, sliced

¼ cup coarsely broken chocolate-covered pretzels

1 tablespoon peanut butter, melted

1 Spoon yogurt into bowl. Top with cereal, banana slices and pretzels.

2 Drizzle melted peanut butter over top. Serve immediately.

1 Serving: Calories 500; Total Fat 14g (Saturated Fat 4.5g, Trans Fat 0g); Cholesterol 10mg; Sodium 520mg; Total Carbohydrate 81g (Dietary Fiber 5g); Protein 14g **% Daily Value:** Vitamin A 20%; Vitamin C 6%; Calcium 30%; Iron 30% **Exchanges:** 1 Starch, 3½ Other Carbohydrate, 1 Skim Milk, ½ High-Fat Meat, 1½ Fat **Carbohydrate Choices:** 5½

Start Happy Tips

To melt the peanut butter, place it in a small microwavable bowl and microwave uncovered on High 30 to 45 seconds, stirring every 15 seconds, until smooth.

If you can't find chocolate-covered pretzels, make your own by dipping pretzels into melted chocolate.

Easy Cereal Toppers

What's for breakfast? It seems like creativity in the morning is not always an option. But because it is considered by many to be the most important meal of the day, why not think ahead and plan to serve some yummy new combinations using favorite cereals. Your family will look at morning in a whole new way. Simply start with a bowl of any cereal or even mix two or three varieties. Topped in a different way, cereal takes on a brand-new look! Here are some ideas to get you started.

1 **Berry-Yogurt Cereal:** Fresh blueberries or raspberries and a sprinkle of shredded orange peel with Greek yogurt and a drizzle of honey.

2 **Maple-Fruit Cereal:** Sliced fresh strawberries and sliced banana with milk and a drizzle of maple syrup.

3 **Cranberry-Walnut Cereal:** Dried cranberries and walnuts with plain or vanilla soymilk.

4 **Brown Sugar–Apple Cereal:** Chopped fresh apple or pear and brown sugar with vanilla yogurt.

5 **Cherry-Almond Cereal:** Fresh pitted cherries or dried cherries and sliced almonds with almond milk.

6 **Figgy Coconut Cereal:** Chopped dried figs and chopped pecans with coconut milk.

rainbow breakfast bento box

prep time: 15 Minutes ⁂ **start to finish:** 15 Minutes ⁂ variable

Small bowls, cookie cutters
   or paper baking cups

Box or lunch container

Trix® cereal

Colorful fruit (such as
   raspberries, blueberries,
   cherries, and cut-up
   kiwifruit, pineapple or
   apricots)

1 Place small bowls in box.

2 Arrange cereal and fruit in bowl, using photo as a guide.

3 Serve immediately, or store covered in refrigerator up to
1 day before serving.

Nutrition not calculated because of recipe variables.

Start Happy Tips

This fun bento box contains both fruity
cereal and lots of fresh fruit. Pack a
colorful box for a morning—or any time of
day—energy boost.

Use a Trix cereal box to make your bento
box!

Sodium 190mg
Potassium 50mg
Total Carbohydrate 21g
Dietary Fiber 1g
Sugars 10g
Other Carbohydrate 15g
Protein 1g

berry breakfast quinoa

prep time: 10 Minutes ❋ **start to finish:** 10 Minutes ❋ 4 Servings

¼ cup milk

2 containers (6 oz each) French vanilla, strawberry or harvest peach low-fat yogurt

4 teaspoons chia seed

1 cup cooled cooked quinoa (¼ cup uncooked)

2 cups fresh fruit (mixed berries or chopped peaches)

¼ cup coarsely chopped toasted almonds or pecans*

⅛ teaspoon ground cinnamon

1 In medium bowl, stir together milk, yogurt and chia seed until blended. Divide mixture evenly among 4 glasses. Spoon ¼ cup cooled cooked quinoa on top of yogurt layer in each glass.

2 Top each with a layer of fruit and almonds. Sprinkle with cinnamon. Let stand 5 minutes, or cover and refrigerate overnight.

*To toast almonds or pecans, sprinkle in ungreased skillet. Cook over medium heat 5 to 7 minutes, stirring frequently until nuts begin to brown, then stirring constantly until nuts are light brown.

1 Serving: Calories 260; Total Fat 8g (Saturated Fat 1.5g, Trans Fat 0g); Cholesterol 5mg; Sodium 80mg; Total Carbohydrate 40g (Dietary Fiber 4g); Protein 8g **% Daily Value:** Vitamin A 10%; Vitamin C 15%; Calcium 15%; Iron 8% **Exchanges:** 2 Starch, ½ Fruit, 1½ Fat **Carbohydrate Choices:** 2½

Start Happy Tips

Chia seed is a delicious addition to this recipe. It thickens the yogurt mixture and adds a nice crunch.

Quinoa (KEEN-wah) has the highest protein content of all the grains. Its flavor is mild, like that of rice or couscous. Rinse the grain before cooking to remove any lingering traces of its bitter-tasting coating.

caribbean steel-cut oats with fruit and yogurt

prep time: 40 Minutes ❉ **start to finish:** 40 Minutes ❉ **4 Servings**

1¾ cups water

1 can (14 oz) reduced-fat (lite) coconut milk

¾ teaspoon ground cinnamon

⅛ teaspoon salt, if desired

1 cup steel-cut oats (from 24-oz container)

1 tablespoon honey

1 container (6 oz) French vanilla low-fat yogurt

1 large mango, seed removed, peeled and chopped (about 1½ cups)

1 cup fresh raspberries

1 In 2-quart saucepan, mix water, coconut milk, ½ teaspoon of the cinnamon and the salt. Heat to boiling over medium-high heat. Stir in oats. Reduce heat to low; simmer uncovered 30 to 35 minutes, stirring occasionally, until oats are tender yet slightly chewy. Remove from heat. Stir in honey.

2 Divide oats evenly among 4 bowls. Top each with generous 2 tablespoons yogurt, about ⅓ cup mango and ¼ cup raspberries. Sprinkle evenly with remaining ¼ teaspoon cinnamon.

1 Serving: Calories 330; Total Fat 8g (Saturated Fat 6g, Trans Fat 0g); Cholesterol 0mg; Sodium 230mg; Total Carbohydrate 57g (Dietary Fiber 7g); Protein 7g **% Daily Value:** Vitamin A 20%; Vitamin C 35%; Calcium 10%; Iron 10% **Exchanges:** 1 Starch, 1 Fruit, 1½ Other Carbohydrate, ½ Skim Milk, 1½ Fat **Carbohydrate Choices:** 4

camper's fruity oatmeal

prep time: 10 Minutes ❄ **start to finish:** 10 Minutes ❄ 6 Servings

3 cups old-fashioned oats

½ cup sweetened dried cranberries

½ teaspoon salt

5 cups water

1 can (15 oz) sliced peaches in syrup, drained, chopped if desired

2 tablespoons chopped almonds

Brown sugar, if desired

1 In resealable food-storage plastic bag, mix oats, cranberries and salt.

2 In 2-quart saucepan, heat water to boiling. Stir in oat mixture. Cook over medium heat about 5 minutes, stirring occasionally, until thick and creamy. Stir in peaches and almonds. Sprinkle with brown sugar.

1 Serving: Calories 270; Total Fat 4g (Saturated Fat 0.5g, Trans Fat 0g); Cholesterol 0mg; Sodium 200mg; Total Carbohydrate 50g (Dietary Fiber 6g); Protein 7g **% Daily Value:** Vitamin A 4%; Vitamin C 0%; Calcium 4%; Iron 10% **Exchanges:** 2 Starch, 1½ Other Carbohydrate, ½ Fat **Carbohydrate Choices:** 3

Start Happy Tips

Any combination of dried fruit and nuts can be used to make this oatmeal. If you're out picking berries, add those, too!

Pack single-serve coffee bags, tea bags and cocoa mixes for instant camper's drinks. The same hot water can be used to prepare all the beverages.

banana–chocolate chip gran-oatmeal

prep time: 5 Minutes ❄ **start to finish:** 5 Minutes ❄ 1 Serving

2 oats 'n honey crunchy granola bars (1 pouch from 8.9-oz box)

⅓ cup 1% low-fat or fat-free (skim) milk

2 tablespoons semisweet chocolate chips

¾ banana, sliced

1 In microwavable bowl, place granola bars. Add milk. Microwave uncovered on High 25 to 30 seconds or until milk is warm.

2 Using spoon, break bars in milk into granola pieces. Top with chocolate chips and banana.

1 Serving: Calories 420; Total Fat 14g (Saturated Fat 5g, Trans Fat 0g); Cholesterol 5mg; Sodium 200mg; Total Carbohydrate 64g (Dietary Fiber 5g); Protein 8g **% Daily Value:** Vitamin A 4%; Vitamin C 10%; Calcium 10%; Iron 10% **Exchanges:** 2½ Starch, 2 Other Carbohydrate, 2½ Fat **Carbohydrate Choices:** 4

tropical fruit 'n ginger oatmeal

prep time: 15 Minutes ❄ **start to finish:** 45 Minutes ❄ 4 Servings

2¼ cups water

¾ cup steel-cut oats

2 teaspoons finely chopped gingerroot

⅛ teaspoon salt

½ medium banana, mashed

1 container (6 oz) vanilla thick-and-creamy low-fat yogurt

1 medium mango, seed removed, peeled and chopped (1 cup)

½ cup sliced fresh strawberries

2 tablespoons shredded coconut, toasted*

2 tablespoons chopped walnuts

1 In 1½-quart saucepan, heat water to boiling. Stir in oats, gingerroot and salt. Reduce heat to low; simmer gently uncovered 25 to 30 minutes, without stirring, until oats are tender yet slightly chewy.

2 Stir banana into oatmeal. Divide among 4 bowls. Top each serving with yogurt, mango, strawberries, coconut and walnuts. Serve immediately.

*To toast coconut, sprinkle in an ungreased skillet and cook over medium-low heat 6 to 14 minutes, stirring frequently until browning begins, then stirring constantly until golden brown.

1 Serving: Calories 220; Total Fat 6g (Saturated Fat 2g, Trans Fat 0g); Cholesterol 0mg; Sodium 105mg; Total Carbohydrate 38g (Dietary Fiber 4g); Protein 5g **% Daily Value:** Vitamin A 20%; Vitamin C 35%; Calcium 10%; Iron 6% **Exchanges:** 1½ Starch, 1 Fruit, 1 Fat **Carbohydrate Choices:** 2½

Start Happy Tip

Trim the calories for this breakfast meal by skipping the banana, using fat-free yogurt and omitting the coconut for a savings of about 50 calories per serving.

apple crisp refrigerator oatmeal

prep time: 10 Minutes ❄ **start to finish:** 8 Hours 10 Minutes ❄ 1 Serving

Oatmeal

- ¼ cup old-fashioned oats
- 1 container (6 oz) apple crisp low-fat yogurt
- 1 teaspoon chia seed, if desired

Toppings, if desired

- ¼ cup chopped Granny Smith apple
- ⅛ teaspoon ground cinnamon
- 2 tablespoons chopped walnuts

1 In half-pint canning jar (or other resealable container), pour oats and yogurt. Top with chia seed; carefully stir to mix thoroughly. Cover; refrigerate about 8 hours.

2 When ready to serve, sprinkle with toppings.

1 Serving: Calories 240; Total Fat 3g (Saturated Fat 1g, Trans Fat 0g); Cholesterol 10mg; Sodium 90mg; Total Carbohydrate 47g (Dietary Fiber 2g); Protein 7g **% Daily Value:** Vitamin A 15%; Vitamin C 0%; Calcium 20%; Iron 4% **Exchanges:** 1½ Starch, 1½ Other Carbohydrate, ½ Fat **Carbohydrate Choices:** 3

Start Happy Tip

Chia seed is a delicious addition to this dish and is classified as a super-food. In addition, it helps to thicken dishes. Also try chia seed in smoothies for its thickening power.

cranberry-apple gran-oatmeal

prep time: 5 Minutes ❋ **start to finish:** 5 Minutes ❋ 1 Serving

2   oats 'n honey crunchy granola bars (1 pouch from 8.9-oz box)

⅓   cup 1% low-fat or fat-free (skim) milk

2   tablespoons sweetened dried cranberries

¼   apple, chopped

1 In microwavable bowl, place granola bars. Top with milk. Microwave uncovered on High 25 to 30 seconds or until milk is warm.

2 Using spoon, break bars in milk into granola pieces. Top with cranberries and chopped apple.

1 Serving: Calories 300; Total Fat 8g (Saturated Fat 1.5g, Trans Fat 0g); Cholesterol 5mg; Sodium 200mg; Total Carbohydrate 52g (Dietary Fiber 4g); Protein 6g **% Daily Value:** Vitamin A 4%; Vitamin C 4%; Calcium 10%; Iron 6% **Exchanges:** 1½ Starch, 2 Other Carbohydrate, 1½ Fat **Carbohydrate Choices:** 3½

"superpower" overnight oatmeal

prep time: 5 Minutes ❄ **start to finish:** 8 Hours 5 Minutes ❄ 1 Serving

Oatmeal

- 1 container (5.3 oz) 100-calorie fat-free Greek yogurt (any flavor)
- ¼ cup old-fashioned or quick-cooking oats
- 1 teaspoon chia seed

Stir-ins

(see ideas below)

1 In container with tight-fitting cover, mix yogurt, oats and chia seed. Add desired stir-ins.

2 Cover; refrigerate at least 8 hours but no longer than 3 days before eating.

1 Serving: Calories 190; Total Fat 2g (Saturated Fat 0g, Trans Fat 0g); Cholesterol 0mg; Sodium 45mg; Total Carbohydrate 29g (Dietary Fiber 3g); Protein 13g **% Daily Value:** Vitamin A 4%; Vitamin C 0%; Calcium 15%; Iron 8% **Exchanges:** ½ Starch, 1 Other Carbohydrate, ½ Skim Milk, 1 Very Lean Meat **Carbohydrate Choices:** 2

Stir-ins

Almond Power Oatmeal: Stir in ¼ cup toasted almonds.*
Calories 330 (Calories from Fat 120); Total Fat 13g (Saturated Fat 1g, Trans Fat 0g); Cholesterol 0mg; Sodium 55mg; Potassium 240mg; Total Carbohydrate 31g (Dietary Fiber 6g); Protein 21g

Banana Power Oatmeal: Stir in ¼ cup banana slices.
Calories 220 (Calories from Fat 20); Total Fat 2g (Saturated Fat 0g, Trans Fat 0g); Cholesterol 0mg; Sodium 55mg; Potassium 210mg; Total Carbohydrate 34g (Dietary Fiber 4g); Protein 16g

Blackberry Power Oatmeal: Stir in ¼ cup blackberries.
Calories 200 (Calories from Fat 20); Total Fat 2.5g (Saturated Fat 0g, Trans Fat 0g); Cholesterol 0mg; Sodium 55mg; Potassium 135mg; Total Carbohydrate 29g (Dietary Fiber 5g); Protein 16g

Blueberry Power Oatmeal: Stir in ¼ cup blueberries.
Calories 210 (Calories from Fat 20); Total Fat 2g (Saturated Fat 0g, Trans Fat 0g); Cholesterol 0mg; Sodium 55mg; Potassium 105mg; Total Carbohydrate 31g (Dietary Fiber 4g); Protein 16g

Honey Power Oatmeal: Stir in 1 tablespoon honey.
Calories 260 (Calories from Fat 20); Total Fat 2g (Saturated Fat 0g, Trans Fat 0g); Cholesterol 0mg; Sodium 60mg; Potassium 90mg; Total Carbohydrate 43g (Dietary Fiber 3g); Protein 16g

Pomegranate Power Oatmeal: Stir in ¼ cup pomegranate seeds.
Calories 230 (Calories from Fat 25); Total Fat 2.5g (Saturated Fat 0g, Trans Fat 0g); Cholesterol 0mg; Sodium 60mg; Potassium 180mg; Total Carbohydrate 34g (Dietary Fiber 4g); Protein 16g

*To toast almonds, sprinkle in ungreased skillet. Cook over medium heat 5 to 7 minutes, stirring frequently until almonds begin to brown, then stirring constantly until almonds are light brown.

indulgent overnight oatmeal swap

prep time: 5 Minutes ❄ **start to finish:** 8 Hours 5 Minutes ❄ 1 Serving

Oatmeal

1 container (6 oz) fat-free yogurt (any flavor)

¼ cup old-fashioned or quick-cooking oats

Stir-ins

(see ideas below)

1 In container with tight-fitting cover, mix yogurt and oats. Add desired stir-ins.

2 Cover; refrigerate at least 8 hours but no longer than 3 days before eating.

1 Serving: Calories 210; Total Fat 1.5g (Saturated Fat 0g, Trans Fat 0g); Cholesterol 0mg; Sodium 95mg; Total Carbohydrate 38g (Dietary Fiber 2g); Protein 10g **% Daily Value:** Vitamin A 0%; Vitamin C 0%; Calcium 30%; Iron 6% **Exchanges:** 2 Starch, ½ Skim Milk **Carbohydrate Choices:** 2½

Stir-ins

Bananas Foster Overnight Oatmeal: Stir in ½ sliced banana and 1 tablespoon chocolate chips.

Calories 280 (Calories from Fat 40); Total Fat 4.5g (Saturated Fat 2g, Trans Fat 0g); Cholesterol 0mg; Sodium 0mg; Potassium 320mg; Total Carbohydrate 50g (Dietary Fiber 4g); Protein 8g

German Chocolate Cake Overnight Oatmeal: Stir in 1 tablespoon chocolate chips and 1 tablespoon unsweetened coconut.

Calories 250 (Calories from Fat 70); Total Fat 8g (Saturated Fat 5g, Trans Fat 0g); Cholesterol 0mg; Sodium 0mg; Potassium 140mg; Total Carbohydrate 38g (Dietary Fiber 3g); Protein 8g

Peanut Butter Cup Overnight Oatmeal: Stir in 1 tablespoon each chocolate chips and peanut butter chips.

Calories 270 (Calories from Fat 70); Total Fat 8g (Saturated Fat 3g, Trans Fat 0g); Cholesterol 0mg; Sodium 30mg; Potassium 150mg; Total Carbohydrate 42g (Dietary Fiber 3g); Protein 9g

S'mores Overnight Oatmeal: Stir in 1 tablespoon chocolate chips and 2 tablespoons miniature marshmallows.

Calories 240 (Calories from Fat 40); Total Fat 4.5g (Saturated Fat 2g, Trans Fat 0g); Cholesterol 0mg; Sodium 5mg; Potassium 110mg; Total Carbohydrate 42g (Dietary Fiber 2g); Protein 8g

s'mores hot cereal

prep time: 10 Minutes ❄ **start to finish:** 10 Minutes ❄ 1 Serving

3 tablespoons dry chocolate- or regular-flavor hot wheat cereal

½ cup milk

¼ cup water

2 tablespoons miniature marshmallows

2 tablespoons semisweet chocolate chips

¼ cup Golden Grahams® cereal

1 Make hot wheat cereal as directed on package, using milk and water.

2 Immediately stir in marshmallows and chocolate chips. Sprinkle with cereal. Serve immediately.

1 Serving: Calories 350; Total Fat 10g (Saturated Fat 5g, Trans Fat 0g); Cholesterol 10mg; Sodium 250mg; Total Carbohydrate 58g (Dietary Fiber 2g); Protein 9g **% Daily Value:** Vitamin A 8%; Vitamin C 0%; Calcium 40%; Iron 60% **Exchanges:** 1½ Starch, 2 Other Carbohydrate, ½ Low-Fat Milk, 1½ Fat **Carbohydrate Choices:** 4

Start Happy Tip

Because this hot breakfast cereal can be made so quickly, it's easy to have even on hurried mornings. For a touch of fruit, add some sliced strawberries or a wedge of cantaloupe on the side.

dulce de leche cheerios® parfaits

prep time: 10 Minutes ✳ **start to finish:** 10 Minutes ✳ 4 Parfaits

2 medium ripe bananas, sliced (2 cups)

4 containers (6 oz each) French vanilla low-fat yogurt

2 cups Dulce de Leche Cheerios cereal

1 cup sliced fresh strawberries, if desired

1 In each of 4 parfait glasses, layer ¼ cup of the bananas, half container of the yogurt and ¼ cup of the cereal; repeat layers.

2 Top each parfait with ¼ cup strawberries. Serve immediately.

1 Parfait: Calories 300; Total Fat 2.5g (Saturated Fat 1g, Trans Fat 0g); Cholesterol 10mg; Sodium 170mg; Total Carbohydrate 61g (Dietary Fiber 3g); Protein 7g **% Daily Value:** Vitamin A 20%; Vitamin C 25%; Calcium 25%; Iron 35% **Exchanges:** 3½ Other Carbohydrate, 1 Skim Milk **Carbohydrate Choices:** 4

Start Happy Tip

This fruit combination is declious, but you could use any fresh fruit you have on hand. Why not try peaches with blueberries?

crunchy-topped strawberry-kiwi parfaits

prep time: 10 Minutes ❊ **start to finish:** 20 Minutes ❊ **4 Parfaits**

2 cups Banana Nut Cheerios® cereal

¼ cup sliced almonds

1½ cups creamy vanilla or creamy peach low-fat yogurt (from 2-lb container)

1 cup sliced fresh strawberries

2 medium kiwifruit, peeled, cut into chunks

1 Heat oven to 350°F. In ungreased 13x9-inch pan, place cereal and almonds. Bake 6 to 10 minutes, stirring occasionally, until light brown. Cool about 5 minutes.

2 In each of 4 parfait glasses, alternate layers of yogurt, strawberries, kiwifruit and toasted cereal mixture. Serve immediately.

1 Parfait: Calories 230; Total Fat 4.5g (Saturated Fat 0.5g, Trans Fat 0g); Cholesterol 5mg; Sodium 150mg; Total Carbohydrate 41g (Dietary Fiber 3g); Protein 5g **% Daily Value:** Vitamin A 15%; Vitamin C 60%; Calcium 20%; Iron 20% **Exchanges:** 1½ Starch, ½ Fruit, ½ Other Carbohydrate, 1 Fat **Carbohydrate Choices:** 3

Start Happy Tip

Strawberries provide vitamin C and many other nutrients. So these luscious berries not only taste good, but they are good for you too!

very berry parfaits

prep time: 10 Minutes ❄ start to finish: 10 Minutes ❄ 2 Parfaits

1 cup Berry Burst Cheerios® cereal (any flavor)

½ cup fresh blueberries, raspberries or sliced strawberries

1 container (6 oz) thick-and-creamy low-fat yogurt (any berry flavor)

1 Place cereal in resealable food-storage plastic bag; seal bag. Using rolling pin, slightly crush cereal.

2 In 2 (about 1-cup each) parfait or drinking glasses, layer half of the berries and half of the yogurt. Top each parfait with half of the crushed cereal.

1 Parfait: Calories 120; Total Fat 0.5g (Saturated Fat 0g, Trans Fat 0g); Cholesterol 0mg; Sodium 130mg; Total Carbohydrate 24g (Dietary Fiber 2g); Protein 3g **% Daily Value:** Vitamin A 15%; Vitamin C 45%; Calcium 15%; Iron 15% **Exchanges:** 1 Starch, ½ Fruit **Carbohydrate Choices:** 1½

Start Happy Tip
Blueberries provide antioxidants, which are believed to reduce the risk of cancer and heart disease.

mixed-berry cream parfaits

prep time: 10 Minutes ※ **start to finish:** 10 Minutes ※ 4 Parfaits

¾ cup fresh blueberries

¾ cup fresh blackberries

¾ cup fresh raspberries

2 cups creamy vanilla or creamy strawberry low-fat yogurt (from 2-lb container)

2 roasted almond crunchy granola bars (1 pouch from 8.9-oz box)

1 Divide berries among 4 parfait glasses or dessert dishes. Top each with ½ cup yogurt.

2 While granola bars are still in the pouch, break into coarse pieces with hands. Sprinkle granola pieces over fruit and yogurt. Serve immediately.

1 Parfait: Calories 190; Total Fat 3g (Saturated Fat 1g, Trans Fat 0g); Cholesterol 0mg; Sodium 105mg; Total Carbohydrate 36g (Dietary Fiber 4g); Protein 5g **% Daily Value:** Vitamin A 10%; Vitamin C 25%; Calcium 15%; Iron 4% **Exchanges:** 1 Fruit, 1 Other Carbohydrate, ½ Skim Milk, ½ Fat **Carbohydrate Choices:** 2½

Start Happy Tip

Make these delicious parfaits in plastic cups or small dishes, then grab a plastic spoon on your way out the door!

ambrosia breakfast parfaits

prep time: 10 Minutes ❄ **start to finish:** 10 Minutes ❄ 4 Parfaits

2 cups Honey Nut Cheerios cereal or Multigrain Cheerios® cereal

2 cups French vanilla low-fat yogurt (from 2-lb container)

1 can (8 oz) crushed pineapple in juice, drained

1 medium banana, sliced

1 can (11 oz) mandarin orange segments in light syrup, drained

¼ cup flaked coconut, toasted*

4 fresh strawberries, sliced

1 Place ¼ cup cereal in each of 4 parfait glasses.

2 In small bowl, stir together yogurt and pineapple. Spoon ¼ cup yogurt mixture on top of cereal in each glass. Top each with ¼ cup cereal, then with ¼ of the banana slices

3 Spoon remaining yogurt mixture onto banana in each; top each with orange segments. Sprinkle with coconut. Garnish with strawberries.

*To toast coconut, sprinkle in an ungreased skillet and cook over medium-low heat 6 to 14 minutes, stirring frequently until browning begins, then stirring constantly until golden brown.

1 Serving: Calories 310 (Calories from Fat 35); Total Fat 4g (Saturated Fat 2g, Trans Fat 0g); Cholesterol 0mg; Sodium 200mg; Total Carbohydrate 62g (Dietary Fiber 3g, Sugars 44g); Protein 6g **% Daily Value:** Vitamin A 30%; Vitamin C 50%; Calcium 20%; Iron 20% **Exchanges:** ½ Starch, 1 Fruit, 2 Other Carbohydrate, ½ Skim Milk, 1 Fat **Carbohydrate Choices:** 4

granola

prep time: 10 Minutes ⁑ **start to finish:** 1 Hour 10 Minutes ⁑ 8 Servings (½ cup each)

3 cups old-fashioned or quick-cooking oats

1 cup whole almonds

1 teaspoon ground cinnamon

⅓ cup real maple syrup or honey

½ cup dried cherries

½ cup dried blueberries

1 Heat oven to 300°F. Spread oats and almonds evenly in ungreased 15x10x1-inch pan. Sprinkle evenly with cinnamon; drizzle with syrup. Toss to coat; spread mixture evenly in pan.

2 Bake 15 minutes. Remove from oven. Stir well to mix so granola dries evenly. Spread mixture evenly in pan. Bake 15 minutes longer or until mixture is dry and lightly toasted. Cool completely in pan, about 30 minutes.

3 Place granola in container with tight-fitting lid or resealable food-storage plastic bag. Add dried fruit; stir to distribute. Cover tightly. Store granola at room temperature up to 1 month.

1 Serving: Calories 330; Total Fat 11g (Saturated Fat 1g, Trans Fat 0g); Cholesterol 0mg; Sodium 0mg; Total Carbohydrate 50g (Dietary Fiber 7g); Protein 8g **% Daily Value:** Vitamin A 0%; Vitamin C 0%; Calcium 8%; Iron 15% **Exchanges:** 2 Starch, 1½ Other Carbohydrate, 2 Fat **Carbohydrate Choices:** 3

Start Happy Tip

Make this granola to suit your taste. Walnuts or pecans can be added or substituted for the almonds, and dried cranberries or golden raisins can be used.

green tea granola

prep time: 15 Minutes ❈ start to finish: 1 Hour 55 Minutes ❈ 20 Servings (½ cup each)

6 cups Fiber One® Honey Clusters® cereal

1 cup cashew halves

1 cup sesame sticks

¼ cup packed brown sugar

½ cup strong brewed green tea (2 bags per ½ cup hot water)

2 tablespoons honey

2 tablespoons canola or vegetable oil

½ cup chopped dried mangoes

½ cup sweetened dried cranberries

1 Heat oven to 250°F. Spray 15x10x1-inch pan with cooking spray. In large bowl, mix cereal, cashews and sesame sticks.

2 In 1-quart saucepan, mix brown sugar, tea, honey and oil. Cook over medium heat 3 to 4 minutes, stirring constantly, until brown sugar is melted. Pour mixture over cereal mixture; toss to coat well. Spread mixture in pan.

3 Bake 30 minutes. Stir well. Bake 10 minutes longer. Stir in mangoes and cranberries. Cool completely in pan, about 1 hour. Store granola in tightly covered container.

1 Serving: Calories 170; Total Fat 5g (Saturated Fat 0.5g, Trans Fat 0g); Cholesterol 0mg; Sodium 115mg; Total Carbohydrate 27g (Dietary Fiber 4g); Protein 2g **% Daily Value:** Vitamin A 4%; Vitamin C 0%; Calcium 4%; Iron 10% **Exchanges:** 1 Starch, 1 Other Carbohydrate, ½ Fat **Carbohydrate Choices:** 2

Start Happy Tip

Replacing saturated fats with unsaturated fats from nuts may help lower blood cholesterol. But since fats are high in calories, keep portions small.

triple-berry oatmeal-flax muesli

prep time: 5 Minutes ✳ **start to finish:** 40 Minutes ✳ 6 Servings

2¾ cups old-fashioned oats or rolled barley flakes

½ cup sliced almonds

2 containers (6 oz each) banana crème or French vanilla low-fat yogurt

1½ cups milk

¼ cup ground flaxseed or flaxseed meal

½ cup fresh blueberries

½ cup fresh raspberries

½ cup sliced fresh strawberries

1 Heat oven to 350°F. On ungreased cookie sheet, spread oats and almonds. Bake 18 to 20 minutes, stirring occasionally, until light golden brown. Cool 15 minutes.

2 In large bowl, mix yogurt and milk until well blended. Stir in oats, almonds and flaxseed. Top each serving with berries.

1 Serving: Calories 320; Total Fat 10g (Saturated Fat 2g, Trans Fat 0g); Cholesterol 5mg; Sodium 60mg; Total Carbohydrate 46g (Dietary Fiber 8g); Protein 13g **% Daily Value:** Vitamin A 8%; Vitamin C 10%; Calcium 20%; Iron 15% **Exchanges:** 2 Starch, 1 Other Carbohydrate, 1 High-Fat Meat **Carbohydrate Choices:** 3

Start Happy Tip

If you like soy milk, go ahead and substitute it for the regular milk.

lemon muesli

prep time: 10 Minutes ✳ **start to finish:** 8 Hours 10 Minutes ✳ 3 Servings

½ cup fat-free (skim) milk

1 cup old-fashioned oats

½ cup lemon or orange fat-free yogurt

1 tablespoon packed brown sugar

2 tablespoons raisins or chopped dried fruit

½ medium banana, chopped

3 tablespoons ground flaxseed or flaxseed meal

1 Pour milk over oats in medium bowl. Cover; refrigerate at least 8 hours but no longer than 12 hours.

2 Just before serving, stir in yogurt, brown sugar, raisins and banana. Divide among 3 bowls. Sprinkle each with flaxseed.

1 Serving: Calories 250 (Calories from Fat 40); Total Fat 4.5g (Saturated Fat 0.5g, Trans Fat 0g); Cholesterol 0mg; Sodium 50mg; Total Carbohydrate 44g (Dietary Fiber 5g); Protein 9g **% Daily Value:** Vitamin A 0%; Vitamin C 2%; Calcium 15%; Iron 10% **Exchanges:** 2½ Starch, ½ Fruit **Carbohydrate Choices:** 3

Start Happy Tip

Look for the flaxseed or flaxseed meal at the health or natural foods store. This is also a great location to purchase the dried fruit and oats.

chex® breakfast-to-go

prep time: 10 Minutes ❊ **start to finish:** 25 Minutes ❊ **7 Servings (½ cup each)**

- 2 tablespoons sugar
- ¼ teaspoon ground cinnamon
- 3 tablespoons butter
- ½ cup Corn Chex® cereal
- ½ cup Rice Chex® cereal
- ½ cup Wheat Chex® cereal
- ½ cup Honey Nut Cheerios cereal
- ⅓ cup toasted sliced almonds*
- ½ cup dried banana chips
- ¼ cup dried blueberries or raisins

1 In small bowl, mix sugar and cinnamon; set aside.

2 In medium microwavable bowl, microwave butter uncovered on High about 30 seconds or until melted. Stir in cereals and almonds until evenly coated. Microwave uncovered on High 2 minutes, stirring after 1 minute.

3 Stir in sugar mixture and banana chips until evenly coated. Microwave uncovered on High 1 minute. Spread on paper towels; cool about 15 minutes.

4 Place in serving bowl. Stir in blueberries. Store mixture in tightly covered container.

Oven Directions: Heat oven to 300°F. In small bowl, mix sugar and cinnamon; set aside. In ungreased 13x9-inch pan, melt butter in oven. Stir in cereals and almonds until evenly coated. Bake uncovered 10 minutes. Stir in sugar mixture and banana chips until evenly coated. Bake 10 to 15 minutes longer or until banana chips just begin to brown. Spread on paper towels; cool about 15 minutes. Place in serving bowl. Stir in blueberries. Store mixture in tightly covered container.

*To toast almonds, sprinkle in ungreased skillet. Cook over medium heat 5 to 7 minutes, stirring frequently until almonds begin to brown, then stirring constantly until almonds are light brown.

1 Serving: Calories 180; Total Fat 9g (Saturated Fat 5g, Trans Fat 0g); Cholesterol 15mg; Sodium 130mg; Total Carbohydrate 22g (Dietary Fiber 3g); Protein 2g **% Daily Value:** Vitamin A 6%; Vitamin C 0%; Calcium 4%; Iron 20% **Exchanges:** 1 Starch, ½ Other Carbohydrate, 1½ Fat **Carbohydrate Choices:** 1½

Start Happy Tips

Store this hearty morning mix in small food-storage plastic bags for on-the-run mornings.

Layer the mix with your favorite yogurt in a disposable covered container for a parfait-to-go!

eggs,
bacon
&
more

skillet eggs with summer squash hash

prep time: 35 Minutes ❋ **start to finish:** 1 Hour 15 Minutes ❋ 4 Servings

2 medium yellow summer squash (1 lb)

2 medium zucchini (1 lb)

1 teaspoon salt

1 tablespoon olive oil

¼ cup chopped red onion

1 small tomato, chopped (½ cup)

½ cup diced cooked 95% fat-free ham

1 tablespoon chopped fresh dill weed

1 teaspoon grated lemon peel

4 eggs

⅛ teaspoon pepper

1 Shred yellow squash and zucchini; place in large colander. Stir in salt; let stand in sink 30 minutes to drain.

2 Gently rinse squash to remove excess salt. Squeeze squash mixture to remove as much liquid as possible. Set aside.

3 In 12-inch nonstick skillet, heat oil over medium-high heat. Add onion; cook 2 minutes, stirring frequently. Stir in squash mixture. Cook 8 minutes, stirring occasionally, until vegetables are crisp-tender. Add tomato, ham, dill and lemon peel; cook and stir 1 minute longer. Reduce heat to medium.

4 Spread squash mixture evenly in skillet. Make 4 (2½-inch-wide) indentations in mixture with back of spoon. Break eggs, one at a time, into custard cup or saucer; slide into indentations. Sprinkle eggs with pepper. Cover; cook 8 to 10 minutes or until whites and yolks are firm, not runny.

1 Serving: Calories 260; Total Fat 13g (Saturated Fat 3.5g, Trans Fat 0g); Cholesterol 225mg; Sodium 1550mg; Total Carbohydrate 10g (Dietary Fiber 2g); Protein 24g **% Daily Value:** Vitamin A 15%; Vitamin C 30%; Calcium 6%; Iron 15% **Exchanges:** 2 Vegetable, 2 Very Lean Meat, 1 Medium-Fat Meat, 1½ Fat **Carbohydrate Choices:** ½

Start Happy Tip

Add 1 cup finely chopped red bell pepper with the zucchini and squash for a dish that's rich in vitamin C, beta-carotene and about 10 calories more per serving.

breakfast egg scramble with brie

prep time: 20 Minutes ✳ start to finish: 20 Minutes ✳ 4 Servings

10 eggs
2 tablespoons milk
2 tablespoons butter
5 oz Canadian bacon, finely chopped (about 1 cup)
2 cups loosely packed fresh baby spinach
4 oz Brie cheese, rind removed, cut into ½-inch pieces
4 English muffins, split, toasted

1 In large bowl, beat eggs and milk with fork or whisk. Set aside.

2 In 12-inch nonstick skillet, melt butter over medium heat. Add Canadian bacon and spinach; cook and stir 1 minute or just until spinach begins to wilt.

3 Pour egg mixture over spinach mixture. Add cheese; cook 3 to 5 minutes longer, stirring occasionally, until eggs are set but slightly moist. Spoon ½ cup egg mixture onto each muffin half.

1 Serving: Calories 540; Total Fat 31g (Saturated Fat 14g, Trans Fat 0g); Cholesterol 595mg; Sodium 1180mg; Total Carbohydrate 28g (Dietary Fiber 2g); Protein 36g **% Daily Value:** Vitamin A 50%; Vitamin C 4%; Calcium 25%; Iron 25% **Exchanges:** 1½ Starch, ½ Vegetable, 4½ Lean Meat, 3½ Fat **Carbohydrate Choices:** 2

Start Happy Tips

For the best flavor, Brie should be very ripe. Select a round of Brie that is plump; the rind might have some pale edges. Use Brie within a few days, as it does not keep well.

This classy egg dish is great for brunch, paired with your favorite fresh fruits.

sausage-wrapped stuffed chiles

prep time: 45 Minutes ❊ **start to finish:** 1 Hour 15 Minutes ❊ 10 Servings

20 canned whole jalapeño chiles

3 cups shredded sharp Cheddar cheese (12 oz)

2 cups shredded Monterey Jack cheese (8 oz)

1 lb bulk mild pork sausage

2 cups Original Bisquick® mix

2 eggs, beaten

1 package (6 oz) seasoned coating mix for pork

1 Heat oven to 375°F. Spray 15x10x1-inch pan with cooking spray.

2 Cut lengthwise slit on one side of each chile, leaving other side intact; remove seeds. Stuff each chile with about 2 teaspoons Cheddar cheese. Pinch edges to close; set aside.

3 In large bowl, mix remaining Cheddar cheese, the Monterey Jack cheese, sausage and Bisquick mix. Shape about 2 rounded tablespoonfuls of sausage mixture into ¼-inch-thick patties. Place 1 stuffed chile in center of each patty; wrap mixture around chile. Dip into eggs; roll in coating mix. Place in pan.

4 Bake 30 minutes or until golden.

1 Serving: Calories 490; Total Fat 30g (Saturated Fat 15g, Trans Fat 1g); Cholesterol 110mg; Sodium 1900mg; Total Carbohydrate 31g (Dietary Fiber 1g); Protein 23g **% Daily Value:** Vitamin A 25%; Vitamin C 4%; Calcium 40%; Iron 15% **Exchanges:** ½ Starch, 1½ Other Carbohydrate, 3 High-Fat Meat, 1 Fat **Carbohydrate Choices:** 2

Start Happy Tip

Unbaked sausage-wrapped chiles can be refrigerated up to 2 hours before baking or frozen up to 1 month. If frozen, add about 5 minutes to the baking time.

scrambled eggs with havarti and wine

prep time: 20 Minutes ❄ **start to finish:** 20 Minutes ❄ 4 Servings

8 eggs

¼ cup dry white wine or nonalcoholic wine

¼ teaspoon salt

¼ teaspoon pepper

2 tablespoons chopped fresh parsley

2 medium green onions, sliced (2 tablespoons)

2 tablespoons butter

4 oz Havarti cheese with dill weed, cut into ½-inch cubes

Additional chopped fresh parsley or dill weed, if desired

1 In medium bowl, beat eggs, wine, salt, pepper, 2 tablespoons parsley and the onions thoroughly with fork or whisk until well mixed.

2 In 10-inch nonstick skillet, heat butter over medium heat just until butter begins to sizzle. Pour egg mixture into skillet. Sprinkle cheese evenly over eggs.

3 As mixture begins to set at bottom and side, gently lift cooked portions with spatula so that thin, uncooked portion can flow to bottom. Avoid constant stirring. Cook 3 to 4 minutes or until eggs are thickened throughout but still moist. Garnish with additional parsley.

1 Serving: Calories 320; Total Fat 27g (Saturated Fat 14g, Trans Fat 0.5g); Cholesterol 470mg; Sodium 530mg; Total Carbohydrate 2g (Dietary Fiber 0g); Protein 19g **% Daily Value:** Vitamin A 25%; Vitamin C 2%; Calcium 20%; Iron 8% **Exchanges:** 2½ Medium-Fat Meat, 3 Fat **Carbohydrate Choices:** 0

Start Happy Tip

When this recipe made a showing in our test kitchens, people raved. It's luscious, creamy and sophisticated—perfect for a special brunch as well as a light, elegant dinner. Serve the eggs with hash browns and brown-and-serve sausage links or bacon, and some warmed scones or muffins.

home-style scrambled eggs

prep time: 15 Minutes ❊ **start to finish:** 20 Minutes ❊ 4 Servings

6 eggs

¾ teaspoon salt

3 tablespoons water

¼ cup butter

1 cup refrigerated diced potatoes with onions or frozen hash brown potatoes

1 small zucchini, chopped (1 cup)

1 medium tomato, seeded, chopped (¾ cup)

1 In medium bowl, beat eggs, salt and water with fork or whisk. In 10-inch skillet, melt butter over medium heat. Add potatoes, zucchini and tomato; cook, stirring occasionally, until hot.

2 Pour egg mixture over vegetable mixture. As mixture begins to set at bottom and side, gently lift cooked portions with spatula so that thin, uncooked portion can flow to bottom. Avoid constant stirring. Cook 3 to 5 minutes or until eggs are thickened throughout but still moist.

1 Serving: Calories 260; Total Fat 20g (Saturated Fat 10g, Trans Fat 0g); Cholesterol 350mg; Sodium 690mg; Total Carbohydrate 10g (Dietary Fiber 1g); Protein 11g **% Daily Value:** Vitamin A 20%; Vitamin C 10%; Calcium 4%; Iron 6% **Exchanges:** ½ Starch, ½ Vegetable, 1 Medium-Fat Meat, 3 Fat **Carbohydrate Choices:** ½

Start Happy Tip

Do your scrambled eggs end up looking more like rice or peas than the fluffy, moist thick eggs from a restaurant? The trick is to stir them as little as possible while they cook.

breakfast skillet

prep time: 25 Minutes ❋ **start to finish:** 40 Minutes ❋ 4 Servings

¾ lb bacon, cut into 1-inch pieces

3 cups refrigerated cooked shredded hash brown potatoes (from 20-oz bag)

3 eggs

1 can (4.5 oz) chopped green chiles, drained

¾ cup shredded Cheddar cheese (3 oz)

1 medium tomato, chopped (¾ cup)

1 In 10-inch nonstick skillet, cook bacon over medium heat 5 to 7 minutes, stirring occasionally, until crisp. (Drain, reserving 2 tablespoons drippings and bacon in pan.)

2 Add potatoes to skillet; spread evenly. Cook 8 to 10 minutes, stirring occasionally, until brown.

3 In small bowl, beat eggs and chiles with fork or whisk. Pour egg mixture evenly over potatoes. Reduce heat to low; cover and cook 8 to 10 minutes or until eggs are firm. Sprinkle with cheese and tomato; cover and cook 2 to 4 minutes or until cheese is melted.

1 Serving: Calories 420; Total Fat 21g (Saturated Fat 9g, Trans Fat 0g); Cholesterol 210mg; Sodium 890mg; Total Carbohydrate 35g (Dietary Fiber 3g); Protein 21g **% Daily Value:** Vitamin A 15%; Vitamin C 20%; Calcium 15%; Iron 8% **Exchanges:** 1½ Starch, ½ Other Carbohydrate, 2½ High-Fat Meat **Carbohydrate Choices:** 2

Start Happy Tips

For a little more spice, try using pepper Jack cheese instead of Cheddar.

If desired, garnish with chopped green onions.

broccoli, potato and chorizo scramble

prep time: 20 Minutes ✳ **start to finish:** 20 Minutes ✳ 6 Servings (1 cup each)

6 eggs

¼ cup milk

¼ teaspoon dried oregano leaves

1 clove garlic, chopped

1 bag (19 oz) frozen roasted potatoes with broccoli and cheese sauce

½ lb fully cooked chorizo sausage links, casing removed, chopped

1 can (4.5 oz) chopped green chiles, drained

½ cup shredded Cheddar cheese (2 oz)

Chunky-style salsa, if desired

1 In small bowl, beat eggs and milk with fork or whisk; stir in oregano and garlic. Set aside. Cook frozen vegetables as directed on bag; set aside.

2 In 12-inch skillet, cook chorizo over medium heat 2 to 3 minutes, stirring frequently, until hot. Stir in cooked vegetables and chiles; blend well.

3 Pour egg mixture over chorizo mixture. Reduce heat to medium-low; cook uncovered about 4 minutes. As mixture begins to set at bottom and side, gently lift cooked portions with spatula so that thin, uncooked portion can flow to bottom. Avoid constant stirring. Cook until eggs are thickened throughout but still moist.

4 Sprinkle cheese over egg mixture. Reduce heat to low. Cover; cook 3 to 5 minutes or until center is set and cheese is melted. Serve with salsa.

1 Serving: Calories 350; Total Fat 24g (Saturated Fat 9g, Trans Fat 0g); Cholesterol 255mg; Sodium 980mg; Total Carbohydrate 13g (Dietary Fiber 1g); Protein 20g **% Daily Value:** Vitamin A 10%; Vitamin C 15%; Calcium 10%; Iron 10% **Exchanges:** ½ Starch, ½ Low-Fat Milk, ½ Vegetable, 2 Medium-Fat Meat, 2 Fat **Carbohydrate Choices:** 1

Start Happy Tip

Chorizo can be purchased in bulk form without casing.

bacon and cheese blintzes

prep time: 35 Minutes ⁑ **start to finish:** 35 Minutes ⁑ 5 Servings (2 blintzes each)

½ cup Original Bisquick mix

½ cup milk

¼ cup butter, melted

8 eggs

4 tablespoons butter

¼ cup whipping cream or half-and-half

1 package (3 oz) cream cheese, cut into small pieces

½ cup chopped green onions (8 medium)

¼ teaspoon salt

⅛ teaspoon freshly ground pepper

8 slices bacon, crisply cooked, crumbled

½ cup shredded Cheddar cheese (2 oz)

1 In small bowl, beat Bisquick mix, milk, melted butter and 2 of the eggs with whisk until blended. In 6- to 7-inch skillet or crepe pan, heat 1 tablespoon of the butter over medium heat until bubbly. For each crepe, pour 2 tablespoons batter into skillet. Immediately tilt and rotate skillet until batter covers bottom; cook until light brown. Run wide spatula around edge to loosen; turn and cook other side until light brown. Stack crepes with waxed paper between each; keep covered.

2 In medium bowl, beat remaining 6 eggs and the whipping cream with fork or whisk until blended. Stir in cream cheese, ¼ cup of the onions, the salt and pepper. In 12-inch skillet, heat 1 tablespoon of the butter over medium heat just until it begins to sizzle. Add egg mixture; cook 3 to 4 minutes, stirring frequently but not constantly, until eggs are thickened throughout but still moist.

3 To make blintzes, spoon 3 tablespoons egg mixture in center of each crepe. Sprinkle with bacon. Fold sides and ends of crepe over filling to form rectangle.

4 In same skillet, melt 1 tablespoon of the butter over medium heat. Add 5 blintzes, seam side down, to skillet; cook 1 to 2 minutes, turning once, until golden brown. Remove from skillet to serving platter. Repeat with remaining 1 tablespoon butter and 5 blintzes. Sprinkle blintzes with Cheddar cheese and remaining onions.

1 Serving: Calories 550; Total Fat 46g (Saturated Fat 24g, Trans Fat 1.5g); Cholesterol 405mg; Sodium 940mg; Total Carbohydrate 12g (Dietary Fiber 0g); Protein 21g **% Daily Value:** Vitamin A 30%; Vitamin C 0%; Calcium 20%; Iron 10% **Exchanges:** 1 Other Carbohydrate, 2 Medium-Fat Meat, 1 High-Fat Meat, 5½ Fat **Carbohydrate Choices:** 1

Start Happy Tip

Blintzes are similar to thin crepe-like pancakes but with a heartier texture. You can stuff blintzes with a sweet or savory filling for a breakfast, brunch, dinner or dessert dish.

gluten-free rosemary-potato frittata

prep time: 35 Minutes ❋ **start to finish:** 35 Minutes ❋ 8 Servings

10 grape tomatoes, cut in half

Olive oil cooking spray

2 teaspoons chopped fresh rosemary leaves

6 eggs

¼ cup milk

¼ cup Bisquick® Gluten Free mix

¼ teaspoon salt

¼ teaspoon pepper

1 tablespoon olive oil

2 small unpeeled red potatoes, cut into cubes (1 cup)

4 oz fresh spinach leaves, stems removed, chopped (about 5 cups loosely packed)

½ cup gluten-free shredded Parmesan cheese (2 oz)

Additional chopped fresh rosemary leaves, if desired

1 Spray tomatoes with cooking spray. In 10-inch nonstick skillet with sloping sides, cook tomatoes and 1 teaspoon of the rosemary over medium-high heat 4 to 5 minutes or until browned. Remove from heat; place in small bowl.

2 In medium bowl, beat eggs and milk with fork or whisk until blended. Stir in Bisquick mix, salt and pepper. Set aside.

3 In same skillet, heat oil over medium heat. Add potatoes; cook about 6 minutes, stirring frequently, until tender. Add spinach and remaining 1 teaspoon rosemary; cook 1 to 2 minutes or until spinach is wilted. Reduce heat to low. Spread potatoes and spinach in skillet; top with tomatoes.

4 Pour egg mixture over top. Stir well with rubber spatula. Cover; cook 14 to 15 minutes, lifting edges occasionally to allow uncooked egg mixture to flow to bottom of skillet, until bottom is lightly browned and set.

5 Sprinkle cheese over top. Cover; cook 1 minute longer. Garnish with additional rosemary.

1 Serving: Calories 140; Total Fat 8g (Saturated Fat 2.5g, Trans Fat 0g); Cholesterol 145mg; Sodium 300mg; Total Carbohydrate 8g (Dietary Fiber 1g); Protein 8g **% Daily Value:** Vitamin A 45%; Vitamin C 8%; Calcium 15%; Iron 6% **Exchanges:** ½ Other Carbohydrate, ½ Vegetable, 1 Medium-Fat Meat, ½ Fat **Carbohydrate Choices:** ½

Start Happy Tip

If you are cooking gluten free, always read labels to be sure each recipe ingredient is gluten free. Products and ingredient sources can change.

smoked salmon and herb frittata

prep time: 30 Minutes ☼ **start to finish:** 30 Minutes ☼ 4 Servings

6 eggs

2 tablespoons half-and-half or milk

2 tablespoons chopped fresh chives (½-inch pieces)

1 tablespoon coarsely chopped fresh dill weed

¼ teaspoon freshly ground pepper

1 package (3 oz) sliced smoked salmon, cut into 1½-inch pieces

2 teaspoons olive oil

1 package (3 oz) cream cheese, softened

Lemon wedges

1 In medium bowl, beat eggs, half-and-half, chives, dill and pepper with fork or whisk. Gently fold in salmon.

2 In 9- to 10-inch nonstick skillet with sloping sides, heat oil over low heat. Pour egg mixture into skillet. Using 2 teaspoons, drop cream cheese over egg mixture.

3 Cover; cook 12 to 15 minutes or until lightly browned and bottom is set, lifting edges occasionally to allow uncooked egg mixture to flow to bottom of skillet. Cut into 8 wedges. Garnish with lemon wedges.

1 Serving: Calories 240; Total Fat 19g (Saturated Fat 8g, Trans Fat 0g); Cholesterol 350mg; Sodium 330mg; Total Carbohydrate 2g (Dietary Fiber 0g); Protein 15g **% Daily Value:** Vitamin A 15%; Vitamin C 0%; Calcium 8%; Iron 6% **Exchanges:** ½ Lean Meat, 1½ Medium-Fat Meat, 2 Fat **Carbohydrate Choices:** 0

Start Happy Tips

A frittata is an Italian-style omelet with ingredients stirred in that is cooked slowly over low heat. Be creative, substituting your favorite seasonings and ingredients.

This frittata can be served warm or cold.

potato-crusted frittata

prep time: 20 Minutes ⁕ **start to finish:** 40 Minutes ⁕ 6 Servings

1 box (4.5 oz) seasoned roasted garlic and herb skillet potatoes

Water and vegetable oil called for on potato box

1 package (8 oz) sliced fresh mushrooms (about 3 cups)

1 medium onion, chopped (½ cup)

1 medium green or red bell pepper, seeded, chopped

½ cup shredded Cheddar cheese (2 oz)

6 eggs

¼ cup whipping cream or half-and-half

1 Heat oven to 375°F. Make potatoes as directed on box in ovenproof 10-inch nonstick skillet, using water and oil.

2 Meanwhile, in another 10-inch nonstick skillet, cook mushrooms, onion and bell pepper over medium-high heat about 5 minutes, stirring frequently, until vegetables begin to soften.

3 When potatoes are done, sprinkle cooked vegetables and cheese over top. In medium bowl, beat eggs and cream with whisk; pour over cheese.

4 Bake about 20 minutes or until eggs are set. Run spatula around side of frittata to loosen. Carefully turn upside down onto platter; cut into 6 wedges.

1 Serving: Calories 290; Total Fat 18g (Saturated Fat 7g, Trans Fat 0g); Cholesterol 235mg; Sodium 440mg; Total Carbohydrate 20g (Dietary Fiber 2g); Protein 11g **% Daily Value:** Vitamin A 10%; Vitamin C 15%; Calcium 10%; Iron 6% **Exchanges:** 1 Starch, ½ Vegetable, 1 Medium-Fat Meat, 2½ Fat **Carbohydrate Choices:** 1

Start Happy Tip
Serve this breakfast dish with a side of fresh fruit to complete the meal.

classic omelet

prep time: 10 Minutes ☀ **start to finish:** 40 Minutes ☀ 4 Omelets

8 eggs

Salt and pepper, if desired

8 teaspoons butter

Cheese Omelet: Before folding omelet, sprinkle with ¼ cup shredded Cheddar, Monterey Jack or Swiss cheese, or ¼ cup crumbled blue cheese.

Denver Omelet: Before adding eggs to pan, cook 2 tablespoons chopped fully cooked ham, 1 tablespoon finely chopped bell pepper and 1 tablespoon finely chopped onion in butter about 2 minutes, stirring frequently. Continue as directed in Step 2.

Ham and Cheese Omelet: Before folding omelet, sprinkle with 2 tablespoons shredded Cheddar, Monterey Jack or Swiss cheese and 2 tablespoons finely chopped fully cooked ham.

1 For each omelet, in small bowl, beat 2 of the eggs until fluffy. Add salt and pepper to taste. In 8-inch nonstick omelet pan or skillet, heat 2 teaspoons of the butter over medium-high heat just until butter is hot and sizzling. As butter melts, tilt pan to coat bottom.

2 Quickly pour eggs into pan. While rapidly sliding pan back and forth over heat, quickly and continuously stir with spatula to spread eggs over bottom of pan as they thicken. Let stand over heat a few seconds to lightly brown bottom of omelet. Do not overcook; omelet will continue to cook after folding. If desired, add filling (see Omelet Fillings, page 129) before folding.

3 To remove from pan, first run spatula under one edge of omelet, folding about one-third of it to the center. Transfer to plate by tilting pan, letting flat, unfolded edge of omelet slide out onto plate. Using edge of pan as a guide, flip folded edge of omelet over the flat portion on the plate.

4 Repeat with remaining butter and eggs. If desired, omelets can be kept warm on platter in 200°F oven while preparing remaining omelets.

1 Omelet: Calories 220; Total Fat 18g (Saturated Fat 7g, Trans Fat 0g); Cholesterol 445mg; Sodium 170mg; Total Carbohydrate 1g (Dietary Fiber 0g); Protein 13g **% Daily Value:** Vitamin A 15%; Vitamin C 0%; Calcium 6%; Iron 6% **Exchanges:** 2 Medium-Fat Meat, 1½ Fat **Carbohydrate Choices:** 0

Start Happy Tip

For about 8 grams of fat and 130 calories per serving, substitute ½ cup fat-free egg product for 2 egg each omelet (2 eggs).

Omelet Fillings

Wake up those taste buds with one of these tasty fillings. For cooked fillings, make them first, then keep warm while cooking the omelets. Some fillings are difficult to measure, but in general, for each omelet, plan to use ¼ to ⅓ cup filling. Add filling to one side of the omelet, then fold the remaining side over the filling.

1 **Avocado, Bacon and Cheddar Filling:** Avocado slices, crisply cooked crumbled bacon and shredded Cheddar cheese.

2 **Buffalo Chicken and Green Onion Filling:** Heat 1 cup cut-up cooked chicken with ⅓ cup bottled buffalo wing sauce until warm. Spoon onto omelets; sprinkle with sliced green onions.

3 **Caprese Filling:** Tomato slices, thinly sliced fresh mozzarella and fresh basil leaves.

4 **Chorizo and Black Bean Salsa Filling:** Crumble and cook ½ pound bulk fresh chorizo sausage in skillet; cook and stir until no longer pink. Stir in ¼ cup each drained black beans and salsa; heat through.

5 **Crab, Artichoke and Corn Filling:** Layer each omelet with about ¼ cup chopped cooked crabmeat or imitation crabmeat pieces, 1 or 2 sliced marinated artichoke hearts from jar, drained, and 2 to 3 tablespoons whole kernel corn from 11-ounce can, drained.

6 **Cucumber and Greek Yogurt Filling:** Thinly sliced cucumbers, Greek yogurt and chopped fresh or dried dill.

7 **Greek Spinach and Feta Filling:** Fresh spinach leaves, red onion slices, sliced pitted kalamata olives and crumbled feta cheese.

8 **Italian Turkey Sausage and Bell Pepper Filling:** Remove casings from 4 Italian turkey sausages. Crumble sausage in skillet and cook with ½ cup each chopped bell pepper and onion until sausage is no longer pink and vegetables are tender.

9 **Sun-Dried Tomato and Goat Cheese Filling:** Chopped sun-dried tomatoes in oil, drained, crumbled goat cheese and chopped chives.

10 **Swiss, Mushroom and Thyme Filling:** In small nonstick skillet, melt 1 teaspoon butter over medium heat. Stir in 1½ cups sliced mushrooms and ½ teaspoon dried thyme leaves. Cook 4 to 6 minutes or until tender, stirring occasionally. Spoon onto omelets; sprinkle with shredded Swiss cheese.

veggie-stuffed omelet

prep time: 15 Minutes ✳ **start to finish:** 15 Minutes ✳ 1 Omelet

1 teaspoon olive or vegetable oil

2 tablespoons chopped red bell pepper

1 tablespoon chopped onion

¼ cup sliced mushrooms

1 cup loosely packed fresh baby spinach leaves, rinsed

½ cup fat-free egg product or 2 eggs, beaten

1 tablespoon water

Dash salt

Dash pepper

1 tablespoon shredded reduced-fat Cheddar cheese

1 In 8-inch nonstick skillet, heat oil over medium-high heat. Add bell pepper, onion and mushrooms to oil. Cook 2 minutes, stirring frequently, until onion is tender. Stir in spinach; continue cooking and stirring just until spinach wilts. Remove vegetables from pan to small bowl.

2 In medium bowl, beat egg product, water, salt and pepper with fork or whisk until well mixed. Reheat same skillet over medium-high heat. Quickly pour egg mixture into pan. While rapidly sliding pan back and forth over heat, quickly and continuously stir with spatula to spread eggs over bottom of pan as they thicken. Let stand over heat a few seconds to lightly brown bottom of omelet. Do not overcook; omelet will continue to cook after folding.

3 Place cooked vegetable mixture over half of omelet; top with cheese. With spatula, fold other half of omelet over vegetables. Gently slide out of pan onto plate. Serve immediately.

1 Omelet: Calories 140 (Calories from Fat 50); Total Fat 5g (Saturated Fat 1g, Trans Fat 0g); Cholesterol 0mg; Sodium 470mg; Total Carbohydrate 6g (Dietary Fiber 2g, Sugars 3g); Protein 16g **% Daily Value:** Vitamin A 100%; Vitamin C 30%; Calcium 15%; Iron 20% **Exchanges:** 1 Vegetable, 2 Very Lean Meat, 1 Fat **Carbohydrate Choices:** ½

Start Happy Tip

To make 2 omelets, double all of the ingredients and cook the egg mixture in 2 batches. Keep the first omelet warm by placing it on a warm plate. Topping each omelet with about 1 tablespoon salsa or hot sauce adds an extra burst of flavor.

huevos rancheros

prep time: 1 Hour ✳ **start to finish:** 1 Hour ✳ 6 Servings

½ lb bulk uncooked chorizo or pork sausage

Vegetable oil

6 corn tortillas (6 to 7 inch)

1¼ cups chunky-style salsa

6 fried eggs

1½ cups shredded Cheddar cheese (6 oz)

1 In 8-inch skillet, cook sausage over medium heat 8 to 10 minutes, stirring occasionally, until no longer pink; drain and keep warm.

2 In same skillet, heat ⅛ inch oil over medium heat just until hot. Cook 1 tortilla at a time in oil about 1 minute, turning once, until crisp; drain.

3 In 1-quart saucepan, heat salsa, stirring occasionally, until hot.

4 Spread 1 tablespoon salsa over each tortilla to soften. Place 1 fried egg on each tortilla. Top each with 1 tablespoon salsa, some sausage, another tablespoon salsa and ¼ cup cheese.

1 Serving: Calories 490; Total Fat 36g (Saturated Fat 14g, Trans Fat 0g); Cholesterol 250mg; Sodium 1150mg; Total Carbohydrate 16g (Dietary Fiber 2g); Protein 24g **% Daily Value:** Vitamin A 15%; Vitamin C 0%; Calcium 20%; Iron 10% **Exchanges:** 1 Starch, 1 Medium-Fat Meat, 2 High-Fat Meat, 3 Fat **Carbohydrate Choices:** 1

huevos rancheros tarts

prep time: 20 Minutes ❊ **start to finish:** 40 Minutes ❊ 4 Servings

1 can (8 oz) refrigerated crescent dinner rolls

½ teaspoon dried oregano leaves

½ teaspoon chipotle chili powder

¼ teaspoon kosher (coarse) salt

4 eggs

1 can (14.5 oz) fire-roasted tomatoes, undrained

¼ cup chopped onion

1 clove garlic, peeled

4 tablespoons chopped fresh cilantro

1 can (15 oz) black beans, drained, rinsed

½ cup crumbled queso fresco cheese

Avocado slices, if desired

1 Heat oven to 375°F. Line cookie sheet with cooking parchment paper. Separate dough into 4 rectangles on cookie sheet. Firmly press perforations to seal. For each rectangle, roll edges toward center to form 3½-inch-diameter round with ½-inch rim. Press rim firmly to seal.

2 In small bowl, mix oregano leaves, ¼ teaspoon of the chipotle chili powder and the salt. Sprinkle over dough rounds. Break 1 egg in center of each dough round. (Egg may run over slightly.)

3 Bake 16 to 18 minutes or until egg whites and yolks are firm, not runny.

4 Meanwhile, in blender, place tomatoes, onion, garlic, 2 tablespoons of the cilantro and the remaining ¼ teaspoon chipotle chili powder. Cover; blend until smooth. In 2-quart saucepan, heat tomato mixture over medium-high heat 4 to 5 minutes or until hot.

5 Remove and reserve ¾ cup mixture from saucepan; cover to keep warm. Add beans to remaining mixture in saucepan. Cook over medium-high heat 5 minutes, stirring frequently, mashing beans slightly with back of wooden spoon until slightly thickened.

6 For each serving, place about ⅓ cup bean mixture on plate with egg tart. Serve with reserved sauce, cheese, avocado slices and remaining 2 tablespoons cilantro.

1 Serving: Calories 450; Total Fat 22g (Saturated Fat 9g, Trans Fat 0g); Cholesterol 195mg; Sodium 1330mg; Total Carbohydrate 45g (Dietary Fiber 5g); Protein 18g **% Daily Value:** Vitamin A 20%; Vitamin C 2%; Calcium 20%; Iron 20% **Exchanges:** 2½ Starch, ½ Other Carbohydrate, 1 Very Lean Meat, ½ Medium-Fat Meat, 3½ Fat **Carbohydrate Choices:** 3

Start Happy Tip

Queso fresco is a creamy, white Mexican cheese that crumbles easily and can be found in the cheese aisle of most supermarkets. Shredded Monterey Jack cheese can be substituted.

easy mini breakfast sausage pies

prep time: 15 Minutes ❋ **start to finish:** 1 Hour 5 Minutes ❋ 6 Servings (2 mini pies each)

¾ lb bulk pork sausage

1 medium onion, chopped (½ cup)

1 can (4 oz) mushrooms pieces and stems, drained

½ teaspoon salt

3 tablespoons chopped fresh sage leaves

1 cup shredded Cheddar cheese (4 oz)

½ cup Original Bisquick® mix

½ cup milk

2 eggs

1 Heat oven to 375°F. Spray 12 regular-size muffin cups with cooking spray.

2 In 10-inch skillet, cook sausage and onion over medium-high heat 5 to 7 minutes, stirring frequently, until sausage is no longer pink; drain. Cool 5 minutes. Stir in mushrooms, salt, sage and cheese.

3 In medium bowl, stir Bisquick mix, milk and eggs with fork or whisk until blended. Spoon slightly less than 1 tablespoon Bisquick mixture into each muffin cup. Top with about ¼ cup sausage mixture. Spoon 1 tablespoon Bisquick mixture onto sausage mixture in each muffin cup.

4 Bake about 30 minutes or until toothpick inserted in center comes out clean and tops of pies are golden brown. Cool 5 minutes. With thin knife, loosen sides of pies from muffin cups; remove from pan and place top side up on cooling rack. Cool 10 minutes longer before serving.

1 Serving: Calories 250; Total Fat 17g (Saturated Fat 8g, Trans Fat 0.5g); Cholesterol 105mg; Sodium 920mg; Total Carbohydrate 10g (Dietary Fiber 1g); Protein 14g **% Daily Value:** Vitamin A 6%; Vitamin C 0%; Calcium 15%; Iron 6% **Exchanges:** ½ Starch, ½ Vegetable, 1½ High-Fat Meat, 1 Fat **Carbohydrate Choices:** ½

mexican hash brown breakfast cupcakes

prep time: 20 Minutes ❋ **start to finish:** 55 Minutes ❋ 6 Servings (2 cupcakes each)

1 box (5.2 oz) seasoned hash brown potato mix for skillets

Hot water and salt called for on potato box

1 small red onion, diced

1 can (4.5 oz) chopped green chiles

½ cup shredded Cheddar cheese (2 oz)

2 eggs, beaten

1 medium avocado, pitted, peeled and sliced

1 cup sour cream

Fresh cilantro leaves, if desired

1 Heat oven to 375°F. Spray 12 regular-size muffins cups with cooking spray.

2 Make potatoes as directed on box, omitting margarine but using hot water and salt. When done, place in large bowl.

3 Using same skillet, cook onion over medium heat, stirring occasionally, until soft. Add onion, green chiles and cheese to potatoes in bowl. Stir in eggs. Divide mixture evenly among muffin cups, about ⅓ cup each. Press down into cups.

4 Bake 25 to 30 minutes or until tops are golden brown and crispy. Cool 5 minutes. Serve cupcakes with avocado, sour cream and cilantro.

1 Serving: Calories 290; Total Fat 17g (Saturated Fat 7g, Trans Fat 0g); Cholesterol 100mg; Sodium 410mg; Total Carbohydrate 25g (Dietary Fiber 3g); Protein 7g **% Daily Value:** Vitamin A 10%; Vitamin C 8%; Calcium 10%; Iron 4% **Exchanges:** 1½ Starch, 3½ Fat **Carbohydrate Choices:** 1½

Start Happy Tip

Substitute your favorite veggies in these savory cupcakes. Just be sure to cook them first in a skillet, and then mix them in with the potato mixture.

bacon breakfast cupcakes

prep time: 15 Minutes ❋ **start to finish:** 1 Hour 30 Minutes ❋ 12 Servings

1 bag (20 oz) refrigerated shredded hash brown potatoes

2 tablespoons vegetable oil

½ teaspoon salt

¼ teaspoon pepper

6 eggs

2 tablespoons milk

¾ cup crumbled crisply cooked bacon

¾ cup shredded Cheddar cheese (3 oz)

Sriracha sauce

1 Heat oven to 400°F. Place foil baking cup in each of 12 regular-size muffin cups. Generously spray with cooking spray.

2 In large bowl, mix potatoes, oil, salt and pepper. Divide mixture evenly among muffin cups; press lightly.

3 Bake 45 to 55 minutes or until golden brown.

4 In medium bowl, beat eggs and milk. Stir in bacon and cheese. Firmly press potatoes in muffin cups with bottom of ¼-cup dry measuring cup. Top each with slightly less than ¼ cup egg mixture.

5 Bake 13 to 16 minutes longer or until knife inserted in center of egg comes out clean. Cool 5 minutes. Serve with sauce.

1 Serving: Calories 190; Total Fat 9g (Saturated Fat 3.5g, Trans Fat 0g); Cholesterol 105mg; Sodium 450mg; Total Carbohydrate 17g (Dietary Fiber 1g); Protein 8g **% Daily Value:** Vitamin A 4%; Vitamin C 6%; Calcium 6%; Iron 4% **Exchanges:** 1 Starch, ½ Vegetable, ½ High-Fat Meat, 1 Fat **Carbohydrate Choices:** 1

Start Happy Tips

If you don't have Sriracha sauce, serve the cupcakes with your favorite hot sauce or ketchup.

Get a head start by cooking the bacon and shredding the cheese the night before.

mini breakfast quiches with potato crust

prep time: 20 Minutes ❋ **start to finish:** 1 Hour ❋ 6 Servings (2 mini quiches each)

1 box (4.5 oz) seasoned traditional recipe skillet potatoes

Water and vegetable oil called for on potato box

½ cup crumbled cooked bacon

½ cup shredded Swiss cheese (2 oz)

3 eggs

1 cup whipping cream

1 Heat oven to 350°F. Spray 12 regular-size muffin cups with cooking spray.

2 Make potatoes as directed on box, using water and oil. Divide potato mixture evenly among muffin cups, pressing in bottom and up side of each cup to form crust. Sprinkle bacon and cheese evenly in cups.

3 In medium bowl, beat eggs and cream. Pour filling evenly in cups, about ¼ cup each.

4 Bake 25 to 30 minutes or until knife inserted in center comes out clean. Let stand 10 minutes before serving.

1 Serving: Calories 360; Total Fat 28g (Saturated Fat 12g, Trans Fat 0.5g); Cholesterol 165mg; Sodium 590mg; Total Carbohydrate 19g (Dietary Fiber 1g); Protein 10g **% Daily Value:** Vitamin A 10%; Vitamin C 0%; Calcium 10%; Iron 4% **Exchanges:** 1½ Starch, ½ Medium-Fat Meat, 4½ Fat **Carbohydrate Choices:** 1

Start Happy Tip

Instead of the bacon, try substituting ¼ cup cooked spinach, drained. Or vary the flavors by substituting your favorite fillings, such as ham and Cheddar cheese. The quiches will be just as delicious!

balsamic–brown sugar bacon

prep time: 15 Minutes ✴ **start to finish:** 1 Hour 5 Minutes ✴ 8 Servings

½ lb bacon (8 slices)
¼ cup packed brown sugar
2 tablespoons balsamic vinegar

1 Heat oven to 350°F. Line cookie sheet with foil; place wire rack on foil.

2 Arrange bacon in single layer on rack. Bake 20 minutes. Meanwhile, in small bowl, stir together brown sugar and balsamic vinegar.

3 Turn bacon over; spoon brown sugar and vinegar mixture over bacon slices. Bake 10 to 15 minutes longer or until golden brown. Remove bacon from rack. Cool completely, about 15 minutes.

1 Serving: Calories 70; Total Fat 3.5g (Saturated Fat 1g, Trans Fat 0g); Cholesterol 10mg; Sodium 190mg; Total Carbohydrate 8g (Dietary Fiber 0g); Protein 3g **% Daily Value:** Vitamin A 0%; Vitamin C 0%; Calcium 0%; Iron 0% **Exchanges:** ½ Other Carbohydrate, ½ High-Fat Meat **Carbohydrate Choices:** ½

Start Happy Tips

The unique flavor of this bacon can be attributed to the balsamic vinegar. Balsamic vinegar is imported from Italy and has a full-bodied, slightly sweet flavor and rich reddish brown color. It is available in most supermarkets.

Light or dark brown sugar can be used in this recipe. The dark brown sugar will give the bacon a deeper, more caramelized flavor.

honey-mustard bacon

prep time: 15 Minutes ✳ **start to finish:** 1 Hour 5 Minutes ✳ **8 Servings**

½ lb bacon (8 slices)

¼ cup honey mustard

1 Heat oven to 350°F. Line cookie sheet with foil; place wire rack on foil.

2 Brush both sides of bacon slices with honey mustard. Arrange bacon in single layer on rack. Bake 20 minutes.

3 Turn bacon over. Bake 10 to 15 minutes longer or until golden brown. Remove bacon from rack. Cool completely, about 15 minutes.

1 Serving: Calories 45; Total Fat 3.5g (Saturated Fat 1g, Trans Fat 0g); Cholesterol 10mg; Sodium 200mg; Total Carbohydrate 0g (Dietary Fiber 0g); Protein 3g **% Daily Value:** Vitamin A 0%; Vitamin C 0%; Calcium 0%; Iron 0% **Exchanges:** ½ High-Fat Meat **Carbohydrate Choices:** 0

Start Happy Tips

If you don't have the honey mustard, just mix 1 tablespoon honey with 2 tablespoons Dijon mustard for a quick homemade substitute.

Honey mustard's blend of sweet and piquant flavors adds a new dimension to bacon.

praline bacon

prep time: 15 Minutes ✳ **start to finish:** 1 Hour 5 Minutes ✳ 8 Servings

½ lb bacon (8 slices)

¼ cup packed brown sugar

¼ cup finely chopped pecans

1 Heat oven to 350°F. Line cookie sheet with foil; place wire rack on foil.

2 Arrange bacon in single layer on rack. Bake 20 minutes. Meanwhile, in small bowl, stir together brown sugar and pecans.

3 Turn bacon over; sprinkle with brown sugar mixture. Bake 10 to 15 minutes longer or until golden brown. Remove bacon from rack. Cool completely, about 15 minutes.

1 Serving: Calories 90; Total Fat 6g (Saturated Fat 1.5g, Trans Fat 0g); Cholesterol 10mg; Sodium 190mg; Total Carbohydrate 7g (Dietary Fiber 0g); Protein 3g **% Daily Value:** Vitamin A 0%; Vitamin C 0%; Calcium 0%; Iron 0% **Exchanges:** ½ Other Carbohydrate, ½ High-Fat Meat, ½ Fat **Carbohydrate Choices:** ½

Start Happy Tip

Praline most commonly refers to pecans or almonds coated with caramelized sugar. This treat is thought to have originated in Louisiana where spices are not an uncommon addition to this sweet, crunchy delight.

breakfast kabobs with yogurt dip

prep time: 25 Minutes ❊ **start to finish:** 25 Minutes ❊ 4 Servings

8 wooden skewers (8 inch)

2 oz thinly sliced hard salami, folded into quarters

4 oz Muenster cheese, cubed

2 cups cantaloupe cubes

1 cup fresh strawberries, halved

4 slices (½ inch thick) French bread, cut into cubes

1 cup creamy harvest peach, creamy strawberry or creamy strawberry-banana low-fat yogurt (from 2-lb container)

1 Onto wooden skewers, thread salami, cheese, fruit and bread.

2 Serve kabobs with yogurt as a dip.

1 Serving: Calories 350; Total Fat 14g (Saturated Fat 8g, Trans Fat 0g); Cholesterol 45mg; Sodium 680mg; Total Carbohydrate 39g (Dietary Fiber 2g); Protein 17g **% Daily Value:** Vitamin A 60%; Vitamin C 90%; Calcium 35%; Iron 10% **Exchanges:** 1 Starch, 1 Fruit, ½ Skim Milk, 1½ High-Fat Meat **Carbohydrate Choices:** 2½

Start Happy Tip

Thread the kabobs the night before, leaving a little space between each ingredient. Cover tightly and refrigerate.

meat 'n pepper breakfast kabobs

prep time: 55 Minutes ⁑ **start to finish:** 55 Minutes ⁑ 6 Servings

Kabobs

- 6 wooden skewers
- 6 pork sausage links, cut into thirds
- 1 fully cooked ham steak (½ lb), cut into 18 pieces
- 1 large green, red or yellow bell pepper, cut into 18 pieces

Sauce

- ¾ cup barbecue sauce
- ¼ cup seedless raspberry jam
- ¼ teaspoon chipotle chili powder

1 Heat oven to 375°F. Line 15x10x1-inch pan with foil. Spray wire rack with cooking spray; place in pan.

2 Onto skewers, thread sausage, ham and bell pepper pieces. Place on rack in pan.

3 In small microwavable bowl, stir together sauce ingredients. Microwave uncovered on High 30 seconds or until jam is melted and sauce is warm. Brush over kabobs, turning to coat all sides.

4 Bake 30 to 35 minutes, turning and brushing with sauce every 10 minutes, until sausage is thoroughly cooked and bell pepper is tender. Serve immediately.

1 Serving: Calories 200; Total Fat 7g (Saturated Fat 2g, Trans Fat 0g); Cholesterol 30mg; Sodium 920mg; Total Carbohydrate 24g (Dietary Fiber 0g); Protein 10g **% Daily Value:** Vitamin A 4%; Vitamin C 20%; Calcium 2%; Iron 6% **Exchanges:** ½ Starch, 1 Other Carbohydrate, 1 High-Fat Meat **Carbohydrate Choices:** 1½

Colorful Meat 'n Pepper Breakfast Kabobs: Use 2 or 3 colors of bell peppers. When available, try orange or purple bell peppers.

Sausage 'n Pepper Breakfast Kabobs: Eliminate the ham and increase the number of sausage links to 12.

Start Happy Tip

Use your favorite flavor and brand of barbecue sauce for this recipe.

greens, eggs and ham biscuits

prep time: 20 Minutes ❊ **start to finish:** 1 Hour 5 Minutes ❊ 8 Sandwiches

1 bag (6 oz) washed fresh baby spinach

1 tablespoon olive oil

1½ cups shredded Cheddar cheese (6 oz)

12 eggs

¼ cup milk

¼ teaspoon salt

¼ teaspoon pepper

1 can (16.3 oz) large refrigerated homestyle buttermilk biscuits (8 biscuits)

2 teaspoons butter, melted

2 teaspoons yellow cornmeal

8 oz very thinly sliced cooked ham (from deli)

½ cup lightly packed fresh basil leaves

Hot sauce, if desired

1 Heat oven to 350°F. Spray bottom only of 11x7-inch (2-quart) glass baking dish with cooking spray.

2 In 12-inch skillet, heat oil over medium-high heat. Add spinach; cook and stir 3 to 4 minutes or until spinach is wilted. Drain spinach, if needed. Layer spinach in bottom of baking dish. Sprinkle cheese evenly over spinach.

3 In large bowl, beat eggs, milk, salt and pepper; pour over cheese in baking dish. Cover with foil.

4 Bake 40 to 45 minutes or until set and knife inserted in center comes out clean.

5 Meanwhile, separate dough into 8 biscuits. Brush tops with melted butter; sprinkle with cornmeal. Place on ungreased cookie sheet.

6 During last 15 minutes of egg bake time, bake biscuits until golden brown.

7 Meanwhile, in 12-inch skillet, lightly brown sliced ham over medium-high heat.

8 Cut baked egg mixture into 4 rows by 2 rows to make 8 squares. Split warm biscuits; place ham on bottom half of each biscuit. Top each with egg square and fresh basil. Cover with biscuit tops. Serve with hot sauce.

1 Sandwich: Calories 460; Total Fat 27g (Saturated Fat 12g, Trans Fat 0g); Cholesterol 320mg; Sodium 1230mg; Total Carbohydrate 28g (Dietary Fiber 1g); Protein 24g **% Daily Value:** Vitamin A 50%; Vitamin C 6%; Calcium 20%; Iron 20% **Exchanges:** ½ Starch, 1 Other Carbohydrate, ½ Vegetable, 1 Lean Meat, ½ Medium-Fat Meat, 1½ High-Fat Meat, 2 Fat **Carbohydrate Choices:** 2

Start Happy Tip

Canadian bacon can be used in place of the deli ham.

breakfast tacos

prep time: 20 Minutes ⁕ **start to finish:** 20 Minutes ⁕ 6 Tacos

4 eggs

¼ teaspoon garlic salt

¼ teaspoon pepper

¼ cup chopped green or red bell pepper

4 medium green onions, chopped (¼ cup)

1 tablespoon butter

½ cup shredded pepper Jack cheese (2 oz)

6 taco shells

1 cup shredded lettuce

1 small avocado, pitted, peeled and sliced

¼ cup chunky-style salsa

1 In small bowl, beat eggs, garlic salt and pepper thoroughly with fork or whisk. Stir in bell pepper and onions.

2 In 8-inch skillet, heat butter over medium heat. Pour egg mixture into skillet. As mixture begins to set at bottom and side, gently lift cooked portions with spatula so that thin, uncooked portion can flow to bottom. Avoid constant stirring. Cook 3 to 4 minutes or until eggs are thickened throughout but still moist. Gently stir in cheese.

3 Heat taco shells as directed on package. Place lettuce in taco shells. Spoon eggs onto lettuce. Top with avocado and salsa.

1 Taco: Calories 230; Total Fat 16g (Saturated Fat 5g, Trans Fat 1g); Cholesterol 155mg; Sodium 250mg; Total Carbohydrate 13g (Dietary Fiber 3g); Protein 9g **% Daily Value:** Vitamin A 10%; Vitamin C 10%; Calcium 15%; Iron 8% **Exchanges:** 1 Starch, 1 High-Fat Meat, 1 Fat **Carbohydrate Choices:** 1

cheesy egg breakfast tacos

prep time: 20 Minutes ✳ **start to finish:** 20 Minutes ✳ 8 Tacos

Tacos

- 4 eggs
- ¾ cup creamy three-cheese cooking sauce (from 18-oz can)
- ¼ cup sliced green onions (4 medium)
- 2 tablespoons butter
- 8 taco shells that stand on their own (from 4.7-oz box)
- 1 cup shredded Monterey Jack cheese with jalapeño peppers (4 oz)

Garnishes, if desired

- Avocado, cubed
- Chunky-style salsa
- Sour cream

1 In medium bowl, beat eggs and cooking sauce with whisk until well mixed. Stir in green onions.

2 In 10-inch nonstick skillet, heat butter over medium heat just until butter begins to sizzle. Pour egg mixture into skillet. As mixture begins to set at bottom and side, gently lift cooked portions with spatula so that thin, uncooked portion can flow to bottom. Avoid constant stirring. Cook 3 to 4 minutes or until eggs are thickened throughout but still moist.

3 Meanwhile, heat taco shells as directed on box.

4 Spoon about ¼ cup of the egg mixture and 2 tablespoons cheese into each taco shell. Top with avocado, salsa and sour cream.

1 Taco: Calories 180; Total Fat 13g (Saturated Fat 5g, Trans Fat 0g); Cholesterol 120mg; Sodium 340mg; Total Carbohydrate 11g (Dietary Fiber 0g); Protein 6g **% Daily Value:** Vitamin A 15%; Vitamin C 0%; Calcium 6%; Iron 2% **Exchanges:** ½ Other Carbohydrate, ½ Medium-Fat Meat, ½ High-Fat Meat, 1½ Fat **Carbohydrate Choices:** 1

Start Happy Tips

You won't need the whole can of cooking sauce. Cover and refrigerate the remaining sauce for another use. Or heat the remaining sauce until hot, and spoon it over the eggs in the taco shells before adding the cheese.

Diced green or red bell pepper can be substituted for the green onions.

sausage-cheese pancake sandwiches

prep time: 20 Minutes ❄ **start to finish:** 20 Minutes ❄ 4 Sandwiches

1 cup Original Bisquick mix

½ cup milk

3 eggs

2 tablespoons maple-flavored syrup

4 fully cooked pork sausage patties

1 tablespoon milk

1 teaspoon butter

4 slices (⅔ oz each) process American cheese

1 Heat griddle or skillet over medium heat or to 375°F. Grease griddle with vegetable oil if necessary (or spray with cooking spray before heating).

2 In small bowl, stir Bisquick mix, ½ cup milk, 1 of the eggs and the syrup with spoon until blended. For each pancake, pour 2 tablespoons batter onto hot griddle (make 8 pancakes total). Cook until edges are dry. Turn; cook other sides until golden.

3 Meanwhile, heat sausage patties as directed on package. In small bowl, beat remaining 2 eggs and 1 tablespoon milk. In 8-inch nonstick skillet, melt butter over medium heat. Add eggs; cook, stirring occasionally, until set.

4 For each sandwich, place 1 sausage patty on 1 pancake; top with one-fourth of the eggs, 1 slice cheese and another pancake.

1 Sandwich: Calories 440; Total Fat 29g (Saturated Fat 12g, Trans Fat 1g); Cholesterol 215mg; Sodium 1050mg; Total Carbohydrate 28g (Dietary Fiber 0g); Protein 17g **% Daily Value:** Vitamin A 10%; Vitamin C 0%; Calcium 20%; Iron 10% **Exchanges:** 2 Starch, 1½ High-Fat Meat, 3 Fat **Carbohydrate Choices:** 2

Start Happy Tips

Try slices of Canadian bacon or fully cooked ham instead of the sausage patties, if you like.

You can make the pancakes ahead, stack with waxed paper between each pancake, and then wrap and freeze until you need them. Pop them in the toaster to heat.

canadian bacon bagel sandwiches

prep time: 10 Minutes ✳ **start to finish:** 10 Minutes ✳ 2 Sandwiches

4 teaspoons spicy brown or country-style Dijon mustard

2 everything-flavored thin bagels

2 slices (1 oz each) Canadian bacon (from 6-oz package)

2 large slices tomato

½ cup loosely packed fresh spinach leaves

2 thin slices (⅔ oz each) reduced-fat Swiss cheese

1 Heat contact grill or panini maker 5 minutes. Spread 1 teaspoon mustard on cut sides of each bagel. On bagel bottoms, place 1 slice Canadian bacon, 1 slice tomato, ¼ cup spinach and 1 slice cheese. Cover with bagel tops.

2 Place sandwiches on grill. Close grill, pressing down lightly; cook 2 to 3 minutes or until sandwiches are hot and cheese is melted. Serve immediately.

1 Sandwich: Calories 230; Total Fat 7g (Saturated Fat 3.5g, Trans Fat 0g); Cholesterol 25mg; Sodium 920mg; Total Carbohydrate 26g (Dietary Fiber 6g); Protein 16g **% Daily Value:** Vitamin A 25%; Vitamin C 6%; Calcium 20%; Iron 10% **Exchanges:** 1½ Starch, ½ Vegetable, 1½ Lean Meat, ½ Fat **Carbohydrate Choices:** 2

Start Happy Tip

If you like, for a heartier sandwich, use 2 slices of Canadian bacon per sandwich for about 140 more calories.

florentine eggs on english muffins

prep time: 15 Minutes ❄ **start to finish:** 15 Minutes ❄ 2 Servings

¼ cup plain fat-free Greek yogurt (from 6-oz container)

1 tablespoon reduced-fat mayonnaise

½ teaspoon Dijon mustard

2 eggs

1 English muffin, split, toasted

½ cup fresh baby spinach leaves

2 slices tomato

Dash pepper

1 In small microwavable bowl, mix yogurt, mayonnaise and mustard. Microwave uncovered on High 20 to 40 seconds or until warm. Stir; cover to keep warm.

2 In 10-inch skillet, heat 2 to 3 inches water to boiling. Reduce heat to medium-low so water is simmering. Break 1 cold egg into custard cup or small glass bowl. Holding cup close to water, carefully slide egg into water. Repeat with second egg, not allowing eggs to touch. Quickly spoon hot water over each egg until film forms over yolk. Cook uncovered 3 to 5 minutes or until whites and yolks are firm, not runny.

3 Meanwhile, spread about 2 tablespoons sauce on each muffin half. Top each with half of the spinach and 1 tomato slice.

4 With slotted spoon, remove eggs from water; place on tomato. Top with remaining sauce; sprinkle with pepper.

1 Serving: Calories 180; Total Fat 8g (Saturated Fat 2.5g, Trans Fat 0g); Cholesterol 190mg; Sodium 260mg; Total Carbohydrate 16g (Dietary Fiber 1g); Protein 11g **% Daily Value:** Vitamin A 25%; Vitamin C 4%; Calcium 10%; Iron 10% **Exchanges:** 1 Starch, 1 Medium-Fat Meat, ½ Fat **Carbohydrate Choices:** 1

Start Happy Tip

Spinach is an excellent source of the important nutrients folic acid and vitamin C. Spinach is also a good source of iron.

eggs benedict

prep time: 30 Minutes ⁙ **start to finish:** 30 Minutes ⁙ 6 Servings

3 egg yolks

1 tablespoon lemon juice

½ cup cold butter (do not use margarine or vegetable oil spreads)

3 English muffins, split, toasted

7 teaspoons butter, softened

6 thin slices Canadian bacon or cooked ham

6 whole eggs

   Paprika, if desired

1 In 1½-quart saucepan, vigorously stir 3 egg yolks and the lemon juice with whisk. Add ¼ cup of the cold butter. Heat over very low heat, stirring constantly with whisk, until butter is melted. Add remaining ¼ cup cold butter. Continue stirring vigorously until butter is melted and sauce is thickened. (Be sure butter melts slowly so egg yolks have time to cook and thicken sauce without curdling.) If sauce curdles (mixture begins to separate), add about 1 tablespoon boiling water and beat vigorously with whisk or hand beater until smooth. Keep sauce warm.

2 Spread each toasted muffin half with 1 teaspoon of the softened butter. Keep warm.

3 In 10-inch skillet, melt remaining teaspoon softened butter over medium heat. Add bacon; cook until light brown on both sides. Keep warm.

4 Heat 2 to 3 inches water to boiling in skillet or saucepan (use large enough skillet or saucepan so eggs do not touch during cooking). Reduce heat so water is simmering. Break 1 whole egg into custard cup or small glass bowl. Holding cup close to water, carefully slide egg into water. Repeat with remaining eggs, not allowing eggs to touch. Quickly spoon hot water over each egg until film forms over yolk. Cook uncovered 3 to 5 minutes or until whites and yolks are firm, not runny. Remove eggs with slotted spoon.

5 To serve, place 1 slice bacon on each muffin half; top with 1 poached egg. Spoon warm sauce over eggs. Sprinkle with paprika.

1 Serving: Calories 380; Total Fat 30g (Saturated Fat 16g, Trans Fat 1g); Cholesterol 340mg; Sodium 670mg; Total Carbohydrate 14g (Dietary Fiber 1g); Protein 15g **% Daily Value:** Vitamin A 20%; Vitamin C 0%; Calcium 10%; Iron 10% **Exchanges:** 1 Other Carbohydrate, 2 Medium-Fat Meat, 4 Fat **Carbohydrate Choices:** 1

cheddar bread breakfast panini

prep time: 20 Minutes ❄ **start to finish:** 2 Hours 45 Minutes ❄ 8 Servings

3¾ cups Original Bisquick mix

¾ cup shredded sharp Cheddar cheese (3 oz)

1½ cups milk

¼ teaspoon ground red pepper (cayenne)

7 eggs

¼ cup whipping cream or milk

2 teaspoons butter

¼ teaspoon salt

½ teaspoon black pepper

8 slices (¾ oz each) Cheddar cheese

Olive oil cooking spray

1 cup loosely packed fresh baby spinach leaves

1 Heat oven to 350°F. Spray 8x4-inch loaf pan with cooking spray.

2 In medium bowl, stir Bisquick mix and ¾ cup cheese. Add milk, red pepper and 1 of the eggs; stir 2 minutes. Spoon into pan. Bake 50 minutes or until toothpick inserted in center comes out clean. Cool completely, at least 1 hour 30 minutes.

3 In medium bowl, beat remaining 6 eggs and the whipping cream with whisk. In 10-inch nonstick skillet, melt butter over medium heat. Add egg mixture; cook, stirring occasionally, until almost set. Sprinkle with salt and black pepper; remove from heat.

4 Heat closed contact grill 5 minutes. Cut loaf diagonally into 8 (½-inch) slices. Place 1 cheese slice on each of 4 bread slices. Spoon scrambled eggs on top; top each with another cheese slice. Top with remaining bread slices. Spray tops with cooking spray.

5 Place sandwiches on grill. Close grill; cook 2 to 3 minutes or until bread is toasted and cheese is melted. Add spinach to each sandwich before serving. To serve, cut each sandwich in half.

1 Serving: Calories 490; Total Fat 28g (Saturated Fat 13g, Trans Fat 2g); Cholesterol 215mg; Sodium 1050mg; Total Carbohydrate 40g (Dietary Fiber 1g); Protein 19g **% Daily Value:** Vitamin A 25%; Vitamin C 0%; Calcium 30%; Iron 15%
Exchanges: 1½ Starch, 1 Other Carbohydrate, 1 Medium-Fat Meat, 1 High-Fat Meat, 3 Fat
Carbohydrate Choices: 2½

hash brown–egg cups

prep time: 15 Minutes ❄ **start to finish:** 1 Hour ❄ 2 Servings

¾ cup shredded Cheddar cheese (3 oz)

2 cups refrigerated shredded hash-brown potatoes (from 20-oz bag)

¼ cup chopped green onions (4 medium)

½ teaspoon seasoned salt

⅛ teaspoon pepper

2 eggs

⅛ teaspoon Italian seasoning

1 Heat oven to 400°F. Spray 2 (2-cup) ovenproof bowls or ramekins with cooking spray.

2 Reserve 2 tablespoons of the cheese for topping. In medium bowl, mix remaining cheese, the potatoes, onions, ¼ teaspoon of the seasoned salt and the pepper. Press mixture in bottom and up side of each bowl, leaving indentation in center.

3 Bake 25 to 30 minutes or until golden brown and crisp.

4 Remove bowls from oven. Break egg into center of each cup. Sprinkle evenly with remaining ¼ teaspoon seasoned salt, the Italian seasoning and reserved 2 tablespoons cheese. Return to oven; bake 8 to 12 minutes longer or until eggs are set and of desired doneness.

1 Serving: Calories 430; Total Fat 20g (Saturated Fat 11g, Trans Fat 0g); Cholesterol 255mg; Sodium 720mg; Total Carbohydrate 43g (Dietary Fiber 5g); Protein 21g **% Daily Value:** Vitamin A 15%; Vitamin C 15%; Calcium 25%; Iron 10% **Exchanges:** 3 Starch, 1½ High-Fat Meat, 1 Fat **Carbohydrate Choices:** 3

Start Happy Tip

For a soft center, remove the egg cups at the minimum cooking time; leave them in longer for a firm or "hard" cooked egg.

open face spinach-and-egg biscuits

prep time: 35 Minutes ❄ **start to finish:** 55 Minutes ❄ 8 servings (1 biscuit each)

1 package (12 oz) frozen spinach soufflé, thawed

2¾ cups Original Bisquick mix

¾ cup shredded Parmesan cheese (3 oz)

¼ teaspoon ground mustard

2 tablespoons butter

8 eggs

2 tablespoons butter, softened

1½ teaspoons spicy brown mustard

¼ lb thinly sliced cooked ham (from deli)

1 Heat oven to 425°F. In medium bowl, mix spinach soufflé, Bisquick mix, cheese and ground mustard with fork just until dry ingredients are moistened. On lightly floured surface, knead dough 8 to 10 times. Pat dough until ¾ inch thick; cut with 3-inch round cutter. On ungreased cookie sheet, place rounds 1 inch apart. Bake 13 to 16 minutes or until golden brown.

2 Meanwhile, in 12-inch nonstick skillet, melt 1 tablespoon of the butter over medium-high heat. Break egg into custard cup; carefully slide into skillet. Repeat with 3 more eggs. Immediately reduce heat to medium-low. Cook 4 minutes, spooning butter over eggs, until film forms over top and whites and yolks are firm, not runny. If desired, season to taste with salt and pepper. Repeat with remaining 1 tablespoon butter and 4 eggs.

3 In small bowl, mix 2 tablespoons softened butter and the brown mustard. Split 4 biscuits; spread cut sides with butter mixture. (Reserve remaining 4 biscuits for later use.) Top each biscuit half with ham and 1 fried egg.

1 Serving: Calories 400 (Calories from Fat 240); Total Fat 22g (Saturated Fat 9g, Trans Fat 1.5g); Cholesterol 255mg; Sodium 140mg; Total Carbohydrate 32g (Dietary Fiber 1g); Protein 18g **% Daily Value:** Vitamin A 50%; Vitamin C 0%; Calcium 25%; Iron 15% **Exchanges:** 2 Starch, ½ Vegetable, 1 Lean Meat, 2 Fat **Carbohydrate Choices:** 2

sausage–french toast panini

prep time: 25 Minutes ❋ **start to finish:** 25 Minutes ❋ 6 Sandwiches

 1 package (10 oz) frozen
   uncooked pork sausage
   patties (6 patties),
   thawed
 2 eggs
 ½ cup milk
 1 tablespoon Dijon
   mustard
 6 English muffins, split
12 slices provolone cheese
 6 slices Canadian bacon
   (3 oz)

1 Heat panini pan over medium heat or heat contact grill 5 minutes. Press sausage patties into thinner patties, about 3 to 4 inches in diameter. Cook sausage in panini pan 2 to 3 minutes on each side, or cook in contact grill 2 to 3 minutes, or until thoroughly cooked. Wipe surface of pan or grill. Spray weighted top of panini pan with cooking spray.

2 In small bowl, beat eggs, milk and mustard with whisk. Dip muffin halves in egg mixture, soaking well. Place 1 cheese slice and 1 sausage patty on each of 6 muffin halves; top with bacon and second slice of cheese. Cover with remaining muffin halves.

3 Place 3 sandwiches on panini pan; place weighted top over muffins. Cook 2 minutes or until browned. Turn; cook 2 minutes longer or until browned and hot in center. Repeat with remaining sandwiches. Or cook sandwiches in contact grill 2 to 3 minutes.

1 Sandwich: Calories 370; Total Fat 18g (Saturated Fat 9g, Trans Fat 0g); Cholesterol 120mg; Sodium 970mg; Total Carbohydrate 27g (Dietary Fiber 2g); Protein 23g **% Daily Value:** Vitamin A 8%; Vitamin C 0%; Calcium 35%; Iron 15% **Exchanges:** 2 Starch, 2 Medium-Fat Meat, 1½ Fat **Carbohydrate Choices:** 2

Start Happy Tips

You can substitute your favorite cheese for the provolone. Use your favorite English muffins; ours were about 4 inches in diameter.

If you don't have a panini pan or contact grill, just use a regular nonstick skillet. You can weigh down the sandwiches with a plate topped with a couple full cans of food.

breakfast panini

prep time: 10 Minutes ❄ **start to finish:** 10 Minutes ❄ 2 Sandwiches

2 eggs

½ teaspoon salt-free seasoning blend

2 tablespoons chopped fresh chives

2 whole wheat thin bagels

2 slices tomato

2 thin slices onion

4 very thin slices reduced-sodium cooked ham (from deli)

2 thin slices reduced-fat Cheddar cheese

1 Spray 8-inch skillet with cooking spray; heat over medium heat.

2 In medium bowl, beat eggs, seasoning blend and chives with whisk until well mixed. Pour into skillet. As eggs begin to set at bottom and side, gently lift cooked portions with spatula so that thin, uncooked portion can flow to bottom. Avoid constant stirring. Cook 3 to 4 minutes or until eggs are thickened throughout but still moist and creamy. Remove from heat.

3 Heat contact grill or panini maker 5 minutes. For each sandwich, divide cooked eggs evenly between bagel bottoms. Top each with 1 tomato slice, 1 onion slice, 2 ham slices and 1 cheese slice. Cover with bagel tops.

4 Place sandwiches on grill. Close grill, pressing down lightly; cook 2 to 3 minutes or until sandwiches are hot and cheese is melted. Serve immediately.

1 Sandwich: Calories 300; Total Fat 11g (Saturated Fat 4.5g, Trans Fat 0g); Cholesterol 205mg; Sodium 490mg; Total Carbohydrate 32g (Dietary Fiber 3g); Protein 18g **% Daily Value:** Vitamin A 15%; Vitamin C 4%; Calcium 15%; Iron 15% **Exchanges:** 1½ Starch, ½ Other Carbohydrate, 1 Very Lean Meat, 1 Lean Meat, 1½ Fat **Carbohydrate Choices:** 2

Start Happy Tip

Spread each cut side of bagels with 1½ teaspoons reduced-fat mayonnaise and 1 teaspoon Dijon mustard for an additional 25 calories per sandwich.

pancakes, waffles & french toast

strawberries 'n cream pancakes

prep time: 40 Minutes ❄ **start to finish:** 40 Minutes ❄ 4 Servings (3 pancakes with topping each)

1 container (8 oz) sour cream

2 tablespoons turbinado sugar (raw sugar)

2 cups Original Bisquick mix

2 tablespoons granulated sugar

2 tablespoons wheat germ

2 teaspoons baking powder

1¾ cups buttermilk

2 teaspoons vanilla

1 egg

2 tablespoons butter, melted

1½ cups finely chopped fresh strawberries

Powdered sugar

Sliced fresh strawberries, if desired

1 In small bowl, mix sour cream and turbinado sugar until blended. Refrigerate until serving time.

2 In medium bowl, stir Bisquick mix, granulated sugar, wheat germ and baking powder. Add buttermilk, vanilla and egg; stir with fork or whisk until blended. Stir in melted butter. Gently fold in chopped strawberries.

3 Heat griddle or skillet over medium-high heat (375°F). Brush griddle with vegetable oil if necessary (or spray with cooking spray before heating). For each pancake, pour about 3 tablespoons batter onto hot griddle; spread to 4-inch round. Cook until bubbles form on top and edges are dry. Turn; cook other side until golden brown.

4 Sprinkle pancakes with powdered sugar. Serve with sour cream mixture; top with sliced strawberries.

1 Serving: Calories 600; Total Fat 30g (Saturated Fat 14g, Trans Fat 2g); Cholesterol 100mg; Sodium 1180mg; Total Carbohydrate 67g (Dietary Fiber 3g); Protein 13g **% Daily Value:** Vitamin A 15%; Vitamin C 30%; Calcium 45%; Iron 15% **Exchanges:** 3 Starch, ½ Fruit, ½ Other Carbohydrate, ½ Low-Fat Milk, 5 Fat **Carbohydrate Choices:** 4½

Start Happy Tip

To test griddle, sprinkle with a few drops of water. If bubbles jump around, heat is just right.

pancakes

prep time: 20 Minutes ❋ **start to finish:** 20 Minutes ❋ 9 (4-inch) Pancakes

1 egg
1 cup all-purpose or whole wheat flour
1 tablespoon sugar
3 teaspoons baking powder
¼ teaspoon salt
¾ cup milk
2 tablespoons vegetable oil or melted butter

1 In medium bowl, beat egg with whisk until fluffy. Stir in remaining ingredients just until flour is moistened (batter will be slightly lumpy); do not overmix or pancakes will be tough. For thinner pancakes, stir in additional 1 to 2 tablespoons milk.

2 Heat griddle or skillet over medium-high heat (375°F). Brush griddle with vegetable oil if necessary (or spray with cooking spray before heating).

3 For each pancake, pour slightly less than ¼ cup batter onto hot griddle. Cook 2 to 3 minutes or until bubbles form on top and edges are dry. Turn; cook other side until golden brown.

1 Pancake: Calories 110; Total Fat 5g (Saturated Fat 1.5g, Trans Fat 0g); Cholesterol 25mg; Sodium 250mg; Total Carbohydrate 13g (Dietary Fiber 0g); Protein 3g **% Daily Value:** Vitamin A 2%; Vitamin C 0%; Calcium 10%; Iron 6% **Exchanges:** 1 Starch, ½ Fat **Carbohydrate Choices:** 1

Berry Pancakes: Stir ½ cup fresh or frozen (thawed and well drained) blackberries, blueberries or raspberries into batter.

Buttermilk Pancakes: Substitute 1 cup buttermilk for the ¾ cup milk. Decrease baking powder to 1 teaspoon. Add ½ teaspoon baking soda.

Orange-Cranberry Pancakes: Substitute orange juice for the milk. Stir in ¼ cup dried cranberries and ¼ cup chopped dried apples after mixing ingredients in step 1.

Whole-Grain Strawberry Pancakes: Make pancakes with whole wheat flour. Top each serving with ¼ cup strawberry yogurt and ½ cup sliced fresh strawberries.

Start Happy Tip

Pancakes are ready to turn when they are bubbly on top, puffed and dry around edges. The second side never browns as easily as the first.

candied ginger–pumpkin pancakes

prep time: 40 Minutes ❄ **start to finish:** 40 Minutes ❄ 16 Pancakes

2 cups Original Bisquick mix

2 teaspoons pumpkin pie spice

1½ cups buttermilk

1 cup canned pumpkin (not pumpkin pie mix)

2 eggs

¼ cup toasted* pecan halves, finely chopped

1 tablespoon finely chopped crystallized ginger

Pecan halves, if desired

Maple-flavored syrup, if desired

1 In large bowl, stir Bisquick mix, pumpkin pie spice, buttermilk, pumpkin and eggs with fork or whisk until blended. Stir in chopped pecans and ginger.

2 Heat griddle or skillet over medium heat (350°F). Brush griddle with vegetable oil if necessary (or spray with cooking spray before heating).

3 For each pancake, pour ¼ cup batter onto hot griddle. Cook until bubbles form on top and edges are dry. Turn; cook other side until golden brown. Garnish with pecan halves.

4 Serve pancakes with syrup.

*To toast pecans, sprinkle in ungreased skillet. Cook over medium heat 5 to 7 minutes, stirring frequently until pecans begin to brown, then stirring constantly until pecans are light brown.

1 Pancake: Calories 110; Total Fat 4.5g (Saturated Fat 1g, Trans Fat 0g); Cholesterol 25mg; Sodium 210mg; Total Carbohydrate 13g (Dietary Fiber 1g); Protein 3g **% Daily Value:** Vitamin A 50%; Vitamin C 0%; Calcium 6%; Iron 4% **Exchanges:** 1 Starch, 1 Fat **Carbohydrate Choices:** 1

Start Happy Tip

If you don't have the pumpkin pie spice, you can use 1 teaspoon ground cinnamon and ½ teaspoon each of ground nutmeg and ground ginger instead.

cornbread pancakes with butter pecan syrup

prep time: 30 Minutes ❋ **start to finish:** 30 Minutes ❋ 8 Servings

Syrup

- 2 tablespoons butter
- ⅓ cup chopped pecans
- ¾ cup real maple syrup or maple-flavored syrup

Pancakes

- 1¼ cups all-purpose flour
- ¾ cup cornmeal
- ¼ cup sugar
- 2 teaspoons baking powder
- ½ teaspoon salt
- 1⅓ cups milk
- ¼ cup vegetable oil
- 1 egg, beaten

1 In 1-quart saucepan, melt butter over medium heat. Add pecans; cook, stirring frequently, 2 to 3 minutes, or until browned. Stir in syrup; heat until hot. Remove from heat.

2 Heat griddle or skillet over medium-high heat (375°F). Brush griddle with vegetable oil if necessary (or spray with cooking spray before heating).

3 In large bowl, mix flour, cornmeal, sugar, baking powder and salt. Stir in milk, oil and egg just until blended. For each pancake, pour about ¼ cup batter onto hot griddle. Cook 2 to 3 minutes or until bubbles form on top and edges are dry. Turn; cook other side until golden brown.

4 Serve pancakes with syrup.

1 Serving: Calories 380; Total Fat 15g (Saturated Fat 4g, Trans Fat 0g); Cholesterol 35mg; Sodium 330mg; Total Carbohydrate 56g (Dietary Fiber 1g); Protein 5g **% Daily Value:** Vitamin A 4%; Vitamin C 0%; Calcium 15%; Iron 10% **Exchanges:** 1½ Starch, 2 Other Carbohydrate, 3 Fat **Carbohydrate Choices:** 4

Start Happy Tips

Mix pancake batter in a measuring cup or bowl with a handle and spout. Then you can easily pour batter onto the griddle.

Keep pancakes warm in a single layer on a paper towel–lined cookie sheet in a 200°F oven.

red velvet pancakes

prep time: 30 Minutes ✳ **start to finish:** 30 Minutes ✳ 7 Servings (3 pancakes with topping each)

Topping

- 4 oz (half of 8-oz package) cream cheese, softened
- ¼ cup butter, softened
- 3 tablespoons milk
- 2 cups powdered sugar

Pancakes

- 2 cups Original Bisquick mix
- 2 tablespoon granulated sugar
- 1 tablespoon unsweetened baking cocoa
- 1 cup milk
- 1 to 1½ teaspoons red paste food color*
- 2 eggs

  Powdered sugar, if desired

1 In medium bowl, beat cream cheese, butter and 3 tablespoons milk with electric mixer on low speed until smooth. Gradually beat in 2 cups powdered sugar, 1 cup at a time, on low speed until topping is smooth. Cover; set aside.

2 In large bowl, stir all pancake ingredients except powdered sugar with whisk until well blended.

3 Heat griddle or skillet over medium-high heat (375°F). Brush griddle with vegetable oil if necessary (or spray with cooking spray before heating). For each pancake, pour slightly less than ¼ cup batter onto hot griddle. Cook until bubbles form on top and edges are dry. Turn; cook other side until set.

4 Spoon topping into resealable food-storage plastic bag; seal bag. Cut off tiny corner of bag; squeeze bag to drizzle topping over pancakes. Sprinkle pancakes with powdered sugar.

*For the best results, liquid food color is not recommended for this recipe.

1 Serving: Calories 450; Total Fat 20g (Saturated Fat 10g, Trans Fat 1.5g); Cholesterol 90mg; Sodium 570mg; Total Carbohydrate 62g (Dietary Fiber 1g); Protein 7g **% Daily Value:** Vitamin A 10%; Vitamin C 0%; Calcium 10%; Iron 8% **Exchanges:** 2 Starch, 2 Other Carbohydrate, 4 Fat **Carbohydrate Choices:** 4

Start Happy Tip

For the most tender pancakes, mix just until dry ingredients are moistened. There may still be lumps in the batter.

chocolate chip pancakes

prep time: 20 Minutes ❋ **start to finish:** 20 Minutes ❋ 5 Servings (3 pancakes each)

2 cups Original Bisquick mix

1 cup milk

2 eggs

½ cup miniature semisweet chocolate chips

Maple-flavored syrup, if desired

1 In medium bowl, stir Bisquick mix, milk and eggs with fork or whisk until blended. Stir in chocolate chips.

2 Heat griddle or skillet over medium heat (350°F). Brush griddle with vegetable oil if necessary (or spray with cooking spray before heating). For each pancake, pour slightly less than ¼ cup batter onto hot griddle. Cook until bubbles form on top and edges are dry. Turn; cook other side until golden brown.

3 Serve pancakes with syrup.

1 Serving: Calories 340; Total Fat 14g (Saturated Fat 6g, Trans Fat 2g); Cholesterol 90mg; Sodium 630mg; Total Carbohydrate 44g (Dietary Fiber 2g); Protein 8g **% Daily Value:** Vitamin A 4%; Vitamin C 0%; Calcium 10%; Iron 10% **Exchanges:** 2 Starch, 1 Other Carbohydrate, 2½ Fat **Carbohydrate Choices:** 3

Peanut Butter Chip Pancakes: Substitute peanut butter chips for the chocolate chips.

pecan pancakes with fudge syrup

prep time: 25 Minutes ❄ **start to finish:** 25 Minutes ❄ 4 Servings (3 pancakes and 3 tablespoons syrup each)

Syrup

- 1 cup maple-flavored or real maple syrup
- ¼ cup hot fudge topping

Pancakes

- 1½ cups all-purpose flour
- 2 tablespoons packed brown sugar
- 1 teaspoon baking powder
- ¼ teaspoon baking soda
- ¼ teaspoon salt
- ½ cup chopped pecans
- 1½ cups buttermilk
- 2 eggs, beaten
- 2 tablespoons butter, melted

1 In 1-quart nonstick saucepan, heat syrup and fudge topping over medium heat until warm, stirring until smooth. Keep warm.

2 In medium bowl, mix flour, brown sugar, baking powder, baking soda, salt and pecans. Stir in buttermilk, eggs and butter with fork or whisk just until blended.

3 Heat griddle or skillet over medium-high heat (375°F). Grease griddle with butter or vegetable oil if necessary (or spray with cooking spray before heating). For each pancake, pour about ¼ cup batter onto hot griddle. Cook until bubbles form on top and edges are dry. Turn; cook other side until golden brown.

4 Serve pancakes with warm syrup.

1 Serving: Calories 710; Total Fat 21g (Saturated Fat 7g, Trans Fat 0g); Cholesterol 125mg; Sodium 610mg; Total Carbohydrate 116g (Dietary Fiber 3g); Protein 13g **% Daily Value:** Vitamin A 8%; Vitamin C 0%; Calcium 25%; Iron 20% **Exchanges:** 3½ Starch, 4 Other Carbohydrate, ½ High-Fat Meat, 3 Fat **Carbohydrate Choices:** 8

Start Happy Tip

Serve these tasty pancakes with your favorite sausage links and fresh fruit.

apple crisp pancakes

prep time: 25 Minutes ❄ **start to finish:** 25 Minutes ❄ 12 Pancakes

Streusel Topping

- ¼ cup plus 2 tablespoons packed brown sugar
- ¼ cup all-purpose flour
- ¼ cup old-fashioned or quick-cooking oats
- ½ teaspoon ground cinnamon
- ¼ teaspoon ground nutmeg
- 2 tablespoons plus 2 teaspoons cold butter

Pancakes

- 2 cups Original Bisquick mix
- 1 cup diced peeled Granny Smith apple (¼ inch)
- 1 cup milk
- 2 eggs

Toppings, if desired

- Powdered sugar
- Real maple syrup
- Sweetened whipped cream

1 In medium bowl, mix brown sugar, flour, oats, cinnamon and nutmeg. Using pastry blender or fork, cut in butter until mixture is crumbly. Set aside.

2 In large bowl, stir pancake ingredients until well blended. Heat griddle or 12-inch skillet over medium heat (350°F). Brush griddle with vegetable oil (or spray with cooking spray before heating) to help prevent streusel from sticking to griddle.

3 For each pancake, pour ¼ cup batter onto hot griddle. Sprinkle each pancake evenly with scant 2 tablespoons streusel topping. Cook 2 to 3 minutes or until bubbles form on top and edges are dry. Turn; cook other side until light golden brown around edges, 1 minute to 1 minute 30 seconds. If necessary, scrape off griddle between batches of pancakes.

4 Serve pancakes streusel side up with desired toppings.

1 Pancake: Calories 170; Total Fat 6g (Saturated Fat 2.5g, Trans Fat 0.5g); Cholesterol 35mg; Sodium 270mg; Total Carbohydrate 23g (Dietary Fiber 0g); Protein 3g **% Daily Value:** Vitamin A 4%; Vitamin C 0%; Calcium 6%; Iron 4% **Exchanges:** 1 Starch, ½ Other Carbohydrate, 1 Fat **Carbohydrate Choices:** 1½

white chocolate–berry pancakes

prep time: 20 Minutes ✳ **start to finish:** 20 Minutes ✳ **4 Servings (3 pancakes each)**

2 cups Original Bisquick mix

1 cup milk

2 eggs

½ cup frozen wild blueberries (do not thaw)

½ cup white vanilla baking chips

Butter, if desired

Maple-flavored syrup, if desired

1 In medium bowl, stir Bisquick mix, milk and eggs until blended. Fold in blueberries and white chips.

2 Heat griddle or skillet over medium heat (350°F). Brush griddle with vegetable oil if necessary (or spray with cooking spray before heating). For each pancake, pour about ¼ cup batter onto hot griddle. Cook until bubbles form on top and edges are dry. Turn; cook other side until golden brown.

3 Serve pancakes with butter and syrup.

1 Serving: Calories 450; Total Fat 19g (Saturated Fat 8g, Trans Fat 1.5g); Cholesterol 100mg; Sodium 840mg; Total Carbohydrate 58g (Dietary Fiber 2g); Protein 11g **% Daily Value:** Vitamin A 6%; Vitamin C 0%; Calcium 20%; Iron 10% **Exchanges:** 3½ Starch, ½ Other Carbohydrate, 3½ Fat **Carbohydrate Choices:** 4

Start Happy Tip
Frozen raspberries can be substituted for the blueberries.

banana-buckwheat pancakes

prep time: 20 Minutes ✳ **start to finish:** 20 Minutes ✳ **9 Servings (2 pancakes)**

2 cups Original Bisquick mix

½ cup buckwheat flour

3 tablespoons packed brown sugar

1¼ cups milk

1 cup mashed ripe bananas (2 medium)

2 eggs

Sliced bananas, fresh blueberries and granola, if desired

Real maple syrup, if desired

1 In medium bowl, stir Bisquick mix, flour, brown sugar, milk, mashed bananas and eggs with fork or whisk until blended.

2 Heat griddle or skillet over medium heat (350°F). Brush griddle with vegetable oil if necessary (or spray with cooking spray before heating). For each pancake, pour ¼ cup batter onto hot griddle. Cook until bubbles form on top and edges are dry. Turn; cook other side until golden brown.

3 Top pancakes with sliced bananas, blueberries and granola. Serve with syrup.

1 Serving: Calories 210; Total Fat 6g (Saturated Fat 2g, Trans Fat 0.5g); Cholesterol 45mg; Sodium 360mg; Total Carbohydrate 34g (Dietary Fiber 2g); Protein 5g **% Daily Value:** Vitamin A 2%; Vitamin C 0%; Calcium 8%; Iron 6% **Exchanges:** 1½ Starch, 1 Other Carbohydrate, 1 Fat **Carbohydrate Choices:** 2

oatmeal pancakes with banana-walnut syrup

prep time: 30 Minutes ❋ start to finish: 30 Minutes ❋ 6 Servings (3 pancakes with syrup each)

Syrup

- 2 tablespoons butter
- ¼ cup chopped walnuts
- 2 bananas, sliced
- 1 cup maple-flavored syrup

Pancakes

- 2 cups Original Bisquick mix
- ½ cup old-fashioned or quick-cooking oats
- 2 tablespoons packed brown sugar
- 1¼ cups milk
- 2 eggs

1 In 1½-quart saucepan, melt butter over medium heat. Add walnuts; cook, stirring occasionally, until walnuts and butter just begin to brown. Add bananas; stir to coat with butter. Stir in syrup. Reduce heat to low; cook until warm. Keep warm while making pancakes.

2 In medium bowl, stir pancake ingredients with fork or whisk until blended.

3 Heat griddle or skillet over medium-high heat (375°F). Brush griddle with vegetable oil if necessary (or spray with cooking spray before heating).

4 For each pancake, pour slightly less than ¼ cup batter onto hot griddle. Cook until bubbles form on top and edges are dry. Turn; cook other side until golden brown.

5 Serve pancakes with warm syrup.

1 Serving: Calories 520; Total Fat 15g (Saturated Fat 6g, Trans Fat 1.5g); Cholesterol 85mg; Sodium 590mg; Total Carbohydrate 87g (Dietary Fiber 3g); Protein 9g **% Daily Value:** Vitamin A 6%; Vitamin C 2%; Calcium 15%; Iron 10% **Exchanges:** 3 Starch, ½ Fruit, 2½ Other Carbohydrate, 2½ Fat **Carbohydrate Choices:** 6

Start Happy Tip

If you've got pecans on hand and not walnuts, go ahead and substitute them. Also, the butter can burn quickly, so watch it carefully while it's browning. It should be an even golden brown color.

strawberry cheesecake pancakes

prep time: 25 Minutes ⁛ **start to finish:** 25 Minutes ⁛ 4 Servings

Filling

- 4 oz (half of 8-oz package) ⅓-less-fat cream cheese (Neufchâtel), softened
- 1 box (4-serving size) cheesecake instant pudding and pie filling mix
- 1 cup milk

Topping

- 2 cups sliced fresh strawberries
- ½ cup strawberry syrup

Pancakes

- 1 cup Fiber One® Complete pancake mix (from 28.3-oz box)
- ½ cup graham cracker crumbs
- ¾ cup water

1 In medium bowl, beat cream cheese with electric mixer on medium speed until creamy. Add pudding mix and milk; beat until thick and creamy, scraping side of bowl as necessary. Refrigerate until serving time.

2 In small bowl, mix strawberries and syrup; set aside. In large bowl, mix pancake ingredients just until blended.

3 Heat griddle or skillet over medium-high heat (375°F). Grease griddle with butter or vegetable oil if necessary (or spray with cooking spray before heating). For each pancake, pour ¼ cup batter onto hot griddle and spread slightly to 4½-inch diameter. Cook until bubbles form on top and edges are dry. Turn; cook other side until golden brown.

4 Place 1 pancake on each of 4 serving plates. Top each with ⅓ cup of the filling and ¼ cup of the topping. Top each with second pancake and another ¼ cup topping.

1 Serving: Calories 470; Total Fat 11g (Saturated Fat 5g, Trans Fat 0g); Cholesterol 40mg; Sodium 760mg; Total Carbohydrate 85g (Dietary Fiber 4g); Protein 9g **% Daily Value:** Vitamin A 8%; Vitamin C 40%; Calcium 25%; Iron 10% **Exchanges:** 1 Starch, 1 Fruit, 3½ Other Carbohydrate, 1 High-Fat Meat, ½ Fat **Carbohydrate Choices:** 5½

Start Happy Tip

Look for the strawberry syrup in the grocery store near the other pancake syrups. Or, if you prefer, you can just stir about 2 tablespoons of sugar into the sliced strawberries and omit the syrup.

whole-grain strawberry pancakes

prep time: 30 Minutes ❄ **start to finish:** 30 Minutes ❄ 7 Servings (2 pancakes with toppings each)

1½ cups whole wheat flour

3 tablespoons sugar

1 teaspoon baking powder

½ teaspoon baking soda

½ teaspoon salt

3 eggs or ¾ cup fat-free egg product

1 container (6 oz) vanilla thick-and-creamy low-fat yogurt

¾ cup water

3 tablespoons canola oil

1¾ cups sliced fresh strawberries

1 container (6 oz) strawberry thick-and-creamy low-fat yogurt

1 In large bowl, mix flour, sugar, baking powder, baking soda and salt. In medium bowl, beat eggs, vanilla yogurt, water and oil with whisk until well blended. Pour egg mixture all at once into flour mixture; stir until moistened.

2 Heat griddle or skillet over medium-high heat (375°F). Grease griddle with vegetable oil if necessary (or spray with cooking spray before heating). For each pancake, pour slightly less than ¼ cup batter onto hot griddle. Cook until bubbles form on top and edges are dry. Turn; cook other side until golden brown.

3 Place 2 pancakes on each serving plate. Top each with ¼ cup strawberries and about 1 heaping tablespoon strawberry yogurt.

1 Serving: Calories 270; Total Fat 10g (Saturated Fat 2g, Trans Fat 0g); Cholesterol 85mg; Sodium 380mg; Total Carbohydrate 37g (Dietary Fiber 4g); Protein 7g **% Daily Value:** Vitamin A 6%; Vitamin C 20%; Calcium 15%; Iron 8% **Exchanges:** 1½ Starch, 1 Other Carbohydrate, ½ Medium-Fat Meat, 1½ Fat **Carbohydrate Choices:** 2½

Start Happy Tip

Have a craving for chocolate? Drizzle the pancakes with 2 tablespoons fat-free chocolate syrup before topping with the strawberries and yogurt for an extra 100 calories per serving.

gluten-free pancakes

prep time: 20 Minutes ❋ **start to finish:** 20 Minutes ❋ 10 Pancakes

1 cup Bisquick Gluten Free mix

1 cup milk

2 tablespoons vegetable oil

1 egg

Butter, if desired

Syrup, if desired

1 In large bowl, stir Bisquick mix, milk, oil and egg until well blended.

2 Heat griddle or skillet over medium-high heat (375°F). Brush griddle with vegetable oil if necessary (or spray with cooking spray before heating).

3 For each pancake, pour slightly less than ¼ cup batter onto hot griddle. Cook until edges are dry. Turn; cook other side until golden brown.

4 Serve pancakes with butter and syrup.

1 Pancake: Calories 90; Total Fat 4g (Saturated Fat 1g, Trans Fat 0g); Cholesterol 25mg; Sodium 150mg; Total Carbohydrate 11g (Dietary Fiber 0g); Protein 2g **% Daily Value:** Vitamin A 0%; Vitamin C 0%; Calcium 4%; Iron 0% **Exchanges:** 1 Starch, ½ Fat **Carbohydrate Choices:** 1

Start Happy Tips

If you are cooking gluten free, always read labels to be sure each recipe ingredient is gluten free. Products and ingredient sources can change.

Feel free to add fresh fruit to the pancakes for a bit of added flavor.

nutty cereal dollar pancakes

prep time: 25 Minutes   ⁎   **start to finish:** 25 Minutes   ⁎   6 Servings (6 pancakes with toppings each)

¾ cup Wheaties® cereal, slightly crushed (½ cup)

¼ cup raisins

¼ cup dry-roasted sunflower nuts

2 cups Original Bisquick mix

1½ cups Wheaties cereal, crushed (¾ cup)

1¼ cups milk

2 eggs

⅓ cup very vanilla fat-free yogurt (or any flavor)

¾ cup honey

1 In small bowl, toss ½ cup slightly crushed cereal, the raisins and nuts; set aside. In medium bowl, stir Bisquick mix, ¾ cup crushed cereal, the milk and eggs with fork until blended.

2 Heat griddle or skillet over medium-high heat (375°F). Brush griddle with vegetable oil if necessary (or spray with cooking spray before heating).

3 For each pancake, pour 1 measuring tablespoon batter onto hot griddle. Cook until edges are dry. Turn; cook other side until golden.

4 For each serving, arrange 6 pancakes on plate. Top with 1 tablespoon yogurt and 2½ tablespoons cereal mixture. Drizzle 2 tablespoons honey over all.

1 Serving: Calories 450; Total Fat 12g (Saturated Fat 3g, Trans Fat 1g); Cholesterol 75mg; Sodium 750mg; Total Carbohydrate 79g (Dietary Fiber 2g); Protein 10g **% Daily Value:** Vitamin A 8%; Vitamin C 2%; Calcium 15%; Iron 30% **Exchanges:** 3 Starch, 2 Other Carbohydrate, 2 Fat **Carbohydrate Choices:** 5

Start Happy Tip

You can vary this "emergency" breakfast to use what you have on hand. Instead of topping with the cereal mixture, try these mini pancakes with yogurt, honey, sliced strawberries or bananas.

Pancake, French Toast and Waffle Toppers

Need to add some dazzle to your breakfast table? These toppings can be served over Pancakes (page 170), French Toast (page 217) or Waffles (page 204). Move over maple syrup and butter!

1 Apple-Rum Butter: Beat ½ cup softened butter with electric mixer until light and fluffy. Gradually beat in ½ cup apple butter and 1 teaspoon rum or ¼ teaspoon rum extract to taste.

2 Blackberry-Lime Sauce: In small saucepan, combine 2 cups blackberries or raspberries, ¼ cup water, ¼ cup sugar and 1 tablespoon fresh lime juice. Simmer sauce for 10 to 15 minutes until berries break down and sauce slightly thickens; stir in 1 teaspoon grated lime peel.

3 Cherry and Granola Topping: Top with about ¼ cup vanilla yogurt and ¼ cup frozen (thawed) sweet cherries; sprinkle with 2 tablespoons granola.

4 Maple Yogurt Topping with Candied Nuts and Bananas: Stir ⅛ cup real maple syrup into 8 ounces plain Greek yogurt. Top pancakes, French toast or waffles with maple yogurt; sprinkle with purchased candied or regular walnuts or pecans and sliced bananas.

5 Red, White and Blueberries Topping: Melt ¼ cup raspberry preserves in small saucepan; add about 1 tablespoon orange liqueur or orange juice. Serve pancakes, French toast or waffles with sauce, fresh blueberries and ½ cup crème fraîche or sour cream mixed with 1 tablespoon sugar.

6 Super Sundae Topping: Drizzle pancakes, French toast or waffles with warm chocolate syrup; top with sliced bananas, fresh strawberries, chopped toasted pecans, whipped cream and a maraschino cherry.

raspberry-rhubarb puff pancake

prep time: 25 Minutes ❋ **start to finish:** 25 Minutes ❋ 4 Servings

¾ cup all-purpose flour

¾ cup milk

3 eggs

½ teaspoon vanilla

2 tablespoons butter

¾ cup ricotta cheese

2 tablespoons powdered sugar

1 cup chopped fresh or frozen rhubarb

¼ cup granulated sugar

¼ cup water

2 teaspoons cornstarch

1 cup fresh or frozen (thawed) raspberries

1 Heat oven to 425°F. In medium bowl, beat flour, milk, eggs and vanilla with whisk until combined.

2 In 9½-inch glass deep-dish pie plate, melt butter in oven. Using oven mitts, carefully tilt pie plate to coat bottom with melted butter. Slowly pour batter into hot pie plate. Bake 18 to 20 minutes or until puffed and deep golden brown (do not underbake).

3 Meanwhile, in small bowl, mix cheese and powdered sugar; set aside. In 1-quart saucepan, cook and stir rhubarb, granulated sugar, water and cornstarch over medium-low heat until rhubarb is tender, about 4 minutes. Cool slightly. Stir in raspberries.

4 Remove pancake from oven. Carefully spread cheese filling over top of pancake. Cut into 4 wedges. If necessary, run spatula under pancake to loosen. Serve topped with fruit filling.

1 Serving: Calories 370; Total Fat 15g (Saturated Fat 8g, Trans Fat 0g); Cholesterol 190mg; Sodium 170mg; Total Carbohydrate 45g (Dietary Fiber 3g); Protein 14g **% Daily Value:** Vitamin A 15%; Vitamin C 8%; Calcium 25%; Iron 10% **Exchanges:** 1½ Starch, 1 Fruit, ½ Other Carbohydrate, 1½ Lean Meat, 2 Fat **Carbohydrate Choices:** 3

Start Happy Tip

It's important to make the cheese and fruit fillings while the pancake bakes so they're ready to use as soon as the pancake comes out of the oven. The "puff" will start to deflate quickly.

chocolate, maple and pear pancakes

prep time: 20 Minutes ❋ **start to finish:** 20 Minutes ❋ 3 Servings (3 pancakes and ½ cup sauce each)

1 cup Bisquick Heart Smart® mix

3 tablespoons unsweetened baking cocoa

2 tablespoons sugar

1 teaspoon ground cinnamon

⅔ cup chocolate milk

¼ cup fat-free egg product

2 ripe pears, peeled, thinly sliced

¼ cup maple-flavored syrup

1 In medium bowl, stir Bisquick mix, cocoa, sugar and cinnamon. Stir in milk and egg product until blended.

2 Heat griddle or skillet over medium heat (350°F). Brush griddle with vegetable oil if necessary (or spray with cooking spray before heating). For each pancake, pour slightly less than ¼ cup batter onto hot griddle. Cook until bubbles form on top and edges are dry. Turn; cook other side until golden brown.

3 Meanwhile, in medium microwavable bowl, microwave pears and syrup uncovered on High 2 minutes or until hot and pears are tender.

4 Serve pancakes with pear sauce.

1 Serving: Calories 400; Total Fat 4.5g (Saturated Fat 1g, Trans Fat 0g); Cholesterol 0mg; Sodium 430mg; Total Carbohydrate 83g (Dietary Fiber 6g); Protein 8g **% Daily Value:** Vitamin A 8%; Vitamin C 4%; Calcium 30%; Iron 15% **Exchanges:** 2½ Starch, 3 Other Carbohydrate, ½ Fat **Carbohydrate Choices:** 5½

Start Happy Tip

Chocolate doesn't always mean a very rich and sweet dish. These pancakes are just a bit sweet. The slightly bitter cocoa flavor is complemented by the sweet pear sauce.

orange pancakes with raspberry topping

prep time: 25 Minutes ❋ **start to finish:** 25 Minutes ❋ 4 Servings (2 pancakes and ¼ cup topping each)

Topping

- ½ cup orange juice
- 1 tablespoon cornstarch
- 1 package (10 oz) frozen raspberries in syrup, thawed

Pancakes

- 1 cup all-purpose flour
- 2 tablespoons powdered sugar
- ¼ teaspoon baking soda
- ¼ teaspoon salt
- 2 teaspoons grated orange peel
- ¾ cup milk
- 2 tablespoons butter, melted
- 1 egg
- 2 tablespoons orange juice

Garnish, if desired

- Frozen whipped topping, thawed
- Fresh raspberries

1 In 1-quart saucepan, stir ½ cup orange juice and the cornstarch until smooth. Heat to boiling over medium heat; boil 1 minute. Meanwhile, pour raspberries and syrup in strainer over medium bowl to drain. Stir syrup into juice mixture; cool slightly. Stir in raspberries; set aside.

2 In medium bowl, mix flour, powdered sugar, baking soda, salt and orange peel. Beat in milk, butter, egg and 2 tablespoons orange juice with fork or whisk just until blended.

3 Heat griddle or skillet over medium-high heat (375°F). Brush griddle with butter or vegetable oil if necessary (or spray with cooking spray before heating). For each pancake, pour about ¼ cup batter onto hot griddle. Cook until bubbles form on top and edges are dry. Turn; cook other side until golden brown.

4 Serve pancakes with raspberry topping. Garnish with whipped topping and fresh berries.

1 Serving: Calories 320; Total Fat 8g (Saturated Fat 4.5g, Trans Fat 0g); Cholesterol 70mg; Sodium 300mg; Total Carbohydrate 55g (Dietary Fiber 4g); Protein 7g **% Daily Value:** Vitamin A 10%; Vitamin C 25%; Calcium 8%; Iron 10% **Exchanges:** 2 Starch, 1 Fruit, ½ Other Carbohydrate, 1½ Fat **Carbohydrate Choices:** 3½

Start Happy Tip

Make the fruit topping ahead of time, and store it covered in the refrigerator. Microwave it for a few seconds to take off the chill before serving.

gluten-free cheesecake pancakes

prep time: 20 Minutes   **start to finish:** 8 Hours 20 Minutes   4 Servings (3 pancakes and about ¼ cup syrup each)

Pancakes

- 1 package (3 oz) gluten-free cream cheese
- 1 cup Bisquick Gluten Free mix
- 1 cup milk
- 2 tablespoons vegetable oil
- 1 teaspoon grated lemon peel
- 1 tablespoon lemon juice
- 1 egg

Syrup

- 1 cup sliced fresh strawberries
- ½ cup gluten-free strawberry syrup

1 Cut cream cheese lengthwise into 4 pieces; place on ungreased plate. Cover; freeze 8 hours or overnight.

2 Cut cream cheese into ¼-inch cubes. In large bowl, stir remaining pancake ingredients until blended. Stir in cream cheese.

3 Heat griddle or skillet over medium-high heat (375°F). Brush griddle with vegetable oil if necessary (or spray with cooking spray before heating). For each pancake, pour about ¼ cup batter onto hot griddle. Cook until bubbles form on top and edges are dry. Turn; cook other side until golden brown.

4 In small bowl, mix strawberries and syrup. Serve pancakes with syrup.

1 Serving: Calories 420; Total Fat 17g (Saturated Fat 6g, Trans Fat 0g); Cholesterol 80mg; Sodium 450mg; Total Carbohydrate 59g (Dietary Fiber 1g); Protein 6g **% Daily Value:** Vitamin A 10%; Vitamin C 20%; Calcium 15%; Iron 2% **Exchanges:** 2 Starch, 2 Other Carbohydrate, 3 Fat **Carbohydrate Choices:** 4

Start Happy Tips

If you are cooking gluten free, always read labels to make sure each recipe ingredient is gluten free. Products and ingredient sources can change.

Substitute your favorite fresh fruit and pancake syrup for the strawberries and strawberry syrup.

snickerdoodle pancakes

prep time: 30 Minutes ❋ **start to finish:** 30 Minutes ❋ 7 Servings (2 pancakes and 3 tablespoons sauce each)

Sauce

- 3 tablespoons sugar
- 1 tablespoon cornstarch
- 1¼ cups half-and-half
- 1 tablespoon butter
- 1 teaspoon vanilla

Pancakes

- 2 cups Original Bisquick mix
- ¼ cup sugar
- 1 cup milk
- 2 eggs
- 2 tablespoons ground cinnamon

Garnish, if desired

- Additional ground cinnamon

1 In 1½-quart saucepan, mix 3 tablespoons sugar and the cornstarch. Stir in half-and-half and butter until smooth. Heat to boiling over medium heat, stirring constantly. Boil about 2 minutes or until slightly thickened. Stir in vanilla. Keep warm.

2 In medium bowl, stir pancake ingredients until well blended. Heat griddle or skillet over medium-high heat (375°F). Brush griddle with vegetable oil if necessary (or spray with cooking spray before heating). For each pancake, pour slightly less than ¼ cup batter onto hot griddle. Cook until bubbles form on top and edges are dry. Turn; cook other side until golden brown.

3 Serve pancakes with sauce. Sprinkle with additional cinnamon.

1 Serving: Calories 310; Total Fat 13g (Saturated Fat 6g, Trans Fat 1.5g); Cholesterol 85mg; Sodium 480mg; Total Carbohydrate 41g (Dietary Fiber 2g); Protein 7g **% Daily Value:** Vitamin A 8%; Vitamin C 0%; Calcium 15%; Iron 8% **Exchanges:** 1½ Starch, 1 Other Carbohydrate, ½ Lean Meat, 2 Fat **Carbohydrate Choices:** 3

ham and pineapple pancake sliders

prep time: 25 Minutes ❋ **start to finish:** 25 Minutes ❋ **5 Servings (2 sliders each)**

Sauce

- 1 **can (8 oz) crushed pineapple, undrained**
- ½ **cup pineapple preserves**
- 1 **tablespoon packed brown sugar**
- ½ **teaspoon ground ginger**
- ¼ **to ½ teaspoon crushed red pepper flakes**

Sliders

- 2 **packages (6 oz each) Canadian bacon**
- 2 **cups Original Bisquick mix**
- 1¼ **cups milk**
- 2 **eggs**

1 In 1-quart saucepan, mix sauce ingredients. Heat to boiling. Reduce heat to medium; cook about 2 minutes, stirring constantly, until sauce is slightly thickened. Remove from heat; cool to room temperature.

2 Heat oven to 300°F. Place Canadian bacon in ungreased 15x10x1-inch pan with sides. Place in oven until hot.

3 Meanwhile, in medium bowl, stir Bisquick mix, milk and eggs until blended. Heat griddle or skillet over medium-high heat (375°F). Brush with vegetable oil if necessary (or spray with cooking spray before heating). For each pancake, pour about 2 tablespoons batter onto hot griddle. Cook until bubbles form on top and edges are dry. Turn; cook other side until golden brown.

4 For each slider, place 1 bacon slice on each of 10 pancakes. Top each with spoonful of sauce and second pancake.

1 Serving: Calories 240; Total Fat 7g (Saturated Fat 2.5g, Trans Fat 1g); Cholesterol 60mg; Sodium 760mg; Total Carbohydrate 33g (Dietary Fiber 1g); Protein 11g **% Daily Value:** Vitamin A 2%; Vitamin C 2%; Calcium 8%; Iron 6% **Exchanges:** ½ Starch, 1½ Other Carbohydrate, 1½ Lean Meat, ½ Fat **Carbohydrate Choices:** 2

cinnamon roll pancake stacks

prep time: 25 Minutes ✳ **start to finish:** 25 Minutes ✳ 14 Servings

Icing
- 2 cups powdered sugar
- ¼ cup whipping cream

Filling
- 1 cup packed brown sugar
- ½ cup butter
- 1 tablespoon ground cinnamon

Pancakes
- 2 cups Bisquick Heart Smart mix
- 1⅓ cups milk
- 1 egg
- ½ cup raisins

1 In small bowl, mix icing ingredients with whisk; set aside.

2 In 2-quart saucepan, cook filling ingredients over medium heat, stirring often, until butter is melted and sugar is dissolved. Remove from heat; cover to keep warm.

3 In medium bowl, stir Bisquick mix, milk and egg with fork or whisk until blended. Stir in raisins.

4 Heat griddle or skillet over medium-high heat (375°F). Brush with vegetable oil if necessary (or spray with cooking spray before heating). For each pancake, pour about 2 tablespoons batter onto hot griddle. Cook until bubbles form on top and edges are dry. Turn; cook other side until golden brown.

5 Serve pancakes stacked with filling between each pancake; drizzle with icing.

1 Serving: Calories 300; Total Fat 10g (Saturated Fat 6g, Trans Fat 0g); Cholesterol 40mg; Sodium 230mg; Total Carbohydrate 50g (Dietary Fiber 0g); Protein 3g **% Daily Value:** Vitamin A 6%; Vitamin C 0%; Calcium 15%; Iron 6% **Exchanges:** 1 Starch, 2½ Other Carbohydrate, 2 Fat **Carbohydrate Choices:** 3

whole-grain buttermilk waffles

prep time: 55 Minutes ✳ **start to finish:** 55 Minutes ✳ 4 Servings (two 4-inch waffles each)

1 cup Fiber One original bran cereal

1¼ cups buttermilk

1 egg, slightly beaten

2 tablespoons vegetable oil

1 teaspoon vanilla

¾ cup whole wheat or all-purpose flour

1 tablespoon sugar

½ teaspoon baking powder

½ teaspoon baking soda

¼ teaspoon salt

Maple syrup, if desired

Fresh raspberries, if desired

1 Heat waffle maker. (Waffle makers without a nonstick coating may need to be brushed with vegetable oil or sprayed with cooking spray before batter for each waffle is added.)

2 Place cereal in resealable food-storage plastic bag; seal bag and crush cereal with rolling pin or meat mallet (or crush in food processor). In large bowl, mix crushed cereal and buttermilk; let stand 5 minutes. Stir in egg, oil and vanilla. Stir in remaining ingredients except syrup and raspberries just until smooth. (Batter will be thick.)

3 For each waffle, spread batter onto center of hot waffle maker. (Waffle makers vary in size; check manufacturer's directions for recommended amount of batter.) Close lid of waffle maker.

4 Bake about 5 minutes or until steaming stops and waffle is golden brown. Carefully remove waffle. Serve immediately with maple syrup and raspberries. Repeat with remaining batter.

1 Serving: Calories 270; Total Fat 10g (Saturated Fat 2g, Trans Fat 0g); Cholesterol 55mg; Sodium 520mg; Total Carbohydrate 36g (Dietary Fiber 10g); Protein 8g **% Daily Value:** Vitamin A 6%; Vitamin C 4%; Calcium 20%; Iron 20% **Exchanges:** 1½ Starch, ½ Other Carbohydrate, ½ Skim Milk, 1½ Fat **Carbohydrate Choices:** 2½

Start Happy Tip

Serve waffles immediately, or keep warm in a single layer on a cooling rack or paper towel–lined cookie sheet in a 200°F oven. If you stack them, they'll become soggy.

waffles

prep time: 35 Minutes ❄ **start to finish:** 35 Minutes ❄ 6 (7-inch) Waffles

2 eggs

2 cups all-purpose or whole wheat flour

1 tablespoon sugar

4 teaspoons baking powder

¼ teaspoon salt

1¾ cups milk

½ cup vegetable oil or melted butter

Fresh berries, if desired

1 Heat waffle maker. (Waffle makers without a nonstick coating may need to be brushed with vegetable oil or sprayed with cooking spray before batter for each waffle is added.)

2 In large bowl, beat eggs with whisk until fluffy. Beat in remaining ingredients except berries just until smooth.

3 For each waffle, pour slightly less than ¾ cup batter onto center of hot waffle maker. (Waffle makers vary in size; check manufacturer's directions for recommended amount of batter.) Close lid of waffle maker.

4 Bake about 5 minutes or until steaming stops and waffle is golden brown. Carefully remove waffle. Serve immediately topped with fresh berries. Repeat with remaining batter.

1 Waffle: Calories 380; Total Fat 22g (Saturated Fat 4g, Trans Fat 0g); Cholesterol 75mg; Sodium 480mg; Total Carbohydrate 38g (Dietary Fiber 1g); Protein 9g **% Daily Value:** Vitamin A 4%; Vitamin C 0%; Calcium 25%; Iron 15% **Exchanges:** 2½ Starch, 4 Fat **Carbohydrate Choices:** 2½

Start Happy Tip

For about 7 grams of fat and 255 calories per serving, substitute ½ cup fat-free egg product for the eggs, use fat-free (skim) milk and decrease the oil to 3 tablespoons.

gluten-free waffles

prep time: 50 Minutes ❄ **start to finish:** 50 Minutes ❄ 8 (4-inch) Waffles

1⅓ cups Bisquick Gluten Free mix

1¼ cups milk

3 tablespoons vegetable oil

1 egg

Butter, if desired

Peach preserves, if desired

1 Heat waffle maker. (Waffle makers without a nonstick coating may need to be brushed with vegetable oil or sprayed with cooking spray.)

2 In large bowl, stir Bisquick mix, milk, oil and egg with fork or whisk until blended.

3 For each waffle, pour about ½ cup batter onto center of hot waffle maker. (Waffle makers vary in size; check manufacturer's directions for recommended amount of batter.) Close lid of waffle maker.

4 Bake about 5 minutes or until steaming stops and waffle is golden brown. Carefully remove waffle. Serve immediately with butter and peach preserves. Repeat with remaining batter.

1 Waffle: Calories 150; Total Fat 7g (Saturated Fat 1.5g, Trans Fat 0g); Cholesterol 30mg; Sodium 250mg; Total Carbohydrate 19g (Dietary Fiber 0g); Protein 3g **% Daily Value:** Vitamin A 2%; Vitamin C 0%; Calcium 8%; Iron 0% **Exchanges:** 1 Starch, 1½ Fat **Carbohydrate Choices:** 1

Start Happy Tips

Waffles can be served with syrup or any fresh fruit instead of the peach preserves.

If you're cooking gluten free, always read labels to make sure each recipe ingredient is gluten free. Products and ingredient sources can change.

cornmeal belgian waffles

prep time: 1 Hour ❋ **start to finish:** 1 Hour ❋ **6 Servings (2 waffles with syrup each)**

Waffles

1½ cups Original Bisquick mix

½ cup yellow cornmeal

1⅓ cups milk

3 tablespoons vegetable oil

1 teaspoon vanilla

1 whole egg

2 egg whites

Syrup

1 cup maple-flavored syrup

½ cup walnut halves, toasted*

2 tablespoons butter

1 In medium bowl, stir Bisquick mix, cornmeal, milk, oil, vanilla and whole egg with fork or whisk until blended. In small bowl, beat egg whites with electric mixer on high speed until stiff peaks form. Fold into batter.

2 Heat Belgian waffle maker; brush with vegetable oil. For each waffle, pour ¾ to 1 cup batter onto center of hot waffle maker. Close lid of waffle maker. Bake 4 to 5 minutes or until steaming stops and waffle is golden brown. Carefully remove waffle. Repeat with remaining batter.

3 Meanwhile, in 1-quart saucepan, heat syrup ingredients to simmering over medium heat.

4 Serve waffles with walnut syrup.

*To toast walnuts, sprinkle in ungreased skillet. Cook over medium heat 5 to 7 minutes, stirring frequently until walnuts begin to brown, then stirring constantly until light brown.

1 Serving: Calories 520; Total Fat 23g (Saturated Fat 6g, Trans Fat 1g); Cholesterol 45mg; Sodium 470mg; Total Carbohydrate 70g (Dietary Fiber 1g); Protein 8g **% Daily Value:** Vitamin A 6%; Vitamin C 0%; Calcium 10%; Iron 10% **Exchanges:** 2½ Starch, 2 Other Carbohydrate, 4½ Fat **Carbohydrate Choices:** 4½

cinnamon-cornbread waffles

prep time: 1 Hour 15 Minutes ❋ **start to finish:** 1 Hour 15 Minutes ❋ 7 Servings
(two 3½-inch waffles and ¼ cup syrup each)

Syrup
- 1 cup cinnamon apple pie filling (from 21-oz can)
- 1 cup maple-flavored syrup

Waffles
- 1½ cups Original Bisquick mix
- ½ cup cornmeal
- 1⅓ cups milk
- 2 tablespoons vegetable oil
- 1 teaspoon ground cinnamon
- 1 egg

Garnish
- Ground cinnamon, if desired

1 In medium microwavable bowl, mix syrup ingredients. Microwave uncovered on High 1 to 2 minutes or until warm. Cover to keep warm; set aside.

2 In medium bowl, stir waffle ingredients with spoon until blended.

3 Heat waffle maker. (Waffle makers without a nonstick coating may need to be brushed with vegetable oil or sprayed with cooking spray before batter for each waffle is added.)

4 For each waffle, pour batter onto hot waffle maker. (Waffle makers vary in size; check manufacturer's directions for recommended amount of batter.) Close lid of waffle maker.

5 Bake 4 to 5 minutes or until steaming stops and waffle is golden brown. Carefully remove waffle. Serve immediately with warm apple syrup and a sprinkle of additional cinnamon. Repeat with remaining batter.

1 Serving: Calories 390; Total Fat 9g (Saturated Fat 2.5g, Trans Fat 1g); Cholesterol 35mg; Sodium 370mg; Total Carbohydrate 71g (Dietary Fiber 1g); Protein 5g **% Daily Value:** Vitamin A 4%; Vitamin C 0%; Calcium 10%; Iron 8% **Exchanges:** 2 Starch, 2½ Other Carbohydrate, 1½ Fat **Carbohydrate Choices:** 5

Start Happy Tip
Leftovers? Stack cooled waffles between sheets of waxed paper. Wrap in foil and freeze. To reheat, unwrap the waffles and remove the waxed paper. Microwave uncovered on High, or heat them in the oven for a few minutes, until hot.

bacon waffles with chocolate syrup

prep time: 30 Minutes ❄ **start to finish:** 30 Minutes ❄ **4 Servings**

- 2 cups Original Bisquick mix
- 1⅓ cups milk
- 1 egg
- 2 tablespoons vegetable oil
- 6 slices bacon, chopped, crisply cooked
- 1 cup sliced fresh strawberries
- ¼ cup chocolate-flavor syrup

1 In large bowl, stir together Bisquick mix, milk, egg, oil and bacon until blended.

2 Heat waffle maker. (Waffle makers without a nonstick coating may need to be brushed with vegetable oil or sprayed with cooking spray before batter for each waffle is added.)

3 For each waffle, pour ¾ cup batter onto center of hot waffle maker. (Waffle makers vary in size; check manufacturer's directions for recommended amount of batter.) Close lid of waffle maker.

4 Bake about 5 minutes or until steaming stops and waffle is golden brown. Carefully remove waffle. Serve immediately with strawberries and chocolate syrup. Repeat with remaining batter.

1 Serving: Calories 510; Total Fat 24g (Saturated Fat 6g, Trans Fat 1.5g); Cholesterol 65mg; Sodium 1080mg; Total Carbohydrate 59g (Dietary Fiber 2g); Protein 14g **% Daily Value:** Vitamin A 4%; Vitamin C 20%; Calcium 15%; Iron 15% **Exchanges:** 2½ Starch, 1½ Other Carbohydrate, 1 High-Fat Meat, 3 Fat **Carbohydrate Choices:** 4

Start Happy Tips

Add chopped walnuts, almonds or pecans to the batter for some crunch.

For a little extra decadence, also drizzle waffles with caramel topping.

maple-bacon buttermilk waffles

prep time: 1 Hour 10 Minutes ⁜ **start to finish:** 1 Hour 10 Minutes ⁜ 12 Servings
(one 4-inch waffle and 2 tablespoons syrup each)

2 cups all-purpose flour

¼ cup sugar

1½ teaspoons baking soda

½ teaspoon salt

1¾ cups buttermilk

2 eggs

6 tablespoons butter, melted

1½ teaspoons maple flavor

1 package or jar (3 oz) cooked real bacon pieces or bits

1½ cups real maple or maple-flavored syrup

1 Heat waffle maker. (Waffle makers without a nonstick coating may need to be brushed with vegetable oil or sprayed with cooking spray before batter for each waffle is added.)

2 In large bowl, mix flour, sugar, baking soda and salt. In medium bowl, beat buttermilk, eggs, butter and maple flavor with whisk until well blended. Pour over flour mixture; stir just until moistened.

3 For each waffle, sprinkle about 2 teaspoons bacon pieces on each waffle grid. Spoon batter over bacon. (Waffle makers vary in size; check manufacturer's directions for recommended amount of batter.) Close lid of waffle maker.

4 Bake 3 to 5 minutes or until steaming stops and waffle is golden brown. Serve immediately with syrup. Repeat with remaining bacon and batter.

1 Serving: Calories 250; Total Fat 3g (Saturated Fat 1g, Trans Fat 0g); Cholesterol 45mg; Sodium 530mg; Total Carbohydrate 49g (Dietary Fiber 0g); Protein 7g **% Daily Value:** Vitamin A 0%; Vitamin C 0%; Calcium 8%; Iron 10% **Exchanges:** 1½ Starch, 2 Other Carbohydrate, ½ Fat **Carbohydrate Choices:** 3

Start Happy Tips

If you don't have buttermilk on hand, you can use regular milk plus vinegar. Pour 4 teaspoons white vinegar into a 2-cup measuring cup; add enough milk to equal 1¾ cups.

You can fry your own bacon instead of purchasing already cooked bacon pieces. Cook 6 to 8 strips of bacon until crisp, drain and crumble to equal about ½ cup of pieces.

stuffed cinnamon french toast–waffle sandwiches

prep time: 20 Minutes ✳ **start to finish:** 20 Minutes ✳ 2 Servings

¼ cup hazelnut spread with cocoa

4 slices white bread

¼ cup cream cheese spread

1 egg

3 tablespoons milk

1 teaspoon sugar

¼ teaspoon vanilla

⅛ teaspoon ground cinnamon

1 cup Cinnamon Toast Crunch cereal

Start Happy Tips

The bake time will vary with this recipe depending on the type of waffle maker you use.

To crush the cereal, place it in a resealable food-storage plastic bag; crush with a rolling pin.

1 Spread hazelnut spread on 2 slices of bread. Spread cream cheese on other 2 slices of bread. Press together 1 of each, filling sides together, making 2 sandwiches.

2 In shallow bowl, beat egg, milk, sugar, vanilla and cinnamon with fork or whisk until well mixed. Crush cereal; place in another shallow dish.

3 Heat waffle maker. (Waffle makers without a nonstick coating may need to be brushed with vegetable oil or sprayed with cooking spray before batter for each waffle is added.)

4 For each waffle sandwich, dip both sides of sandwich in egg mixture. Dip both sides in crushed cereal, patting gently to coat. Place on waffle maker. Close lid of waffle maker.

5 Bake 2 to 4 minutes or until browned. Carefully remove waffle sandwich. Repeat with remaining sandwich. To serve, cut sandwiches into quarters.

1 Serving: Calories 590; Total Fat 28g (Saturated Fat 9g, Trans Fat 0.5g); Cholesterol 125mg; Sodium 530mg; Total Carbohydrate 74g (Dietary Fiber 4g); Protein 12g **% Daily Value:** Vitamin A 20%; Vitamin C 4%; Calcium 25%; Iron 40% **Exchanges:** 1½ Starch, 3½ Other Carbohydrate, 1 Medium-Fat Meat, 4½ Fat **Carbohydrate Choices:** 5

pecan–chocolate chip waffles

prep time: 1 Hour 40 Minutes ❋ **start to finish:** 1 Hour 40 Minutes ❋ 18 Servings (one 4-inch waffle and 2 tablespoons syrup each)

3 cups all-purpose flour

1 tablespoon baking powder

¼ cup sugar

⅔ cup finely chopped pecans

⅔ cup miniature semisweet chocolate chips

4 eggs

1 cup butter, melted

2½ cups milk

2 teaspoons vanilla

2¼ cups maple-flavored syrup

Additional coarsely chopped pecans and miniature semisweet chocolate chips, if desired

1 Heat waffle maker. (Waffle makers without a nonstick coating may need to be brushed with vegetable oil or sprayed with cooking spray before batter for each waffle is added.)

2 In large bowl, mix flour, baking powder, sugar, pecans and chocolate chips. In medium bowl, beat eggs, butter, milk and vanilla with whisk. Pour over flour mixture; stir just until moistened.

3 For each waffle, spoon batter onto waffle maker. (Waffle makers vary in size; check manufacturer's directions for recommended amount of batter.) Close lid of waffle maker.

4 Bake about 5 minutes until steaming stops and waffles are deep golden brown. Serve immediately with syrup and topped with additional pecans and chocolate chips. Repeat with remaining batter.

1 Serving: Calories 380; Total Fat 17g (Saturated Fat 9g, Trans Fat 0g); Cholesterol 75mg; Sodium 190mg; Total Carbohydrate 52g (Dietary Fiber 1g); Protein 5g **% Daily Value:** Vitamin A 8%; Vitamin C 0%; Calcium 15%; Iron 10% **Exchanges:** 1½ Starch, 2 Other Carbohydrate, 3 Fat **Carbohydrate Choices:** 3½

Start Happy Tips

These waffles can be baked in a regular or Belgian waffle maker. The yield will vary.

For even more chocolate and nut flavor, spread the baked waffles with purchased hazelnut spread with cocoa, found near the peanut butter in grocery stores.

cinnamon french toast sticks with spicy cider syrup

prep time: 20 Minutes ❄ **start to finish:** 20 Minutes ❄ 10 Servings

Syrup

- 1 cup sugar
- 3 tablespoons all-purpose flour
- ¼ teaspoon ground cinnamon
- ¼ teaspoon ground nutmeg
- 2 cups apple cider
- 2 tablespoons lemon juice
- ¼ cup butter, cut into 8 pieces

French Toast

- ½ cup all-purpose flour
- 1¼ cups milk
- 2 teaspoons ground cinnamon
- 1 teaspoon vanilla
- 2 eggs
- 10 slices firm-textured whole-grain sandwich bread, cut into thirds

1 In 2-quart saucepan, mix sugar, 3 tablespoons flour, ¼ teaspoon cinnamon and the nutmeg. Stir in cider and lemon juice. Cook over medium heat, stirring constantly, until mixture thickens and boils. Boil and stir 1 minute; remove from heat. Stir in butter; cover to keep warm.

2 In small bowl, beat ½ cup flour, the milk, 2 teaspoons cinnamon, the vanilla and eggs with whisk until smooth.

3 Heat griddle or skillet over medium-high heat (375°F). Grease griddle with vegetable oil if necessary (or spray with cooking spray before heating).

4 Dip sticks of bread into batter; drain excess batter back into bowl. Place bread on hot griddle; cook about 4 minutes on each side or until golden brown. Serve French toast sticks with warm syrup.

1 Serving: Calories 280; Total Fat 7g (Saturated Fat 4g, Trans Fat 0g); Cholesterol 50mg; Sodium 200mg; Total Carbohydrate 46g (Dietary Fiber 2g); Protein 7g **% Daily Value:** Vitamin A 6%; Vitamin C 0%; Calcium 8%; Iron 8% **Exchanges:** 2½ Starch, ½ Other Carbohydrate, 1 Fat **Carbohydrate Choices:** 3

Start Happy Tip

Serve with ½ cup of fresh orange segments for only 40 extra calories and a boost of vitamin C.

french toast

prep time: 25 Minutes ❉ **start to finish:** 25 Minutes ❉ 8 Slices

3 eggs

¾ cup milk

1 tablespoon sugar

¼ teaspoon vanilla

⅛ teaspoon salt

8 slices firm-textured sandwich bread, Texas Toast or 1-inch-thick slices French bread

1 In medium bowl, beat eggs, milk, sugar, vanilla and salt with whisk until well mixed. Pour into shallow bowl.

2 Heat griddle or skillet over medium-high heat (375°F). Brush griddle with vegetable oil if necessary (or spray with cooking spray before heating).

3 Dip bread into egg mixture, coating both sides; place on griddle. Cook about 4 minutes on each side or until golden brown.

1 Slice: Calories 230; Total Fat 3.5g (Saturated Fat 1g, Trans Fat 0g); Cholesterol 80mg; Sodium 490mg; Total Carbohydrate 39g (Dietary Fiber 1g); Protein 10g **% Daily Value:** Vitamin A 4%; Vitamin C 0%; Calcium 6%; Iron 15% **Exchanges:** 2 Starch, ½ Other Carbohydrate, ½ Medium-Fat Meat **Carbohydrate Choices:** 2½

Oven French Toast: Heat oven to 450°F. Generously butter 15x10x1-inch pan. Heat pan in oven 1 minute; remove from oven. Arrange dipped bread in hot pan. Drizzle any remaining egg mixture over bread. Bake 5 to 8 minutes or until bottoms are golden brown; turn bread. Bake 2 to 4 minutes longer or until golden brown.

Start Happy Tip

For 2 grams of fat and 95 calories per serving, substitute 1 egg and 2 egg whites for the 3 eggs and use 2/3 cup fat-free (skim) milk. Increase the vanilla to ½ teaspoon.

ham 'n cheese french toast

prep time: 15 Minutes　✳　**start to finish:** 15 Minutes　✳　**6 Servings (2 toast halves each)**

1 cup milk

⅓ cup Original Bisquick mix

2 teaspoons vanilla

4 eggs

6 slices (1 inch thick) day-old ciabatta or French bread

2 tablespoons Dijon mustard

6 oz thinly sliced cooked ham (from deli)

1½ cups shredded mild Cheddar cheese (6 oz)

2 tablespoons butter

Powdered sugar

1　In shallow dish, stir milk, Bisquick mix, vanilla and eggs with fork or whisk until blended. In each slice of bread, cut 3-inch pocket through top crust. Spread about 1 teaspoon mustard in each pocket. Place 1 oz ham and ¼ cup cheese in each pocket.

2　Heat griddle or skillet over medium heat (350°F). Melt butter on griddle. Dip bread into egg mixture, coating both sides. Place bread on hot griddle; cook about 5 minutes, turning once, until golden brown.

3　Cut French toast in half diagonally; sprinkle with powdered sugar.

1 Serving: Calories 390; Total Fat 21g (Saturated Fat 11g, Trans Fat 0.5g); Cholesterol 185mg; Sodium 980mg; Total Carbohydrate 26g (Dietary Fiber 1g); Protein 23g **% Daily Value:** Vitamin A 15%; Vitamin C 0%; Calcium 25%; Iron 15% **Exchanges:** ½ Starch, 1 Other Carbohydrate, 1 Very Lean Meat, 1 Medium-Fat Meat, 1 High-Fat Meat, 1½ Fat **Carbohydrate Choices:** 2

Start Happy Tip

For a sweet and savory taste, serve with your favorite jam or preserves.

berry french toast stratas

prep time: 20 Minutes ❖ **start to finish:** 50 Minutes ❖ 6 Servings (2 stratas and ½ cup fruit each)

3 cups mixed fresh berries (such as blueberries, raspberries or cut-up strawberries)

1 tablespoon granulated sugar

4 cups cubed (¾ inch) whole wheat bread (about 5 slices)

1½ cups fat-free egg product or 6 eggs, beaten

½ cup fat-free (skim) milk

½ cup fat-free half-and-half

2 tablespoons honey

1½ teaspoons vanilla

1 teaspoon ground cinnamon

¼ teaspoon ground nutmeg

½ teaspoon powdered sugar, if desired

1 Heat oven to 350°F. Generously spray 12 regular-size muffin cups with cooking spray.

2 In medium bowl, mix fruit and granulated sugar; set aside.

3 Divide bread cubes evenly among muffin cups. In large bowl, beat remaining ingredients except powdered sugar with whisk until well mixed. Pour egg mixture over bread cubes, pushing down lightly with spoon to soak bread cubes. (If all egg mixture doesn't fit into cups, let cups stand up to 10 minutes, gradually adding remaining egg mixture as bread cubes soak it up.)

4 Bake 20 to 25 minutes or until centers are set. Cool 5 minutes. Remove stratas from muffin cups; place 2 on each of 6 plates. Top each serving with ½ cup fruit mixture; sprinkle evenly with powdered sugar.

1 Serving: Calories 190; Total Fat 1.5g (Saturated Fat 0g, Trans Fat 0g); Cholesterol 0mg; Sodium 280mg; Total Carbohydrate 31g (Dietary Fiber 5g); Protein 11g **% Daily Value:** Vitamin A 15%; Vitamin C 20%; Calcium 10%; Iron 10% **Exchanges:** 1 Starch, ½ Fruit, ½ Other Carbohydrate, 1 Very Lean Meat **Carbohydrate Choices:** 2

blueberry-orange french toast

prep time: 35 Minutes ✳ **start to finish:** 9 Hours ✳ 16 Slices

Syrup

- ⅓ cup sugar
- 1 teaspoon cornstarch
- ¼ cup orange juice
- 2 cups fresh or frozen blueberries

French Toast

- 16 slices (1 inch thick) French bread
- ½ cup orange marmalade
- 6 eggs
- 1½ cups half-and-half
- ¼ cup sugar
- ¼ teaspoon ground nutmeg
- 2 teaspoons vanilla
- ¼ cup butter, melted

1 In 1-quart saucepan, mix ⅓ cup sugar, the cornstarch and orange juice until smooth; stir in blueberries. Heat to boiling over medium heat, stirring often. Boil 3 minutes, stirring often.

2 Spray 15x10x1-inch pan with cooking spray. Cut lengthwise slit in side of each bread slice, cutting to but not through other side. Spread marmalade inside slit. Place in pan.

3 In large bowl, beat eggs, half-and-half, ¼ cup sugar, the nutmeg and vanilla until well blended. Pour over bread; turn slices carefully to coat. Cover; refrigerate 8 hours or overnight.

4 Heat oven to 425°F. Uncover pan; drizzle French toast with melted butter. Bake 20 to 25 minutes or until golden brown. Serve with syrup.

1 Slice: Calories 250; Total Fat 8g (Saturated Fat 3g, Trans Fat 0.5g); Cholesterol 80mg; Sodium 220mg; Total Carbohydrate 38g (Dietary Fiber 1g); Protein 7g **% Daily Value:** Vitamin A 6%; Vitamin C 2%; Calcium 6%; Iron 8% **Exchanges:** 2½ Starch, 1½ Fat **Carbohydrate Choices:** 2½

Start Happy Tips

Use day-old bread to make the French toast.

Prepare the syrup up to 1 day ahead of time, and store it covered in the refrigerator. Microwave it for a few seconds to take off the chill before serving it with the French toast.

apple-cinnamon french toast

prep time: 25 Minutes ❄ **start to finish:** 9 Hours 50 Minutes ❄ 12 Servings (1 square and 2 tablespoons syrup each)

French Toast

- 10 slices whole-grain bread
- 4 medium cooking apples, peeled, cubed (4 cups)
- 8 eggs
- 2½ cups half-and-half
- 1¼ cups sugar
- 1 tablespoon vanilla
- 1 cup chopped pecans
- 3 teaspoons ground cinnamon
- 1 teaspoon ground nutmeg

Syrup

- 1 cup sugar
- 3 tablespoons all-purpose flour
- 2 cups apple cider
- ¼ teaspoon ground cinnamon
- ¼ teaspoon ground nutmeg
- ¼ cup butter

1 Grease 13x9-inch (3-quart) glass baking dish with shortening or cooking spray. Arrange 5 of the bread slices in baking dish, trimming to fit if necessary. Spoon apples evenly over bread; top with remaining 5 bread slices.

2 In large bowl, beat eggs, half-and-half, ¼ cup of the sugar and the vanilla until smooth. Slowly pour mixture over bread. In small bowl, mix remaining 1 cup sugar, the pecans, 3 teaspoons cinnamon and 1 teaspoon nutmeg. Sprinkle over bread. Cover; refrigerate 8 hours or overnight.

3 Heat oven to 350°F. Bake French toast covered 30 minutes. Uncover baking dish; bake 35 to 45 minutes longer or until knife inserted halfway between center and edge comes out clean and top is golden brown. Let stand 10 minutes.

4 Meanwhile, in 2-quart saucepan, mix 1 cup sugar, the flour, cider, and ¼ teaspoon each cinnamon and nutmeg. Heat to boiling. Reduce heat to low. Add butter; cook and stir until melted.

5 Cut French toast into 12 squares. Serve with syrup.

1 Serving: Calories 520; Total Fat 21g (Saturated Fat 8g, Trans Fat 0.5g); Cholesterol 170mg; Sodium 250mg; Total Carbohydrate 70g (Dietary Fiber 4g); Protein 11g **% Daily Value:** Vitamin A 10%; Vitamin C 2%; Calcium 15%; Iron 10% **Exchanges:** 1½ Starch, ½ Fruit, 2½ Other Carbohydrate, 1 Medium-Fat Meat, 3 Fat **Carbohydrate Choices:** 4½

Start Happy Tip

While the French toast is baking, cook some bacon or sausages and toss a fruit salad to complete the meal.

upside-down banana-walnut french toast

prep time: 15 Minutes ✳ **start to finish:** 2 Hours 10 Minutes ✳ 10 Servings

1½ cups packed brown sugar
½ cup butter, melted
¼ cup light corn syrup
½ cup chopped walnuts
3 medium bananas, sliced
1 loaf (about 1 lb) sliced unfrosted firm cinnamon bread
6 eggs
1½ cups milk
1 teaspoon vanilla
   Powdered sugar, if desired

1 Spray 13x9-inch (3-quart) glass baking dish with cooking spray. In large bowl, stir brown sugar, butter, corn syrup and walnuts until smooth. Gently stir in bananas. Spoon mixture into baking dish.

2 Reserve ends of bread loaf for another use; they do not soak up egg mixture very well. Arrange 2 layers of bread on banana mixture, tearing bread to fit if needed.

3 In medium bowl, beat eggs, milk and vanilla with whisk until well blended. Pour over bread. Cover tightly; refrigerate at least 1 hour but no longer than 24 hours.

4 Heat oven to 325°F. Uncover baking dish; bake 45 to 55 minutes or until knife inserted in center comes out clean. Serve portions upside down, spooning sauce from bottom of dish over each serving. Sprinkle with powdered sugar.

1 Serving: Calories 490; Total Fat 19g (Saturated Fat 7g, Trans Fat 1g); Cholesterol 155mg; Sodium 380mg; Total Carbohydrate 72g (Dietary Fiber 2g); Protein 10g **% Daily Value:** Vitamin A 10%; Vitamin C 2%; Calcium 15%; Iron 15% **Exchanges:** 3 Starch, 2 Other Carbohydrate, 3½ Fat **Carbohydrate Choices:** 5

apricot-stuffed french toast

prep time: 15 Minutes ❉ **start to finish:** 1 Hour 10 Minutes ❉ 6 Servings (2 slices each)

1 loaf (8 oz) or ½ loaf (1-lb size) day-old French bread

1 package (3 oz) cream cheese, softened

3 tablespoons apricot preserves

¼ teaspoon grated lemon peel

3 eggs

¾ cup half-and-half or milk

2 tablespoons granulated sugar

1 teaspoon vanilla

⅛ teaspoon salt

⅛ teaspoon ground nutmeg, if desired

2 tablespoons butter, melted

Powdered sugar, if desired

1 Spray 13x9-inch pan with cooking spray. Cut bread crosswise into 12 (1-inch) slices. Cut horizontal slit in side of each bread slice, cutting to but not through other side.

2 In medium bowl, beat cream cheese, preserves and lemon peel with electric mixer on medium speed about 1 minute or until well mixed. Spread about 2 teaspoons cream cheese mixture inside slit in each bread slice. Place stuffed bread slices in pan.

3 In medium bowl, beat eggs, half-and-half, granulated sugar, vanilla, salt and nutmeg with fork or whisk until well mixed. Pour egg mixture over bread slices in pan; turn slices carefully to coat. Cover; refrigerate at least 30 minutes but no longer than 24 hours.

4 Heat oven to 425°F. Uncover pan; drizzle with butter. Bake 20 to 25 minutes or until golden brown. Sprinkle with powdered sugar.

1 Serving: Calories 310; Total Fat 16g (Saturated Fat 8g, Trans Fat 1g); Cholesterol 145mg; Sodium 380mg; Total Carbohydrate 32g (Dietary Fiber 1g); Protein 9g **% Daily Value:** Vitamin A 10%; Vitamin C 0%; Calcium 8%; Iron 10% **Exchanges:** 1 Starch, 1 Other Carbohydrate, 1 High-Fat Meat, 1½ Fat **Carbohydrate Choices:** 2

cinnamon breakfast bread pudding

prep time: 10 Minutes ❄ **start to finish:** 5 Hours ❄ 8 Servings (1 square and ¼ cup syrup each)

6 cups cubed (½ inch) raisin-cinnamon swirl bread

8 eggs

2½ cups milk

½ teaspoon ground cinnamon

¼ teaspoon ground nutmeg

2 cups maple-flavored syrup

1 Grease 13x9-inch (3-quart) glass baking dish with butter or cooking spray. Spread bread cubes evenly in baking dish.

2 In large bowl, beat eggs, milk, cinnamon and nutmeg until well blended. Pour over bread. Cover; refrigerate 4 hours or overnight.

3 Heat oven to 350°F. Uncover baking dish; bake 45 to 50 minutes or until set and top is golden brown. Cut into 8 squares. Serve with syrup.

1 Serving: Calories 400; Total Fat 8g (Saturated Fat 3g, Trans Fat 0g); Cholesterol 195mg; Sodium 260mg; Total Carbohydrate 72g (Dietary Fiber 0g); Protein 10g **% Daily Value:** Vitamin A 8%; Vitamin C 0%; Calcium 15%; Iron 8% **Exchanges:** 1 Starch, 4 Other Carbohydrate, 1 Medium-Fat Meat, ½ Fat **Carbohydrate Choices:** 5

Start Happy Tips

Plain cinnamon bread can be substituted for raisin-cinnamon bread.

A colorful fruit salad would pair well with this breakfast bread pudding.

cream cheese–filled batter-dipped french toast

prep time: 35 Minutes ❊ **start to finish:** 35 Minutes ❊ 8 Servings

5 oz cream cheese, softened

¼ cup orange marmalade

16 diagonally cut slices (½ inch thick) French bread

1 cup Original Bisquick mix

1 teaspoon ground cinnamon

½ teaspoon grated orange peel

⅔ cup milk

½ teaspoon vanilla

1 egg

1 tablespoon powdered sugar

Maple-flavored syrup, if desired

1 In small bowl, mix cream cheese and marmalade until blended. Spread 8 slices of the bread with cream cheese mixture. Top each with 1 of the remaining bread slices, making 8 sandwiches.

2 In shallow dish or pie pan, stir Bisquick mix, cinnamon, orange peel, milk, vanilla and egg with fork or whisk until blended.

3 Heat nonstick griddle or skillet over medium heat (350°F). Dip each sandwich into batter mixture, turning to coat both sides; drain excess batter into dish. Cook on hot griddle 1 to 2 minutes on each side or until golden brown. Sprinkle each sandwich with powdered sugar; serve with syrup.

1 Serving: Calories 550; Total Fat 11g (Saturated Fat 5g, Trans Fat 1g); Cholesterol 50mg; Sodium 1090mg; Total Carbohydrate 92g (Dietary Fiber 4g); Protein 18g **% Daily Value:** Vitamin A 6%; Vitamin C 0%; Calcium 10%; Iron 30% **Exchanges:** 4 Starch, 1½ Other Carbohydrate, ½ Milk, 1 Fat **Carbohydrate Choices:** 6

Start Happy Tip

For an easy substitution, use English muffin bread or swirled cinnamon bread in place of the French bread.

cheesy vegetable crepes

prep time: 35 Minutes ❊ **start to finish:** 50 Minutes ❊ 6 Servings (2 crepes each)

Filling

- 2 tablespoons vegetable oil
- 2 medium zucchini, coarsely chopped (3 to 4 cups)
- ½ cup chopped green bell pepper
- 4 medium green onions, sliced (¼ cup)
- ¼ teaspoon dried minced garlic
- 2 medium tomatoes, coarsely chopped (1½ cups)
- ½ teaspoon salt

Crepes

- 1 cup Original Bisquick mix
- ¾ cup milk
- 2 eggs
- 1 cup grated Parmesan cheese

1 In 10-inch skillet, heat oil over medium heat. Add zucchini, bell pepper, onions and garlic; cook 3 to 5 minutes, stirring occasionally, until vegetables are crisp-tender. Remove from heat. Stir in tomatoes; sprinkle with salt. Cover; let stand 2 to 3 minutes.

2 Lightly grease 6- to 7-inch skillet; heat over medium-high heat. In medium bowl, stir Bisquick mix, milk and eggs with fork or whisk until blended.

3 Heat oven to 350°F. For each crepe, pour 2 tablespoons batter into hot skillet; rotate skillet until batter covers bottom. Cook over medium-high heat until golden brown. Gently loosen edge with spatula; turn and cook other side until golden brown. Stack crepes, placing waxed paper between, as removed from skillet. Keep crepes covered to prevent drying out.

4 Spoon filling onto each crepe. Sprinkle half of cheese over filling on crepes. Roll up crepes; place seam side down in ungreased 11x7-inch (2-quart) glass baking dish. Sprinkle with remaining cheese.

5 Bake 10 to 12 minutes or until hot.

Start Happy Tip

Freeze unfilled crepes for up to 3 months with waxed paper between them. Wrap tightly. Thaw crepes at room temperature about 1 hour or in the refrigerator 6 to 8 hours.

1 Serving: Calories 260; Total Fat 15g (Saturated Fat 5g, Trans Fat 0.5g); Cholesterol 90mg; Sodium 780mg; Total Carbohydrate 19g (Dietary Fiber 2g); Protein 12g **% Daily Value:** Vitamin A 15%; Vitamin C 25%; Calcium 30%; Iron 8% **Exchanges:** ½ Starch, ½ Other Carbohydrate, 1 Vegetable, 1 Medium-Fat Meat, 2 Fat **Carbohydrate Choices:** 1

chocolate crepes with banana-pecan topping

prep time: 35 Minutes ※ **start to finish:** 35 Minutes ※ 8 Servings

⅓ cup whole wheat flour

2 tablespoons packed brown sugar

2 tablespoons unsweetened baking cocoa

⅛ teaspoon salt

⅔ cup fat-free (skim) milk

¼ cup fat-free egg product

1 teaspoon canola oil

½ teaspoon vanilla

4 medium bananas

¼ cup fat-free caramel topping

¼ teaspoon rum extract

¼ cup coarsely chopped pecans, toasted*

1 In medium bowl, mix flour, brown sugar, cocoa and salt. Add milk, egg product, oil and vanilla; stir with whisk until combined.

2 Lightly oil 7- to 8-inch crepe pan or nonstick skillet; heat over medium heat. For each crepe, pour about 2 tablespoons batter into pan. Immediately rotate pan until thin film covers bottom. Cook 30 to 45 seconds or until top is set and dry. Invert pan to remove crepe. Stack crepes between waxed paper; cover to keep warm. Repeat with remaining batter, oiling pan occasionally.

3 Cut bananas in half lengthwise, then crosswise. Lightly oil nonstick grill pan or large nonstick skillet; heat over medium heat. Add bananas; cook 3 to 4 minutes, turning once, until browned and softened.

4 Meanwhile, in 1-quart saucepan, heat caramel topping over low heat until hot. Remove from heat. Stir in rum extract.

5 On each of 8 plates, place 1 crepe (folding as desired). Top evenly with banana pieces, caramel topping and pecans.

*To toast pecans, cook in an ungreased skillet over medium heat for 5 to 7 minutes, stirring frequently, until pecans begin to brown, then stirring constantly until pecans are light brown.

1 Serving: Calories 170; Total Fat 3.5g (Saturated Fat 0g, Trans Fat 0g); Cholesterol 0mg; Sodium 95mg; Total Carbohydrate 30g (Dietary Fiber 3g); Protein 3g **% Daily Value:** Vitamin A 4%; Vitamin C 4%; Calcium 4%; Iron 4% **Exchanges:** 1 Starch, ½ Fruit, ½ Other Carbohydrate, ½ Fat **Carbohydrate Choices:** 2

Start Happy Tip

Top each serving with a tablespoon of miniature semisweet chocolate chips for about 50 calories more.

hearty brunch dishes

spinach-pesto egg bakes

prep time: 15 Minutes   ❄   **start to finish:** 50 Minutes   ❄   4 Servings

¼ cup pine nuts

1 cup frozen cut leaf spinach (from 14-oz bag), thawed, squeezed to drain

1 cup cottage cheese (from 12-oz container)

1 cup shredded Monterey Jack cheese (4 oz)

¼ cup basil pesto

4 eggs, beaten

¼ cup milk

1 medium tomato, chopped (¾ cup)

¼ cup shredded Parmesan cheese (1 oz)

Fresh basil leaves, if desired

1 Heat oven to 375°F. Lightly spray 4 (10-oz) custard cups or ramekins with cooking spray. Place cups on cookie sheet with sides.

2 Sprinkle pine nuts in ungreased 8- to 10-inch heavy skillet. Cook over medium heat 5 to 7 minutes, stirring frequently until nuts begin to brown, then stirring constantly until light brown.

3 In medium bowl, mix spinach, cottage cheese, Monterey Jack cheese, pesto and toasted nuts. Stir in eggs and milk until well blended. Divide spinach mixture evenly among cups.

4 Bake 25 to 30 minutes or until set. Cool 2 minutes. Top each egg bake with tomato and Parmesan cheese. Garnish with basil.

1 Serving: Calories 420; Total Fat 32g (Saturated Fat 12g, Trans Fat 0g); Cholesterol 255mg; Sodium 680mg; Total Carbohydrate 8g (Dietary Fiber 2g); Protein 25g **% Daily Value:** Vitamin A 80%; Vitamin C 4%; Calcium 50%; Iron 10% **Exchanges:** ½ Starch, ½ Vegetable, 2½ Medium-Fat Meat, ½ High-Fat Meat, 3 Fat **Carbohydrate Choices:** ½

Start Happy Tips

Use a yellow tomato instead of red for added interest. Or, if you aren't a tomato fan, these egg bakes can be made without the tomato.

For a quick weekday breakfast, make extra egg bakes and freeze. Reheat them in the microwave about 1 minute or until hot.

gluten-free impossibly easy breakfast bake

prep time: 20 Minutes ❊ **start to finish:** 1 Hour 5 Minutes ❊ 12 Servings

1 package (16 oz) bulk pork sausage

1 medium red bell pepper, chopped (¾ cup)

1 medium onion, chopped (½ cup)

3 cups frozen hash brown potatoes

2 cups shredded Cheddar cheese (8 oz)

¾ cup Bisquick Gluten Free mix

2 cups milk

¼ teaspoon pepper

6 eggs

1 Heat oven to 400°F. Spray 13x9-inch (3-quart) glass baking dish with cooking spray.

2 In 10-inch skillet, cook sausage, bell pepper and onion over medium heat, stirring occasionally, until sausage is no longer pink; drain. In baking dish, mix sausage mixture, potatoes and 1½ cups of the cheese.

3 In medium bowl, stir Bisquick mix, milk, pepper and eggs until blended. Pour over sausage mixture in baking dish.

4 Bake 30 to 35 minutes or until knife inserted in center comes out clean. Sprinkle with remaining ½ cup cheese. Bake about 3 minutes longer or until cheese is melted. Let stand 5 minutes before serving. Cut into squares.

1 Serving: Calories 270; Total Fat 15g (Saturated Fat 7g, Trans Fat 0g); Cholesterol 145mg; Sodium 520mg; Total Carbohydrate 21g (Dietary Fiber 1g); Protein 14g **% Daily Value:** Vitamin A 15%; Vitamin C 15%; Calcium 20%; Iron 6% **Exchanges:** 1 Starch, 1 Vegetable, 1 High-Fat Meat, 1½ Fat **Carbohydrate Choices:** 1½

Start Happy Tip

If you are cooking gluten free, always read labels to be sure each recipe ingredient is gluten free; products and ingredient sources can change.

cheesy sausage and egg bake

prep time: 25 Minutes ⁂ **start to finish:** 1 Hour ⁂ 12 Servings

1 lb bulk pork sausage, cooked, drained

1½ cups sliced fresh mushrooms (4 oz)

8 medium green onions, sliced (½ cup)

2 medium tomatoes, chopped (1½ cups)

2 cups shredded mozzarella cheese (8 oz)

1¼ cups Original Bisquick mix

1½ teaspoons salt

1½ teaspoons chopped fresh or ½ teaspoon dried oregano leaves

½ teaspoon pepper

1 cup milk

12 eggs

1 Heat oven to 350°F. Spray 13x9-inch (3-quart) glass baking dish with cooking spray.

2 Layer sausage, mushrooms, onions, tomatoes and cheese in baking dish.

3 In medium bowl, stir remaining ingredients with fork or whisk until blended. Pour over cheese.

4 Bake 30 to 35 minutes or until golden brown and set. Cut into squares.

1 Serving: Calories 260; Total Fat 16g (Saturated Fat 6g, Trans Fat 0.5g); Cholesterol 240mg; Sodium 750mg; Total Carbohydrate 12g (Dietary Fiber 0g); Protein 17g **% Daily Value:** Vitamin A 15%; Vitamin C 4%; Calcium 20%; Iron 8% **Exchanges:** 1 Starch, 2 High-Fat Meat **Carbohydrate Choices:** 1

Start Happy Tip

Having guests and want to do some prep ahead of time? Cook the sausage, and layer it with the mushrooms, onions, tomatoes and cheese in the baking dish. Cover and refrigerate. Just before baking, pour the Bisquick mixture over the top.

cheesy bacon–hash brown bake

prep time: 10 Minutes ✳ **start to finish:** 45 Minutes ✳ 12 Servings

1 bag (28 oz) frozen potatoes O'Brien with onions and peppers

1 can (18 oz) creamy three-cheese cooking sauce

1 cup shredded Cheddar cheese (4 oz)

½ cup sour cream

⅓ cup sliced green onions (about 5 medium)

1 package (2.5 oz) cooked real bacon pieces

1 Heat oven to 350°F. Spray 13x9-inch (3-quart) glass baking dish or 3-quart casserole dish with cooking spray.

2 Place potatoes in large microwavable bowl. Microwave uncovered on High 6 to 8 minutes, stirring twice, until thawed and potatoes are hot.

3 Stir in remaining ingredients. Spoon into baking dish.

4 Bake 30 to 35 minutes or until hot in center and bubbly around edges. Cut into squares.

1 Serving: Calories 160; Total Fat 9g (Saturated Fat 4.5g, Trans Fat 0g); Cholesterol 25mg; Sodium 410mg; Total Carbohydrate 15g (Dietary Fiber 1g); Protein 7g **% Daily Value:** Vitamin A 8%; Vitamin C 4%; Calcium 8%; Iron 0% **Exchanges:** 1 Starch, ½ High-Fat Meat, 1 Fat **Carbohydrate Choices:** 1

alfredo scrambled egg bake

prep time: 20 Minutes ✳ **start to finish:** 35 Minutes ✳ 6 Servings

1 cup Original Bisquick mix

¼ teaspoon Italian seasoning

6 tablespoons cold butter

1 egg

¼ cup chopped onion

¼ cup chopped green bell pepper

1 package (8 oz) sliced fresh mushrooms (about 3 cups)

12 eggs, beaten

⅓ cup crumbled packaged precooked bacon (from 2.1-oz package)

¾ cup Alfredo pasta sauce

1 Heat oven to 400°F. Spray 8-inch square (2-quart) glass baking dish with cooking spray.

2 In small bowl, stir together Bisquick mix and Italian seasoning. Using pastry blender or fork, cut in 4 tablespoons of the butter until crumbly. Gently stir in 1 egg. Set aside for topping.

3 In 12-inch nonstick skillet, melt remaining 2 tablespoons butter over medium heat. Add onion, bell pepper and mushrooms; cook 3 to 5 minutes, stirring occasionally, until vegetables are crisp-tender. Add beaten eggs; cook, stirring occasionally, until eggs are set. Remove from heat. Gently stir in bacon and Alfredo sauce. Spread in baking dish. Sprinkle with topping.

4 Bake about 15 minutes or until topping is golden brown. Cut into squares.

1 Serving: Calories 490; Total Fat 37g (Saturated Fat 18g, Trans Fat 1.5g); Cholesterol 470mg; Sodium 710mg; Total Carbohydrate 18g (Dietary Fiber 1g); Protein 20g **% Daily Value:** Vitamin A 25%; Vitamin C 6%; Calcium 15%; Iron 10% **Exchanges:** ½ Starch, ½ Other Carbohydrate, ½ Vegetable, 2 Medium-Fat Meat, ½ High-Fat Meat, 4½ Fat **Carbohydrate Choices:** 1

Start Happy Tips

Part of the quick and easy preparation is using precooked bacon slices. Look for packages of these convenient bacon strips with the regular bacon.

Serve this casserole with a bowl of fresh berries or melon and warm breadsticks.

cowboy breakfast bake

prep time: 20 Minutes ❋ **start to finish:** 40 Minutes ❋ 10 Servings

Crust

¾ cup all-purpose flour

¼ cup cornmeal

1 tablespoon sugar

1 teaspoon baking powder

¼ teaspoon salt

⅓ cup milk

2 tablespoons vegetable oil

1 egg

Topping

1 package (12 oz) bulk pork sausage

½ cup sliced red bell pepper

½ cup sliced onion

6 eggs

¼ cup milk

½ teaspoon salt

Dash pepper

1 tablespoon butter

2 cups shredded Cheddar cheese (8 oz)

⅔ cup chunky-style salsa, if desired

1 Heat oven to 400°F. Spray bottom and sides of 13x9-inch pan with cooking spray or grease with shortening.

2 In medium bowl, mix flour, cornmeal, sugar, baking powder and ¼ teaspoon salt. In small bowl, stir together ⅓ cup milk, the oil and 1 egg. Add egg mixture all at once to flour mixture; stir just until moistened. Spread batter in pan. Bake 10 to 13 minutes or until crust is light golden brown.

3 Meanwhile, in 10-inch nonstick skillet, cook sausage, bell pepper and onion over medium-high heat 5 to 7 minutes, stirring occasionally, until sausage is no longer pink; drain. Remove sausage from skillet; keep warm.

4 In medium bowl, beat 6 eggs, ¼ cup milk, ½ teaspoon salt and the pepper with fork or whisk until well mixed.

5 In same skillet, heat butter over medium heat just until butter begins to sizzle. Pour egg mixture into skillet. As mixture begins to set at bottom and side, gently lift cooked portions with spatula so that thin, uncooked portion can flow to bottom. Avoid constant stirring. Cook 3 to 4 minutes or until eggs are thickened throughout but still moist.

6 Arrange eggs over hot crust; top with sausage mixture. Sprinkle with cheese. Bake 5 to 7 minutes or until cheese is melted. Cut into squares. Serve with salsa.

1 Serving: Calories 300; Total Fat 21g (Saturated Fat 9g, Trans Fat 0g); Cholesterol 190mg; Sodium 630mg; Total Carbohydrate 14g (Dietary Fiber 0g); Protein 15g **% Daily Value:** Vitamin A 15%; Vitamin C 8%; Calcium 20%; Iron 8% **Exchanges:** 1 Other Carbohydrate, 2 High-Fat Meat, 1 Fat **Carbohydrate Choices:** 1

muffuletta egg bake

prep time: 15 Minutes ❄ **start to finish:** 1 Hour 5 Minutes ❄ 8 Servings

1⅓ cups chopped cooked ham

⅓ cup coarsely chopped pimiento-stuffed green olives

½ cup chopped drained roasted red bell peppers (from a jar)

½ loaf (1-lb size) unsliced Italian bread, cut into 1-inch cubes (about 5¼ cups)

8 eggs

2½ cups milk

6 slices (about ¾ oz each) provolone cheese

1 tablespoon shredded Parmesan cheese

1 Heat oven to 350°F. Grease 11x7-inch (2-quart) glass baking dish with butter or cooking spray.

2 In small bowl, mix ham, olives and roasted peppers. In baking dish, toss bread cubes and half of ham mixture.

3 In large bowl, beat eggs and milk with whisk until well blended. Pour over ingredients in baking dish. Top evenly with provolone cheese; sprinkle with remaining ham mixture.

4 Bake 40 to 45 minutes or until set and edges are golden brown. Sprinkle with Parmesan cheese. Let stand 5 minutes before serving. Cut into squares.

1 Serving: Calories 290; Total Fat 15g (Saturated Fat 6g, Trans Fat 0g); Cholesterol 245mg; Sodium 830mg; Total Carbohydrate 17g (Dietary Fiber 1g); Protein 21g **% Daily Value:** Vitamin A 20%; Vitamin C 10%; Calcium 25%; Iron 10% **Exchanges:** ½ Starch, ½ Low-Fat Milk, ½ Lean Meat, 1 Medium-Fat Meat, ½ High-Fat Meat, ½ Fat **Carbohydrate Choices:** 1

Start Happy Tips

Italian bread from the bakery or the bread aisle will work for this recipe. Wheat bread also works in place of the Italian bread.

With its combination of savory ingredients, this egg dish pairs well with fruit.

tomato-pesto brunch bake

prep time: 20 Minutes ❊ **start to finish:** 1 Hour 5 Minutes ❊ 12 Servings

2½ cups Original Bisquick mix

½ cup grated Parmesan cheese

¾ cup milk

2 cups shredded mozzarella cheese (8 oz)

3 large tomatoes, cut into thin slices

½ cup refrigerated basil pesto

4 eggs

½ cup whipping cream

1 teaspoon salt

½ teaspoon white pepper

1 Heat oven to 350°F. In medium bowl, stir Bisquick mix, Parmesan cheese and milk until soft dough forms. With fingers dipped in Bisquick mix, press dough in bottom and ½ inch up sides of ungreased 13x9-inch (3-quart) glass baking dish.

2 Sprinkle 1½ cups of the mozzarella cheese over crust. Layer tomatoes over cheese, overlapping if necessary. Spread pesto over tomatoes.

3 In medium bowl, beat eggs, whipping cream, salt and pepper with fork or whisk until blended. Gently pour mixture over tomatoes. Sprinkle with remaining ½ cup mozzarella cheese.

4 Bake 35 to 40 minutes or until top is golden brown. Let stand 5 minutes before serving. Cut into squares.

1 Serving: Calories 300; Total Fat 19g (Saturated Fat 8g, Trans Fat 1g); Cholesterol 100mg; Sodium 780mg; Total Carbohydrate 21g (Dietary Fiber 1g); Protein 12g **% Daily Value:** Vitamin A 15%; Vitamin C 6%; Calcium 30%; Iron 8% **Exchanges:** 1 Starch, ½ Low-Fat Milk, ½ Vegetable, ½ Lean Meat, 3 Fat **Carbohydrate Choices:** 1½

Start Happy Tip

The standing time for this dish, like many egg-based dishes, allows it to set before being cut.

bacon and hash brown egg bake

prep time: 30 Minutes ❋ **start to finish:** 9 Hours 40 Minutes ❋ 12 Servings

1 lb bacon, cut into 1-inch pieces

1 medium onion, chopped (½ cup)

1 medium red bell pepper, chopped (¾ cup)

1 package (8 oz) sliced fresh mushrooms (about 3 cups)

2 tablespoons Dijon mustard

½ teaspoon salt

½ teaspoon pepper

¾ cup milk

12 eggs

1 package (32 oz) frozen hash brown potatoes, thawed

2 cups shredded Cheddar cheese (16 oz)

1 In 12-inch skillet, cook bacon until crisp. Using slotted spoon, remove bacon from skillet to small bowl. Cover; refrigerate. Drain drippings, reserving 1 tablespoon in skillet. Add onion, bell pepper and mushrooms; cook 4 minutes, stirring occasionally, over medium heat. Stir in mustard, salt and pepper; set aside.

2 In large bowl, beat milk and eggs with whisk; set aside.

3 Spray 13x9-inch (3-quart) glass baking dish with cooking spray. Spread half of hash brown potatoes in baking dish. Spread onion mixture evenly over top. Sprinkle with 1 cup of the cheese. Spread remaining potatoes over top. Pour egg mixture over top. Cover; refrigerate 8 hours or overnight.

4 Heat oven to 325°F. Uncover baking dish; bake 50 to 60 minutes or until thermometer inserted in center reads 160°F. Sprinkle with remaining 1 cup cheese and the bacon. Bake 3 to 5 minutes longer or until knife inserted in center comes out clean, top is puffed and cheese is melted. Let stand 5 minutes before serving. Cut into squares.

1 Serving: Calories 410; Total Fat 24g (Saturated Fat 12g, Trans Fat 0g); Cholesterol 265mg; Sodium 740mg; Total Carbohydrate 25g (Dietary Fiber 3g); Protein 22g **% Daily Value:** Vitamin A 20%; Vitamin C 20%; Calcium 25%; Iron 8% **Exchanges:** 1½ Starch, 2½ High-Fat Meat, 1 Fat **Carbohydrate Choices:** 1½

Start Happy Tips

Use Monterey Jack, Colby or Swiss instead of the Cheddar cheese.

Serve with assorted breads and fresh fruit.

rancher's egg casserole

prep time: 10 Minutes ❋ **start to finish:** 2 Hours 10 Minutes ❋ 8 Servings

1⅔ cups Original Bisquick mix

1 tablespoon taco seasoning mix (from 1-oz package)

3⅓ cups milk

8 eggs, slightly beaten

½ cup chopped drained roasted red bell peppers (from a jar)

1 can (4.5 oz) chopped green chiles, drained

1 cup shredded Mexican cheese blend (4 oz)

Chopped grape tomatoes, if desired

Sliced avocados, if desired

Chopped fresh cilantro, if desired

1 Heat oven to 450°F. Generously grease bottom and sides of 13x9-inch (3-quart) glass baking dish with shortening or spray with cooking spray.

2 In small bowl, stir Bisquick mix, taco seasoning mix and ⅓ cup of the milk until soft dough forms. Pat dough in bottom of baking dish. Bake 8 minutes. Cool 30 minutes.

3 Reduce oven temperature to 350°F. In medium bowl, beat eggs, remaining 3 cups milk, the roasted peppers and chiles with fork or whisk until blended. Pour over cooled crust. Cover with foil.

4 Bake 30 minutes. Uncover baking dish; bake 30 to 40 minutes longer or until knife inserted in center comes out clean. Sprinkle with cheese. Let stand 10 minutes before serving. Cut into squares. Garnish with tomatoes, avocado slices and cilantro.

1 Serving: Calories 300; Total Fat 15g (Saturated Fat 7g, Trans Fat 1g); Cholesterol 235mg; Sodium 840mg; Total Carbohydrate 24g (Dietary Fiber 1g); Protein 15g **% Daily Value:** Vitamin A 30%; Vitamin C 20%; Calcium 25%; Iron 10% **Exchanges:** 1½ Starch, 1½ Medium-Fat Meat, 1½ Fat **Carbohydrate Choices:** 1½

mexican breakfast casserole

prep time: 20 Minutes ❊ **start to finish:** 1 Hour 10 Minutes ❊ 12 Servings

1 bag (20 oz) refrigerated cooked shredded hash brown potatoes

1 package (1 oz) taco seasoning mix

1 lb bulk turkey or pork breakfast sausage

1 medium onion, chopped (½ cup)

12 eggs

2 cups shredded Cheddar cheese (8 oz)

¼ cup milk

½ teaspoon salt

¼ teaspoon ground pepper

1½ cups chunky-style medium salsa (from 16-oz jar)

1 Heat oven to 350°F. Spray 13x9-inch (3-quart) glass baking dish with cooking spray.

2 In large bowl, place potatoes and 1 tablespoon of the taco seasoning mix; toss to coat potatoes evenly. Pat in bottom of baking dish.

3 Spray 10-inch skillet with cooking spray. Cook breakfast sausage and onion over medium-high heat 5 to 7 minutes, stirring occasionally, until sausage is no longer pink; drain.

4 Meanwhile, in same large bowl, beat eggs, cheese, milk, salt, pepper and remaining taco seasoning mix with whisk until well mixed. Stir in sausage mixture and salsa. Carefully pour over potatoes in baking dish.

5 Bake about 40 minutes or until eggs are set in center. Let stand 10 minutes before serving. Cut into squares.

1 Serving: Calories 280; Total Fat 16g (Saturated Fat 7g, Trans Fat 0g); Cholesterol 240mg; Sodium 980mg; Total Carbohydrate 15g (Dietary Fiber 1g); Protein 21g **% Daily Value:** Vitamin A 15%; Vitamin C 2%; Calcium 15%; Iron 10% **Exchanges:** ½ Starch, ½ Low-Fat Milk, 2 Lean Meat, 1½ Fat **Carbohydrate Choices:** 1

Start Happy Tip
Yum! This Mexican egg dish will make you say, "*Hola* morning!" Top servings with dollops of sour cream and more salsa, if you like.

cheesy ham breakfast casserole

prep time: 15 Minutes ✳ **start to finish:** 5 Hours 10 Minutes ✳ 6 Servings (2 wedges each)

Casserole

- 5 eggs
- ¾ cup milk
- ½ cup chives-and-onion cream cheese spread (from 8-oz container)
- ½ teaspoon ground mustard
- ¼ teaspoon salt
- ⅛ teaspoon pepper
- 2 cups refrigerated southwest-style shredded hash brown potatoes (from 20-oz bag)
- 1 cup shredded Cheddar cheese (4 oz)
- ¼ cup diced red bell pepper
- ⅔ cup diced cooked ham (from 8-oz package)

Topping

- ½ cup panko crispy bread crumbs
- ¼ cup shredded Parmesan cheese (1 oz)
- 1 tablespoon butter, melted

1 Grease 8- or 9-inch square baking dish with butter or spray with cooking spray.

2 In large bowl, beat eggs, milk and cream cheese until well blended. Stir in remaining casserole ingredients. Pour mixture into baking dish. Cover; refrigerate 4 hours or overnight.

3 Heat oven to 350°F. Uncover baking dish; bake 40 minutes. In small bowl, mix topping ingredients. Sprinkle over casserole. Bake 10 to 15 minutes longer or until set and top is golden brown. Cut into 6 squares; cut each square in half diagonally.

1 Serving: Calories 330; Total Fat 20g (Saturated Fat 10g, Trans Fat 0g); Cholesterol 225mg; Sodium 750mg; Total Carbohydrate 18g (Dietary Fiber 1g); Protein 18g **% Daily Value:** Vitamin A 15%; Vitamin C 6%; Calcium 25%; Iron 6% **Exchanges:** 1 Starch, 2 Medium-Fat Meat, 2 Fat **Carbohydrate Choices:** 1

Start Happy Tip

Refrigerated hash browns are a great fit for this recipe, although frozen hash browns may be used. If using frozen potatoes, make sure to thaw and pat them dry before using.

puffed pancake brunch casserole

prep time: 15 Minutes ❋ **start to finish:** 1 Hour 5 Minutes ❋ 10 Servings

½ cup butter

2 cups Original Bisquick mix

2 cups milk

8 eggs

1 cup shredded Swiss cheese (4 oz)

1 lb cooked ham, cut into cubes (about 3 cups)

1 package (2.1 oz) precooked bacon, chopped

2 cups shredded Cheddar cheese (8 oz)

¼ teaspoon salt

¼ teaspoon ground mustard

Dash ground nutmeg

Chopped fresh parsley, if desired

1 Heat oven to 375°F. Spray 13x9-inch (3-quart) glass baking dish with cooking spray. Place butter in dish; place in oven until melted, about 10 minutes.

2 Meanwhile, in medium bowl, stir together Bisquick mix, 1 cup of the milk and 2 of the eggs with whisk until tiny lumps remain. Pour over melted butter. Layer with Swiss cheese, ham, bacon and Cheddar cheese.

3 In large bowl, beat remaining 1 cup milk, remaining 6 eggs, the salt, mustard and nutmeg. Pour over ingredients in baking dish.

4 Bake 35 to 40 minutes or until golden brown. Let stand 10 minutes before serving. Sprinkle with parsley. Cut into squares.

1 Serving: Calories 460; Total Fat 30g (Saturated Fat 15g, Trans Fat 1.5g); Cholesterol 255mg; Sodium 1430mg; Total Carbohydrate 19g (Dietary Fiber 0g); Protein 29g **% Daily Value:** Vitamin A 15%; Vitamin C 0%; Calcium 30%; Iron 10% **Exchanges:** 1 Starch, ½ Other Carbohydrate, 3 Medium-Fat Meat, ½ High-Fat Meat, 2 Fat **Carbohydrate Choices:** 1

baked puffy cheese omelet

prep time: 10 Minutes ❉ **start to finish:** 55 Minutes ❉ 6 Servings

1¼ cups shredded Mexican cheese blend (5 oz)

3 medium green onions, thinly sliced (3 tablespoons)

⅓ cup Original Bisquick mix

1 cup milk

4 eggs

¼ cup chunky-style salsa

¼ cup peach preserves

Green onion tops, if desired

1 Heat oven to 350°F. Spray 9-inch glass pie plate with cooking spray.

2 Sprinkle 1 cup of the cheese and the sliced onions in pie plate. In medium bowl, stir Bisquick mix, milk and eggs with fork or whisk until well blended. Pour over ingredients in pie plate.

3 Bake 30 to 35 minutes or until knife inserted in center comes out clean. Sprinkle with remaining ¼ cup cheese. Bake 3 to 5 minutes longer or until cheese is melted. Let stand 5 minutes before cutting.

4 Meanwhile, in small bowl, mix salsa and preserves.

5 Cut omelet into wedges. Serve with salsa mixture. Garnish with green onion tops.

1 Serving: Calories 230; Total Fat 12g (Saturated Fat 6g, Trans Fat 0g); Cholesterol 165mg; Sodium 360mg; Total Carbohydrate 17g (Dietary Fiber 0g); Protein 12g **% Daily Value:** Vitamin A 10%; Vitamin C 2%; Calcium 25%; Iron 6% **Exchanges:** ½ Starch, ½ Other Carbohydrate, 1½ Medium-Fat Meat, 1 Fat **Carbohydrate Choices:** 1

Start Happy Tip

Spicy and sweet flavors complement each other, so you may want to use a medium or hot salsa for this topping to balance the sweetness of the peach preserves.

make-ahead alfredo strata

prep time: 10 Minutes ✳ start to finish: 5 Hours 5 Minutes ✳ 8 Servings

1 loaf (1 lb) unsliced rustic Italian bread, cut into 1-inch cubes (8 cups)

1 cup frozen chopped broccoli (from 12-oz bag), thawed, drained

2 cups shredded Italian cheese blend (8 oz)

5 eggs

2 cups milk

1 container (10 oz) refrigerated Alfredo pasta sauce

1 Spray 13x9-inch (3-quart) glass baking dish with cooking spray.

2 In baking dish, layer half of the bread cubes, the broccoli, 1 cup of the cheese and the remaining bread cubes.

3 In large bowl, beat eggs, milk and Alfredo sauce with whisk until well blended. Pour over ingredients in baking dish. Cover; refrigerate 4 hours or overnight.

4 Heat oven to 350°F. Uncover baking dish; sprinkle remaining 1 cup cheese over strata. Bake 45 to 50 minutes or until knife inserted in center comes out clean and cheese is deep golden brown. Let stand 5 minutes before serving. Cut into squares.

1 Serving: Calories 450; Total Fat 25g (Saturated Fat 14g, Trans Fat 1g); Cholesterol 190mg; Sodium 780mg; Total Carbohydrate 35g (Dietary Fiber 2g); Protein 21g **% Daily Value:** Vitamin A 20%; Vitamin C 6%; Calcium 40%; Iron 15% **Exchanges:** 2½ Starch, 1 Medium-Fat Meat, 1 High-Fat Meat, 2 Fat **Carbohydrate Choices:** 2

Make-Ahead Alfredo-Ham Strata: Add 1 cup diced cooked ham to the layers between the broccoli and cheese.

Start Happy Tip

Alfredo sauce from a jar can be used in place of the refrigerated sauce.

basil breakfast strata

prep time: 15 Minutes ※ **start to finish:** 9 Hours 5 Minutes ※ 12 Servings

6 eggs

3½ cups milk

1 teaspoon salt

½ teaspoon pepper

8 cups cubed (1 inch) French bread

2 cups shredded mozzarella cheese (8 oz)

¼ cup basil pesto

½ cup grated Parmesan cheese (2 oz)

1 Spray 13x9-inch (3-quart) glass baking dish with cooking spray.

2 In large bowl, beat eggs with whisk until foamy. Beat in milk until blended; beat in salt and pepper. Set aside.

3 Place bread cubes in baking dish. Sprinkle with mozzarella cheese. Pour egg mixture over top, pressing lightly to moisten bread. Using spoon, swirl pesto through mixture. Sprinkle Parmesan cheese over top. Cover; refrigerate at least 8 hours but no longer than 24 hours.

4 Heat oven to 350°F. Uncover baking dish; bake 40 to 45 minutes or until strata is puffed and knife inserted in center comes out clean. Let stand 5 minutes before serving. Cut into squares.

1 Serving: Calories 240; Total Fat 13g (Saturated Fat 6g, Trans Fat 0g); Cholesterol 125mg; Sodium 600mg; Total Carbohydrate 16g (Dietary Fiber 0g); Protein 15g **% Daily Value:** Vitamin A 8%; Vitamin C 0%; Calcium 30%; Iron 6% **Exchanges:** 1 Starch, 1½ Medium-Fat Meat, 1 Fat **Carbohydrate Choices:** 1

chicken fajita strata

prep time: 30 Minutes ❈ **start to finish:** 4 Hours ❈ 12 Servings

2 tablespoons canola oil

2 teaspoons chili powder

1 teaspoon ground cumin

½ teaspoon salt

1 clove garlic, finely chopped

1 lb boneless skinless chicken breasts, cut into thin strips

1 medium onion, cut into thin wedges

1 medium green bell pepper, cut into strips

1 to 2 medium jalapeño chiles, seeded, finely chopped

12 soft yellow corn tortillas (6 inch; 10 oz), cut into 1-inch strips

½ cup shredded reduced-fat Cheddar cheese (2 oz)

1 cup reduced-fat sour cream

3 tablespoons chopped fresh cilantro

¼ teaspoon ground red pepper (cayenne)

1 carton (8 oz) fat-free egg product (1 cup)

¾ cup fat-free (skim) milk

1 can (10¾ oz) condensed 98% fat-free cream of chicken soup with 45% less sodium

1 medium tomato, chopped (¾ cup)

1 In small bowl, mix oil, chili powder, cumin, salt and garlic. Place chicken in resealable food-storage plastic bag; add chili powder mixture. Seal bag; shake to coat chicken with spices. Refrigerate 30 minutes.

2 Heat 10-inch nonstick skillet over medium-high heat. Add chicken mixture; cook 5 to 7 minutes, stirring frequently, until chicken is no longer pink in center. Transfer chicken from skillet to plate. In same skillet, cook onion, bell pepper and chiles over medium-high heat 5 to 7 minutes, stirring frequently, until crisp-tender.

3 Spray 13x9-inch (3-quart) glass baking dish with cooking spray. Arrange half of the tortilla strips in baking dish. Top with chicken, half of the vegetable mixture and ¼ cup of the cheese. Repeat layers with remaining tortilla strips, vegetables and ¼ cup cheese.

4 In medium bowl, stir sour cream, 2 tablespoons of the cilantro, the red pepper, egg product, milk and soup with whisk. Pour over chicken mixture. Cover; refrigerate 2 hours or overnight.

5 Heat oven to 350°F. Uncover baking dish; bake 48 to 52 minutes or until egg mixture is set. Sprinkle with tomato and remaining 1 tablespoon cilantro. Let stand 5 minutes before serving. Cut into squares.

1 Serving: Calories 210; Total Fat 9g (Saturated Fat 3g, Trans Fat 0g); Cholesterol 35mg; Sodium 380mg; Total Carbohydrate 17g (Dietary Fiber 2g); Protein 15g **% Daily Value:** Vitamin A 20%; Vitamin C 10%; Calcium 10%; Iron 8% **Exchanges:** 1 Starch, ½ Vegetable, 1½ Very Lean Meat, 1½ Fat **Carbohydrate Choices:** 1

asiago vegetable strata

prep time: 30 Minutes ❄ **start to finish:** 5 Hours 25 Minutes ❄ 12 Servings

1 large onion, chopped (1 cup)

2 cups sliced fresh mushrooms (from 8-oz package)

2 cups small fresh broccoli florets

4 plum (Roma) tomatoes, chopped (2 cups)

6 cups cubed (1 inch) 12-grain bread (7 slices)

6 eggs

1½ cups fat-free (skim) milk

¾ teaspoon dried oregano leaves

¼ teaspoon salt

¼ teaspoon black pepper

¼ teaspoon ground red pepper (cayenne)

1 cup shredded Asiago cheese (4 oz)

1 Spray 12-inch skillet with cooking spray; heat over medium-high heat. Add onion, mushrooms and broccoli; cook 5 to 6 minutes, stirring frequently, until crisp-tender. Stir in tomatoes. Remove skillet from heat.

2 Spray 13x9-inch (3-quart) glass baking dish with cooking spray. Arrange bread cubes in baking dish. Spoon vegetable mixture over bread cubes. In medium bowl, beat eggs, milk, oregano, salt, black pepper and red pepper with whisk. Pour egg mixture over vegetables. Sprinkle with cheese. Cover; refrigerate 4 hours or overnight.

3 Heat oven to 350°F. Uncover baking dish; bake 45 to 50 minutes or until set in center (some moisture will appear in center and will dry upon standing). Let stand 5 minutes before serving. Cut into squares.

1 Serving: Calories 160; Total Fat 7g (Saturated Fat 3.5g, Trans Fat 0g); Cholesterol 105mg; Sodium 300mg; Total Carbohydrate 14g (Dietary Fiber 2g); Protein 10g **% Daily Value:** Vitamin A 10%; Vitamin C 15%; Calcium 15%; Iron 6% **Exchanges:** ½ Starch, 1 Vegetable, 1 Medium-Fat Meat, ½ Fat **Carbohydrate Choices:** 1

Start Happy Tip

Add 1 cup chopped turkey pepperoni (about 3 ounces) with the cooked veggies for an additional 210 calories per serving.

smoked salmon breakfast squares

prep time: 20 Minutes ❋ **start to finish:** 5 Hours 10 Minutes ❋ 12 Servings

2 boxes (5.2 oz each) seasoned hash brown potato mix for skillets

1 package (8 oz) cream cheese, cut into ½-inch cubes

6 oz smoked salmon, flaked

1 tablespoon dried chopped onion

1 cup Original Bisquick mix

½ teaspoon pepper

3 cups milk

4 eggs

4 oz pepper Jack cheese, shredded

½ cup chopped green onion tops (green part only)

1 Spray 13x9-inch (3-quart) glass baking dish with cooking spray.

2 Sprinkle 1 box potatoes into baking dish. Place half of the cream cheese cubes and all of the salmon pieces over potatoes. Sprinkle with dried onion. Top with remaining box of potatoes and cream cheese.

3 In large bowl, beat Bisquick mix, pepper, milk and eggs with fork or whisk until blended. Pour over mixture in baking dish. Sprinkle with shredded cheese. Cover; refrigerate at least 4 hours but no longer than 24 hours.

4 Heat oven to 375°F. Uncover baking dish; bake 32 to 38 minutes or until golden brown and knife inserted in center comes out clean. Sprinkle with green onion. Let stand 10 minutes before serving. Cut into squares.

1 Serving: Calories 300; Total Fat 14g (Saturated Fat 7g, Trans Fat 0.5g); Cholesterol 110mg; Sodium 830mg; Total Carbohydrate 29g (Dietary Fiber 2g); Protein 12g **% Daily Value:** Vitamin A 15%; Vitamin C 0%; Calcium 15%; Iron 6% **Exchanges:** 2 Starch, 1 Lean Meat, 2 Fat **Carbohydrate Choices:** 2

Start Happy Tip

Serve this make-ahead breakfast dish with toasted mini bagels and fresh fruit.

sausage and cheese breakfast torte

prep time: 30 Minutes ✳ **start to finish:** 40 Minutes ✳ 10 Servings

1 cup Original Bisquick mix

½ cup yellow cornmeal

2 cups shredded extra-sharp Cheddar cheese (8 oz)

½ cup reduced-sodium chicken broth or water

4 slices applewood-smoked thick-sliced bacon, cut into bite-size pieces

½ lb bulk pork sausage

8 eggs

¼ cup half-and-half

½ teaspoon freeze-dried chopped chives

⅛ teaspoon salt

1 tablespoon butter

⅓ cup crumbled peppercorn feta or plain feta cheese

1 Heat oven to 350°F. Spray 10-inch springform pan with cooking spray.

2 In medium bowl, stir Bisquick mix, cornmeal and 1 cup of the Cheddar cheese. Stir in broth until blended. Using buttered hands, press mixture in bottom of pan. Bake 20 minutes or until crust is set and beginning to brown around edges.

3 Meanwhile, in 12-inch nonstick skillet, cook bacon until crisp. Drain bacon on paper towels; set aside. Discard drippings. In skillet, cook sausage over medium heat until no longer pink; drain. Remove sausage from skillet to bowl.

4 In large bowl, beat eggs, half-and-half, chives and salt with fork or whisk. In same skillet, melt butter over medium heat. Add egg mixture; cook and stir until eggs are just moist (not dry). Remove from heat. Stir in sausage and feta cheese. Spread mixture evenly over crust. Sprinkle with remaining 1 cup Cheddar cheese and the bacon.

5 Bake 8 to 10 minutes or until thoroughly heated and cheese is melted. Run thin metal spatula alongside of torte to loosen from pan; remove side of pan. Cut into wedges; serve immediately.

1 Serving: Calories 320; Total Fat 21g (Saturated Fat 10g, Trans Fat 1g); Cholesterol 215mg; Sodium 650mg; Total Carbohydrate 15g (Dietary Fiber 0g); Protein 17g **% Daily Value:** Vitamin A 10%; Vitamin C 0%; Calcium 20%; Iron 8% **Exchanges:** 1 Starch, 2 High-Fat Meat, 1 Fat **Carbohydrate Choices:** 1

slow cooker layered huevos rancheros

prep time: 35 Minutes ❉ **start to finish:** 2 Hours 35 Minutes ❉ 8 Servings

16 eggs

1 cup half-and-half or milk

½ teaspoon salt

¼ teaspoon pepper

3 tablespoons butter

1 can (10¾ oz) condensed Fiesta nacho cheese soup

2 tablespoons chopped fresh chives

⅔ cup chunky-style salsa

4 soft corn tortillas (6 inch), cut into ¾-inch strips

1 cup pinto beans (from 15-oz can), drained, rinsed

1 cup shredded sharp Cheddar cheese (4 oz)

½ cup sour cream

4 medium green onions, sliced (¼ cup)

1 In large bowl, beat eggs with whisk. Add half-and-half, salt and pepper; beat well. In 12-inch nonstick skillet, melt butter over medium heat. Add egg mixture; cook about 7 minutes, scraping cooked eggs up from bottom of skillet occasionally, until mixture is firm but still moist. Stir in soup and chives.

2 Spray 3- to 4-quart slow cooker with cooking spray. Spread ⅓ cup of the salsa in bottom of slow cooker. Carefully place half of the tortilla strips on salsa to within ½ inch of side of slow cooker. Top with ½ cup of the beans, 3 cups of the egg mixture and ½ cup of the cheese. Layer with remaining salsa, tortilla strips, beans and egg mixture.

3 Cover; cook on High heat setting 2 hours.

4 Sprinkle remaining ½ cup cheese over top. Cover; let stand until cheese is melted. Serve with sour cream and onions.

1 Serving: Calories 410; Total Fat 28g (Saturated Fat 14g, Trans Fat 0.5g); Cholesterol 475mg; Sodium 780mg; Total Carbohydrate 18g (Dietary Fiber 3g); Protein 21g **% Daily Value:** Vitamin A 35%; Vitamin C 2%; Calcium 25%; Iron 10% **Exchanges:** ½ Starch, ½ Other Carbohydrate, ½ Low-Fat Milk, 2 Medium-Fat Meat, 3 Fat **Carbohydrate Choices:** 1

bacon and egg enchiladas

prep time: 20 Minutes ⁛ **start to finish:** 40 Minutes ⁛ **10 Servings**

12 slices bacon

10 eggs

½ cup milk

½ teaspoon onion powder

½ teaspoon ground cumin

2 cans (10 oz each) green or red enchilada sauce

10 flour tortillas (8 inch)

2 cups shredded Mexican cheese blend (8 oz)

Sour cream, if desired

Taco sauce, if desired

1 Heat oven to 350°F. Spray 13x9-inch (3-quart) glass baking dish with cooking spray.

2 In 10-inch skillet, cook bacon over medium heat, turning occasionally, until very crisp. Drain bacon on paper towels. Discard drippings, reserving 1 tablespoon in skillet. Crumble bacon; set aside.

3 In medium bowl, beat eggs, milk, onion powder and cumin with whisk until well blended. Pour into skillet with bacon drippings; cook over medium heat. As mixture begins to set on bottom and side, gently lift cooked portions with spatula so that thin, uncooked portion can flow to bottom. Do not stir. Cook 5 to 7 minutes or until eggs are thickened throughout but still moist. Do not overcook.

4 Pour ½ can of the enchilada sauce in bottom of baking dish; spread evenly. Fill each tortilla with about ⅓ cup eggs, 1 tablespoon bacon and 2 tablespoons cheese; roll up. Place seam side down on enchilada sauce in dish. Pour remaining 1½ cans enchilada sauce over filled tortillas. Top with remaining cheese and bacon.

5 Bake about 20 minutes or until thoroughly heated and bubbly. Serve with sour cream and taco sauce.

Start Happy Tip

Packages or jars of cooked bacon pieces are available in the refrigerated meat section and salad dressing section of the grocery store. They can be used instead of the freshly cooked bacon.

1 Serving: Calories 370; Total Fat 20g (Saturated Fat 8g, Trans Fat 1g); Cholesterol 220mg; Sodium 1060mg; Total Carbohydrate 28g (Dietary Fiber 1g); Protein 19g **% Daily Value:** Vitamin A 10%; Vitamin C 0%; Calcium 25%; Iron 15% **Exchanges:** 1½ Starch, ½ Other Carbohydrate, 1 Medium-Fat Meat, 1 High-Fat Meat, 1 Fat **Carbohydrate Choices:** 2

loaded potato quiche

prep time: 15 Minutes ❄ **start to finish:** 1 Hour 35 Minutes ❄ 8 Servings

Crust

2½	cups Original Bisquick mix
6	tablespoons cold butter
¼	cup boiling water

Filling

1½	cups chopped cooked ham
1½	cups frozen diced hash brown potatoes, thawed
1½	cups shredded sharp Cheddar cheese (6 oz)
3	medium green onions, sliced (3 tablespoons)
5	eggs
¾	cup half-and-half
¼	teaspoon freshly ground pepper
3	slices bacon, crisply cooked, crumbled
	Sour cream, if desired
	Additional sliced green onions, if desired

1 Heat oven to 350°F. Spray 9½-inch glass deep-dish pie plate with cooking spray.

2 Place Bisquick mix in medium bowl. Using pastry blender or fork, cut in butter until crumbly. Add boiling water; stir vigorously until soft dough forms. With fingers dipped in Bisquick mix, press dough on bottom and up side of pie plate, forming edge on rim of plate.

3 Sprinkle ham, potatoes, cheese and 3 tablespoons onions into crust. In medium bowl, beat eggs, half-and-half and pepper until blended. Pour over ingredients in crust.

4 Bake 1 hour 5 minutes or until knife inserted in center comes out clean. Let stand 15 minutes before serving. Cut into wedges; top each with bacon, sour cream and additional onions.

1 Serving: Calories 520; Total Fat 34g (Saturated Fat 16g, Trans Fat 2g); Cholesterol 190mg; Sodium 1170mg; Total Carbohydrate 34g (Dietary Fiber 1g); Protein 20g **% Daily Value:** Vitamin A 15%; Vitamin C 2%; Calcium 20%; Iron 10% **Exchanges:** ½ Starch, 2 Other Carbohydrate, 1 Very Lean Meat, ½ Medium-Fat Meat, 1 High-Fat Meat, 4½ Fat **Carbohydrate Choices:** 2

grilled-asparagus quiche

prep time: 20 Minutes ✳ **start to finish:** 1 Hour 20 Minutes ✳ 8 Servings

1 lb fresh asparagus spears, trimmed

1 tablespoon olive oil

½ teaspoon salt

4 oz thinly sliced pancetta, cut into strips

1¼ cups Original Bisquick mix

3 tablespoons cold butter

3 tablespoons boiling water

1½ cups shredded Swiss cheese (6 oz)

3 eggs

1 cup half-and-half

½ teaspoon freshly ground pepper

⅓ cup chopped drained roasted red bell peppers (from a jar)

1 Heat oven to 350°F. Spray 9-inch glass pie plate with cooking spray.

2 Heat indoor grill pan over medium-high heat. Drizzle asparagus with oil; sprinkle with salt. Place in grill pan. Cook 3 to 4 minutes or until crisp-tender. Cool. Cut into 1½-inch pieces; set aside.

3 In 10-inch nonstick skillet, cook pancetta over medium heat, stirring frequently, until crisp and browned.

4 In medium bowl, place Bisquick mix. Using pastry blender or fork, cut in butter until crumbly. Add boiling water; stir vigorously until soft dough forms. Press dough in bottom and up side of pie plate, forming edge on rim of plate.

5 Sprinkle cheese, asparagus and pancetta into crust. In medium bowl, beat eggs, half-and-half and pepper until blended. Pour over ingredients in crust. Sprinkle with roasted peppers.

6 Bake 45 to 50 minutes or until knife inserted in center comes out clean. Let stand 10 minutes before serving. Cut into wedges.

1 Serving: Calories 340; Total Fat 24g (Saturated Fat 12g, Trans Fat 1g); Cholesterol 120mg; Sodium 680mg; Total Carbohydrate 18g (Dietary Fiber 1g); Protein 13g **% Daily Value:** Vitamin A 20%; Vitamin C 10%; Calcium 25%; Iron 10% **Exchanges:** ½ Starch, ½ Other Carbohydrate, ½ Vegetable, ½ Very Lean Meat, ½ Medium-Fat Meat, ½ High-Fat Meat, 3½ Fat **Carbohydrate Choices:** 1

ragin' cajun quiche

prep time: 10 Minutes   ❄   **start to finish:** 1 Hour   ❄   6 Servings

1¼ cups Original Bisquick mix

¼ cup butter, softened

2 tablespoons hot water

4 oz pepper Jack cheese, shredded (1 cup)

1 cup diced smoked spicy andouille sausage (about 6 oz)

⅓ cup thinly sliced green onions (about 5 medium)

1 cup half-and-half

1½ teaspoons Cajun seasoning

3 eggs

1 Heat oven to 400°F. Spray 9-inch glass pie plate with cooking spray.

2 In medium bowl, stir Bisquick mix and butter until blended (mixture will be crumbly). Add hot water; stir vigorously until soft dough forms. Press dough in bottom and up side of pie plate. Layer cheese, sausage and onions in crust.

3 In medium bowl, beat half-and-half, Cajun seasoning and eggs with fork or whisk until blended. Pour over ingredients in crust.

4 Bake 32 to 38 minutes or until knife inserted in center comes out clean. Let stand 10 minutes before serving. Cut into wedges.

1 Serving: Calories 500; Total Fat 32g (Saturated Fat 16g, Trans Fat 1.5g); Cholesterol 240mg; Sodium 1330mg; Total Carbohydrate 24g (Dietary Fiber 1g); Protein 29g **% Daily Value:** Vitamin A 35%; Vitamin C 4%; Calcium 20%; Iron 15% **Exchanges:** 1 Starch, ½ Low-Fat Milk, 3 Lean Meat, 4 Fat **Carbohydrate Choices:** 1½

Start Happy Tip
Look for Cajun seasoning in the herb and spice section of your grocery store.

gluten-free spinach-mushroom quiche

prep time: 30 Minutes ✳ **start to finish:** 1 Hour 25 Minutes ✳ 8 Servings

Crust

- 1 cup Bisquick Gluten Free mix
- ⅓ cup plus 1 tablespoon shortening
- 3 to 4 tablespoons cold water

Filling

- 1 tablespoon butter
- 1 small onion, chopped (⅓ cup)
- 1½ cups sliced fresh mushrooms (about 4 oz)
- 4 eggs
- 1 cup milk
- ⅛ teaspoon ground red pepper (cayenne)
- ¾ cup coarsely chopped fresh spinach
- ¼ cup chopped red bell pepper
- 1 cup gluten-free shredded Italian cheese blend (4 oz)

1 Heat oven to 425°F. In medium bowl, place Bisquick mix. Using pastry blender or fork, cut in shortening until particles are size of small peas. Sprinkle with cold water, 1 tablespoon at a time, tossing with fork until all flour is moistened and pastry almost leaves side of bowl (1 to 2 teaspoons more water can be added if necessary).

2 Press pastry in bottom and up side of ungreased 9-inch quiche dish or glass pie plate. Bake 12 to 14 minutes or until crust just begins to brown and is set. Reduce oven temperature to 325°F.

3 Meanwhile, in 10-inch skillet, melt butter over medium heat. Add onion and mushrooms; cook about 5 minutes, stirring occasionally, until tender.

4 In medium bowl, beat eggs, milk and red pepper until well blended. Stir in spinach, bell pepper, mushroom mixture and cheese. Pour into partially baked crust.

5 Bake 40 to 45 minutes or until knife inserted in center comes out clean. Let stand 10 minutes before serving. Cut into wedges.

1 Serving: Calories 260; Total Fat 17g (Saturated Fat 6g, Trans Fat 2g); Cholesterol 120mg; Sodium 340mg; Total Carbohydrate 16g (Dietary Fiber 0g); Protein 9g **% Daily Value:** Vitamin A 15%; Vitamin C 6%; Calcium 30%; Iron 2% **Exchanges:** 1 Starch, ½ Vegetable, 1 Medium-Fat Meat, 2 Fat **Carbohydrate Choices:** 1

southwest tamale tart

prep time: 30 Minutes ❊ **start to finish:** 1 Hour 5 Minutes ❊ 6 Servings

1½ cups reduced-fat shredded Cheddar cheese (6 oz)

1 cup Bisquick Heart Smart mix

½ cup cornmeal

1 can (4.5 oz) chopped green chiles, drained

⅓ cup condensed beef broth (from 10½-oz can)

1 can (15 oz) black beans, drained, rinsed

½ cup chopped fresh cilantro

2 small tomatoes, seeded, chopped

Low-fat sour cream, if desired

Chunky-style salsa, if desired

1 Heat oven to 350°F. Spray 9-inch springform pan with cooking spray.

2 In medium bowl, mix 1 cup of the cheese, the Bisquick mix, cornmeal and chiles. Stir in broth. Pat mixture evenly in bottom of pan.

3 In small bowl, mix beans and cilantro. Spoon over mixture in pan to within ½ inch of edge. Sprinkle with remaining ½ cup cheese.

4 Bake 35 minutes. Run knife around edge of pan to loosen tart; remove side of pan. Arrange tomatoes around edge of tart. Cut into wedges; top with sour cream. Serve with salsa.

1 Serving: Calories 240; Total Fat 4g (Saturated Fat 1.5g, Trans Fat 0g); Cholesterol 5mg; Sodium 860mg; Total Carbohydrate 37g (Dietary Fiber 4g); Protein 14g **% Daily Value:** Vitamin A 10%; Vitamin C 10%; Calcium 35%; Iron 15% **Exchanges:** 2½ Starch, ½ Medium-Fat Meat **Carbohydrate Choices:** 2½

Start Happy Tip

If you have beef broth remaining, freeze it in an ice-cube tray. Store the frozen broth cubes in a resealable freezer plastic bag, and use in soups and stews. Pull one out to add extra flavor to meat dishes.

tomato-basil pie

prep time: 20 Minutes ❋ **start to finish:** 1 Hour ❋ 8 Servings

1 tablespoon olive oil

1⅓ cups finely chopped onion

1¼ cups Original Bisquick mix

3 tablespoons cold butter

3 tablespoons boiling water

1½ cups shredded Parmesan cheese (6 oz)

6 large plum (Roma) tomatoes, sliced

2 tablespoons all-purpose flour

½ cup chopped fresh basil leaves

¼ teaspoon salt

½ teaspoon pepper

¾ cup mayonnaise

Additional chopped fresh basil leaves, if desired

1 Heat oven to 400°F. Spray 9-inch glass pie plate with cooking spray.

2 In 12-inch skillet, heat oil over medium-high heat. Add onion; cook 8 minutes, stirring occasionally, until browned. Remove from heat.

3 Place Bisquick mix in medium bowl. Using pastry blender or fork, cut in butter until crumbly. Add boiling water; stir vigorously until soft dough forms. With fingers dipped in Bisquick mix, press dough on bottom and up side of pie plate, forming edge on rim of plate.

4 Sprinkle ½ cup of the cheese into crust. Arrange half of the tomato slices over cheese. Sprinkle with half each of the flour, onion, chopped basil, salt and pepper. Repeat layers. In small bowl, mix mayonnaise and remaining 1 cup cheese; spread over top of pie to within 1 inch of edge.

5 Bake 24 to 26 minutes or until lightly browned. Let stand 10 minutes before serving. Cut into wedges. Garnish with additional basil.

1 Serving: Calories 400; Total Fat 31g (Saturated Fat 10g, Trans Fat 1g); Cholesterol 35mg; Sodium 800mg; Total Carbohydrate 19g (Dietary Fiber 1g); Protein 10g **% Daily Value:** Vitamin A 15%; Vitamin C 6%; Calcium 30%; Iron 6% **Exchanges:** ½ Starch, ½ Other Carbohydrate, ½ Vegetable, 1 Lean Meat, 5½ Fat **Carbohydrate Choices:** 1

gluten-free huevos rancheros breakfast pizza

prep time: 25 Minutes ❊ **start to finish:** 30 Minutes ❊ 6 Servings

Crust

- 1 cup Bisquick Gluten Free mix
- ½ cup cornmeal
- ½ cup water
- 2 eggs, beaten
- 1 cup gluten-free shredded Monterey Jack cheese (4 oz)

Topping

- ½ lb gluten-free bulk chorizo sausage or spicy Italian pork sausage
- 6 eggs, beaten
- 1 cup gluten-free salsa
- ½ cup gluten-free shredded Monterey Jack cheese (2 oz)
- 2 tablespoons chopped fresh cilantro

1 Heat oven to 350°F. Spray 12-inch pizza pan with cooking spray.

2 In medium bowl, stir Bisquick mix, cornmeal, water and 2 eggs. Add 1 cup cheese; stir until blended. Spread in pan. Bake 15 minutes or until set.

3 Meanwhile, in 10-inch nonstick skillet, cook chorizo over medium-high heat, stirring frequently, until thoroughly cooked. Remove chorizo from skillet to small bowl; set aside. Wipe out skillet. Add 6 eggs to skillet; cook over medium-low heat until almost set (eggs will still be moist). Gently stir chorizo into eggs.

4 Spread ½ cup of the salsa over warm crust. Spoon egg mixture over crust, covering completely. Sprinkle with ½ cup cheese. Bake 5 minutes or until cheese is melted. Sprinkle with cilantro. Serve with remaining ½ cup salsa.

1 Serving: Calories 430; Total Fat 24g (Saturated Fat 10g, Trans Fat 0g); Cholesterol 325mg; Sodium 950mg; Total Carbohydrate 31g (Dietary Fiber 1g); Protein 22g **% Daily Value:** Vitamin A 15%; Vitamin C 0%; Calcium 30%; Iron 10% **Exchanges:** 2 Starch, 2½ Medium-Fat Meat, 2 Fat **Carbohydrate Choices:** 2

Start Happy Tips

Chorizo is a spicy pork sausage containing Mexican seasonings such as chili powder and cumin. If you are unable to find it, any other gluten-free spicy pork sausage would make a good substitution.

If you are cooking gluten free, always read labels to make sure each recipe ingredient is gluten free. Products and ingredient sources can change.

pepperoni breakfast pizza

prep time: 20 Minutes ✳ **start to finish:** 25 Minutes ✳ 8 Servings

1½ cups Original Bisquick mix

⅓ cup hot water

8 eggs

¼ cup milk

⅛ teaspoon pepper

1 cup diced pepperoni (from 6-oz package)

2 medium green onions, sliced (2 tablespoons)

1 tablespoon butter

½ cup pizza sauce (from 8-oz can)

1½ cups finely shredded Italian cheese blend (6 oz)

1 tablespoon sliced fresh basil leaves, if desired

1 Heat oven to 425°F. Spray 12-inch pizza pan with cooking spray.

2 In medium bowl, stir Bisquick mix and hot water vigorously until soft dough forms. With fingers dipped in Bisquick mix, press dough in bottom and up side of pan, forming rim at edge.

3 Bake 10 to 15 minutes or until golden brown.

4 Meanwhile, in large bowl, beat eggs, milk and pepper with fork or whisk until blended. Stir in pepperoni and onions. In 12-inch nonstick skillet, melt butter over medium heat. Add egg mixture; cook 3 to 5 minutes, stirring occasionally, until firm but still moist.

5 Spread pizza sauce over partially baked crust. Top evenly with egg mixture. Sprinkle with cheese. Bake 3 to 5 minutes longer or until cheese is melted and pizza is hot. Sprinkle with basil.

1 Serving: Calories 320; Total Fat 21g (Saturated Fat 9g, Trans Fat 1g); Cholesterol 245mg; Sodium 790mg; Total Carbohydrate 18g (Dietary Fiber 1g); Protein 16g **% Daily Value:** Vitamin A 15%; Vitamin C 0%; Calcium 25%; Iron 10% **Exchanges:** 1 Starch, 2 Medium-Fat Meat, 2 Fat **Carbohydrate Choices:** 1

Start Happy Tips

As with any pizza, it's easy to swap the toppings for your family's favorite. Cooked sausage, olives or your favorite cheese are just a few options to try.

Basil leaves that are cut into thin strips is called "chiffonade." To cut, stack the leaves on top of each other, then roll up like a cigar. Slice across the roll to form long shreds.

sausage and egg breakfast pizzas

prep time: 15 Minutes ❊ **start to finish:** 30 Minutes ❊ 4 Pizzas

1 package (8 oz) frozen brown-and-serve pork sausage links, cut into ½-inch pieces

6 eggs, beaten

4 ready-to-serve pizza crusts (6 inch)

1½ cups shredded Cheddar cheese (6 oz)

1 Heat oven to 400°F. Spray 10-inch nonstick skillet with cooking spray; heat over medium heat. Add sausage; cook about 3 minutes, stirring occasionally, until brown. Drain. Remove sausage from skillet; set aside.

2 Pour eggs into same skillet. As mixture begins to set at bottom and side, gently lift cooked portions with spatula so that thin, uncooked portion can flow to bottom. Do not stir. Cook 4 to 5 minutes or until eggs are thickened throughout but still moist.

3 Place pizza crusts on ungreased cookie sheets. Sprinkle evenly with half of the cheese. Top each evenly with eggs and sausage. Sprinkle evenly with remaining cheese.

4 Bake 10 to 12 minutes or until cheese is melted.

1 Pizza: Calories 670; Total Fat 46g (Saturated Fat 19g, Trans Fat 0.5g); Cholesterol 365mg; Sodium 1080mg; Total Carbohydrate 32g (Dietary Fiber 1g); Protein 32g **% Daily Value:** Vitamin A 15%; Vitamin C 0%; Calcium 35%; Iron 20% **Exchanges:** 2 Other Carbohydrate, 1½ Medium-Fat Meat, 3 High-Fat Meat, 3 Fat **Carbohydrate Choices:** 2

Start Happy Tips

For a veggie lift, add chopped tomato, green bell pepper and mushrooms before topping with the final cheese layer.

Sparkling apple cider or your favorite fruit juice goes well with these pizzas.

ham and gorgonzola pizza

prep time: 25 Minutes ❋ **start to finish:** 1 Hour ❋ 6 Servings

Crust

2½ to 3 cups all-purpose flour

1 tablespoon sugar

1 teaspoon salt

1 package regular active or fast-acting dry yeast (2¼ teaspoons)

3 tablespoons olive or vegetable oil

1 cup very warm water (120°F to 130°F)

Topping

1 teaspoon olive oil

⅓ cup refrigerated Alfredo sauce

1 cup cubed cooked ham

½ cup crumbled Gorgonzola or blue cheese (2 oz)

4 medium green onions, sliced (¼ cup)

1 cup shredded mozzarella cheese (4 oz)

½ teaspoon dried oregano leaves

1 In large bowl, mix 1 cup of the flour, the sugar, salt and yeast. Add 3 tablespoons oil and the warm water; mix well. Stir in enough remaining flour until dough is soft and leaves side of bowl. On lightly floured surface, knead dough 4 to 5 minutes or until smooth and springy. Cover loosely with plastic wrap; let rest 10 minutes.

2 Heat oven to 425°F. Spray large cookie sheet or 12-inch pizza pan with cooking spray.

3 Divide dough in half.* Press half of dough into 12-inch round on cookie sheet. Brush dough with 1 teaspoon oil. Bake 10 to 12 minutes or until crust is golden brown.

4 Spread Alfredo sauce on warm crust. Sprinkle with ham, Gorgonzola cheese, onions, mozzarella cheese and oregano. Bake 9 to 11 minutes longer or until cheese is melted. Cut into wedges.

*You can make 2 pizzas right away if you're serving a larger group. Just press and bake the other half of the dough on a second cookie sheet or pizza pan and double the toppings. Or prebake the second crust, only through step 3, then wrap it tightly in plastic wrap and freeze. Unwrap and thaw before topping and baking as directed in step 4.

1 Serving: Calories 460; Total Fat 22g (Saturated Fat 9g, Trans Fat 0g); Cholesterol 45mg; Sodium 1060mg; Total Carbohydrate 45g (Dietary Fiber 2g); Protein 20g **% Daily Value:** Vitamin A 8%; Vitamin C 0%; Calcium 25%; Iron 15% **Exchanges:** 3 Starch, 1 Medium-Fat Meat, 3 Fat **Carbohydrate Choices:** 3

coffee cakes & other breads

lemon curd–filled butter cake

prep time: 25 Minutes ❄ **start to finish:** 2 Hours 20 Minutes ❄ 12 Servings

Lemon Curd

- ¼ cup granulated sugar
- 2 tablespoons cornstarch
- ¾ cup cold water
- 3 egg yolks
- 1 tablespoon grated lemon peel
- 3 tablespoons lemon juice

Cake

- 1 cup butter, softened
- 1 cup granulated sugar
- 5 eggs
- 1¾ cups all-purpose flour
- 2 teaspoons grated lemon peel
- 1½ teaspoons baking powder
- 1 teaspoon vanilla
- ⅓ cup slivered almonds, toasted*
- ½ teaspoon powdered sugar, if desired

1 In 1-quart saucepan, mix ¼ cup granulated sugar and the cornstarch. Stir in water and egg yolks with whisk until well mixed and no lumps remain. Heat to boiling over medium heat, stirring constantly, until mixture begins to thicken. Cook and stir 1 minute; remove from heat. Stir in 1 tablespoon lemon peel and the lemon juice. Refrigerate uncovered 20 minutes, stirring once, until room temperature.

2 Meanwhile, heat oven to 350°F. Grease bottom and side of 9-inch springform pan with shortening; lightly flour. In large bowl, beat butter and 1 cup granulated sugar with electric mixer on medium speed about 1 minute or until smooth. Beat in eggs, one at a time, until just blended, then continue beating on medium speed 2 minutes, scraping bowl once. On low speed, beat in flour, 2 teaspoons lemon peel, the baking powder and vanilla about 30 seconds or until just blended. Spread half of cake batter (about 2 cups) in bottom of pan.

3 Spoon cooled lemon curd evenly onto batter, spreading to ½ inch of edge. Drop remaining batter by tablespoonfuls around edge of curd and pan; spread batter evenly and toward center to cover curd. Sprinkle almonds over top.

4 Bake 45 to 55 minutes or until center is set, cake is firm to the touch and top is golden brown. Cool in pan on cooling rack at least 1 hour (center will sink slightly). Run thin knife around side of cake; remove side of pan. Sprinkle with powdered sugar before serving. Store cake covered in refrigerator.

*To toast almonds, sprinkle in ungreased skillet. Cook over medium heat 5 to 7 minutes, stirring frequently until almonds begin to brown, then stirring constantly until almonds are light brown.

1 Serving: Calories 360; Total Fat 20g (Saturated Fat 9g, Trans Fat 1g); Cholesterol 180mg; Sodium 190mg; Total Carbohydrate 37g (Dietary Fiber 0g); Protein 6g **% Daily Value:** Vitamin A 15%; Vitamin C 0%; Calcium 6%; Iron 8% **Exchanges:** 1 Starch, 1½ Other Carbohydrate, 4 Fat **Carbohydrate Choices:** 2½

triple-berry coffee cake

prep time: 15 Minutes ❋ **start to finish:** 1 Hour ❋ 8 Servings

½ cup buttermilk

½ cup packed brown sugar

¼ cup vegetable oil

1 teaspoon almond extract

1 egg

1 cup white whole wheat flour

½ teaspoon baking soda

1 teaspoon ground cinnamon

½ teaspoon salt

1 cup mixed berries (such as blueberries, raspberries and blackberries)*

¼ cup granola, slightly crushed

Powdered sugar, if desired

1 Heat oven to 350°F. Spray bottom and side of 8-inch round cake pan with cooking spray.

2 In large bowl, stir buttermilk, brown sugar, oil, almond extract and egg until smooth. Stir in flour, baking soda, cinnamon and salt just until moistened. Gently fold in ½ cup of the berries. Spoon into pan. Sprinkle with remaining ½ cup berries and the granola.

3 Bake 28 to 36 minutes or until golden brown and top springs back when touched in center. Cool in pan on cooling rack 10 minutes. Sprinkle coffee cake lightly with powdered sugar. Serve warm.

*Frozen berries can be used (do not thaw).

1 Serving: Calories 210; Total Fat 8g (Saturated Fat 1.5g, Trans Fat 0g); Cholesterol 25mg; Sodium 260mg; Total Carbohydrate 30g (Dietary Fiber 2g); Protein 4g **% Daily Value:** Vitamin A 0%; Vitamin C 2%; Calcium 4%; Iron 6% **Exchanges:** 1½ Starch, ½ Other Carbohydrate, 1½ Fat **Carbohydrate Choices:** 2

Glazed Mixed-Berry Coffee Cake: Omit sprinkling with powdered sugar. In small bowl, stir together ¼ cup powdered sugar, ¼ teaspoon almond extract and 1 to 2 teaspoons milk. Drizzle over warm coffee cake.

Start Happy Tip

White whole wheat flour can be used in any recipe. It's the best of both worlds—100% whole grain but with a lighter taste and color. Start substituting 25% or 50% of the all-purpose flour with white whole wheat flour, gradually increasing the proportion as desired.

peach-almond coffee cake

prep time: 10 Minutes ❄ **start to finish:** 40 Minutes ❄ **10 Servings**

⅔ cup soymilk

2 tablespoons vegetable oil

½ teaspoon almond extract

1 egg

2 cups Original Bisquick mix

⅓ cup granulated sugar

1 cup chopped fresh or frozen (thawed and drained) peaches

1 container (6 oz) peach lactose-free yogurt

¼ cup packed brown sugar

¼ cup sliced almonds

1 Heat oven to 375°F. Spray 8-inch round cake pan with cooking spray.

2 In medium bowl, beat soymilk, oil, almond extract and egg with whisk until smooth. Stir in Bisquick mix and granulated sugar just until moistened (batter will be lumpy). Spread batter in pan.

3 In small bowl, mix peaches and yogurt. Spoon onto batter; swirl lightly with knife. Sprinkle with brown sugar and almonds.

4 Bake 25 to 30 minutes or until toothpick inserted in center comes out clean. Serve warm or cool. Store coffee cake covered in refrigerator.

1 Serving: Calories 230; Total Fat 8g (Saturated Fat 1.5g, Trans Fat 0.5g); Cholesterol 20mg; Sodium 320mg; Total Carbohydrate 33g (Dietary Fiber 1g); Protein 4g **% Daily Value:** Vitamin A 4%; Vitamin C 0%; Calcium 10%; Iron 6% **Exchanges:** 1½ Starch, ½ Other Carbohydrate, 1½ Fat **Carbohydrate Choices:** 2

Start Happy Tips

Studies have shown that occasionally eating a small handful of nuts (about ¼ cup) does not cause weight gain. It may be because the satisfaction provided by the fat in the nuts makes people eat less overall.

Serve this crunchy delight as a breakfast treat or as a snack!

mile-high raspberry coffee cake

prep time: 20 Minutes ❊ **start to finish:** 3 Hours ❊ 10 Servings

Topping

- ⅔ cup sliced almonds
- ½ cup all-purpose flour
- ⅓ cup sugar
- 3 tablespoons butter, melted

Coffee Cake

- 3 cups Original Bisquick mix
- 1 cup sugar
- 1 cup creamy vanilla low-fat yogurt (from 2-lb container)
- ½ cup almond meal
- ¼ cup butter, melted
- ¼ cup milk
- 2 teaspoons vanilla
- 2 eggs
- 2 cups frozen raspberries (do not thaw)
- 1 tablespoon all-purpose flour

1 Heat oven to 325°F. Generously spray 9-inch springform pan with cooking spray.

2 In medium bowl, mix almonds, ½ cup flour and ⅓ cup sugar. Gradually stir in 3 tablespoons melted butter until blended. Use fingers to pinch topping into clumps.

3 In large bowl, beat Bisquick mix, 1 cup sugar, the yogurt, almond meal, ¼ cup melted butter, the milk, vanilla and eggs with spoon until well blended. Spread batter in pan. Toss raspberries with 1 tablespoon flour; sprinkle over batter. Sprinkle with topping.

4 Bake 1 hour to 1 hour 10 minutes or until toothpick inserted in center comes out clean. Cool completely on cooling rack, about 1 hour 30 minutes. Run thin knife around side of cake; remove side of pan.

1 Serving: Calories 500; Total Fat 21g (Saturated Fat 8g, Trans Fat 1g); Cholesterol 60mg; Sodium 540mg; Total Carbohydrate 69g (Dietary Fiber 5g); Protein 8g **% Daily Value:** Vitamin A 8%; Vitamin C 10%; Calcium 15%; Iron 10% **Exchanges:** 2½ Starch, 2 Other Carbohydrate, 4 Fat **Carbohydrate Choices:** 4½

strawberry-cream brunch cake

prep time: 20 Minutes ✳ **start to finish:** 1 Hour 35 Minutes ✳ 16 Servings

Filling

- 1 package (8 oz) cream cheese, softened
- ¼ cup sugar
- 2 tablespoons all-purpose flour
- 1 egg

Cake

- 2¼ cups all-purpose flour
- ¾ cup sugar
- ¾ cup cold butter
- ½ teaspoon baking powder
- ½ teaspoon baking soda
- ¼ teaspoon salt
- ¾ cup sour cream
- 1 teaspoon almond extract
- 1 egg
- ½ cup strawberry or raspberry preserves
- ½ cup sliced almonds

1 Heat oven to 350°F. Grease bottom and side of 10-inch springform pan or 11x7-inch (2-quart) glass baking dish with shortening; lightly flour.

2 In small bowl, mix filling ingredients until smooth; set aside.

3 In large bowl, mix 2¼ cups flour and ¾ cup sugar. Using pastry blender or fork, cut in butter until mixture looks like coarse crumbs. Reserve 1 cup of the crumb mixture. Stir baking powder, baking soda, salt, sour cream, almond extract and egg into remaining crumb mixture. Spread batter in bottom and 2 inches up side (about ¼ inch thick) of pan.

4 Pour filling over batter. Carefully spoon preserves evenly over filling. Mix almonds and reserved crumb mixture; sprinkle over preserves.

5 Bake springform pan 50 to 60 minutes, 11x7-inch dish 35 to 45 minutes, or until filling is set and crust is deep golden brown. Cool 15 minutes. Run thin knife around side of cake; remove side of pan. Serve warm, if desired. Store brunch cake covered in refrigerator.

1 Serving: Calories 320; Total Fat 18g (Saturated Fat 10g, Trans Fat 0.5g); Cholesterol 70mg; Sodium 220mg; Total Carbohydrate 35g (Dietary Fiber 1g); Protein 4g **% Daily Value:** Vitamin A 10%; Vitamin C 0%; Calcium 6%; Iron 6% **Exchanges:** 1½ Starch, 1 Other Carbohydrate, 3½ Fat **Carbohydrate Choices:** 2

Start Happy Tip

Cool the cake completely, then wrap it tightly and freeze up to 1 month. To thaw, let the cake stand at room temperature several hours before serving.

raspberry-almond coffee cake

prep time: 20 Minutes ✳ **start to finish:** 1 Hour 5 Minutes ✳ 8 Servings

Coffee Cake

¾	cup milk
½	cup butter, melted
1	teaspoon vanilla
½	teaspoon almond extract
1	egg
1¼	cups all-purpose flour
¾	cup whole wheat flour
½	cup granulated sugar
2	teaspoons baking powder
½	teaspoon salt
1	cup fresh raspberries
¼	cup sliced almonds

Glaze

½	cup powdered sugar
1	tablespoon butter, softened
3	to 4 teaspoons milk
¼	teaspoon almond extract

1 Heat oven to 350°F. Spray 9-inch round or square pan with baking spray; lightly flour.

2 In medium bowl, beat ¾ cup milk, ½ cup melted butter, the vanilla, ½ teaspoon almond extract and the egg with whisk or spoon until well blended. Stir in flours, granulated sugar, baking powder and salt. Gently fold in raspberries. Spread in pan. Sprinkle almonds evenly over batter.

3 Bake 30 to 35 minutes or until top is light golden brown and toothpick inserted in center comes out clean. Cool 10 minutes.

4 Meanwhile, in small bowl, mix glaze ingredients until smooth and thin enough to drizzle.

5 Drizzle glaze over warm coffee cake. Serve warm or cool.

1 Serving: Calories 360; Total Fat 16g (Saturated Fat 9g, Trans Fat 0.5g); Cholesterol 65mg; Sodium 380mg; Total Carbohydrate 47g (Dietary Fiber 3g); Protein 6g **% Daily Value:** Vitamin A 10%; Vitamin C 4%; Calcium 10%; Iron 10% **Exchanges:** 2 Starch, 1 Other Carbohydrate, 3 Fat **Carbohydrate Choices:** 3

Blueberry-Almond Coffee Cake: Make this coffee cake with fresh blueberries or blackberries instead of the raspberries.

blackberry coffee cake

prep time: 25 Minutes ✳ **start to finish:** 3 Hours 10 Minutes ✳ 16 servings

Filling

1¼ cups frozen blackberries, thawed and well drained

½ cup finely chopped pecans

3 tablespoons granulated sugar

1½ teaspoons ground cinnamon

Coffee Cake

2¼ cups all-purpose flour

1 teaspoon baking powder

½ teaspoon baking soda

1¼ cups granulated sugar

1 cup butter, softened

1 teaspoon vanilla

2 eggs

1 container (8 oz) sour cream

Glaze

1½ cups powdered sugar

3 to 4 teaspoons water

1 Heat oven to 350°F. Grease bottom and side of 10-inch angel food (tube) cake pan with shortening; lightly flour. In small bowl, stir together filling ingredients; set aside.

2 In medium bowl, mix flour, baking powder and baking soda; set aside. In large bowl, beat 1¼ cups granulated sugar, the butter, vanilla and eggs with electric mixer on medium speed 2 minutes, scraping bowl occasionally. On low speed, alternately add flour mixture with sour cream, beating just until blended after each addition.

3 Spread one-third of the batter in pan; sprinkle with half of the filling. Spoon another one-third of the batter by tablespoonfuls over filling; sprinkle with remaining filling. Spoon remaining batter over filling; spread evenly.

4 Bake 55 to 65 minutes or until toothpick inserted in center comes out clean. Cool 10 minutes; remove from pan to cooling rack. Cool completely, about 1 hour 30 minutes.

5 In small bowl, mix glaze ingredients until smooth and thin enough to drizzle. Drizzle glaze over coffee cake.

1 Serving: Calories 360; Total Fat 18g (Saturated Fat 9g, Trans Fat 0.5g); Cholesterol 60mg; Sodium 190mg; Total Carbohydrate 46g (Dietary Fiber 1g); Protein 3g **% Daily Value:** Vitamin A 10%; Vitamin C 0%; Calcium 4%; Iron 6% **Exchanges:** 1 Starch, 2 Other Carbohydrate, 3 ½ Fat **Carbohydrate Choices:** 3

Start Happy Tip

Packed with sweet blackberries, this glorious coffee cake is a great make-ahead treat. Wrap it up tightly and tuck it away in your freezer for up to 2 months to serve when unexpected guests drop by.

apple crisp–orange pound cake

prep time: 20 Minutes ❄ **start to finish:** 2 Hours ❄ 8 Servings

Filling

- 2 cups chopped peeled baking apples (about 2 medium)
- ¼ cup apple jelly
- 1 tablespoon all-purpose flour
- ½ teaspoon apple pie spice

Cake and Topping

- 1⅓ cups all-purpose flour
- 1¼ cups sugar
- 1 teaspoon grated orange peel
- ¼ teaspoon baking powder
- ¼ teaspoon salt
- ¾ cup cold butter
- ⅓ cup sour cream
- 2 eggs
- 1 teaspoon vanilla
- ½ cup chopped pecans

1 Heat oven to 350°F. Grease 9-inch round or 8-inch square pan with shortening or cooking spray.

2 In small bowl, mix filling ingredients; set aside. In medium bowl, stir 1⅓ cups flour, the sugar, orange peel, baking powder and salt. Using pastry blender or fork, cut in butter until mixture looks like coarse crumbs. Reserve 1 cup of the crumb mixture for topping. Add sour cream, eggs and vanilla to remaining crumb mixture in bowl; beat with electric mixer on medium speed about 1 minute or until blended. Spread batter in pan.

3 Spoon filling over batter; spread evenly. Sprinkle with reserved crumb mixture and the pecans; pat gently.

4 Bake 1 hour 5 minutes to 1 hour 10 minutes or until light golden brown and toothpick inserted in center comes out with a few moist crumbs clinging. Cool in pan on cooling rack 30 minutes. Serve warm or cool.

1 Serving: Calories 490; Total Fat 26g (Saturated Fat 13g, Trans Fat 0.5g); Cholesterol 105mg; Sodium 240mg; Total Carbohydrate 60g (Dietary Fiber 2g); Protein 5g **% Daily Value:** Vitamin A 15%; Vitamin C 2%; Calcium 4%; Iron 8% **Exchanges:** 1½ Starch, 2½ Other Carbohydrate, 5 Fat **Carbohydrate Choices:** 4

Start Happy Tip

Braeburn apples work well in this cake. Or try another crisp, sweet-tart apple such as Cortland or Gala.

orange–almond streusel muffins

prep time: 15 Minutes ❋ **start to finish:** 30 Minutes ❋ 12 Muffins

Topping

- 1 tablespoon Original Bisquick mix
- 2 tablespoons packed brown sugar
- 2 tablespoons sliced almonds
- 1 tablespoon butter

Muffins

- ⅓ cup packed brown sugar
- 1 teaspoon grated orange peel
- ½ cup orange juice
- ¼ cup vegetable oil
- ½ teaspoon almond extract
- 1 egg
- 2 cups Original Bisquick mix
- ¼ cup sliced almonds

1 Heat oven to 400°F. Place paper baking cup in each of 12 regular-size muffin cups, or grease bottoms only with shortening.

2 In medium bowl, mix all streusel topping ingredients except butter. Using fork, cut in butter until mixture looks like coarse crumbs; set aside.

3 In large bowl, mix all muffin ingredients except Bisquick mix and ¼ cup almonds. Stir in 2 cups Bisquick mix just until moistened. Stir in ¼ cup almonds. Divide batter evenly among muffin cups. Sprinkle with topping.

4 Bake 13 to 15 minutes or until golden brown. Immediately remove muffins from pan to cooling rack. Serve warm.

1 Muffin: Calories 200; Total Fat 11g (Saturated Fat 2.5g, Trans Fat 0.5g); Cholesterol 20mg; Sodium 270mg; Total Carbohydrate 23g (Dietary Fiber 0g); Protein 3g **% Daily Value:** Vitamin A 0%; Vitamin C 4%; Calcium 4%; Iron 6% **Exchanges:** 1 Starch, ½ Other Carbohydrate, 2 Fat **Carbohydrate Choices:** 1½

Start Happy Tip

Serve these muffins warm with honey butter or cream cheese. Add fresh fruit and hot tea for a light breakfast, brunch or snack.

oatmeal–whole wheat–blueberry muffins

prep time: 15 Minutes ✳ **start to finish:** 40 Minutes ✳ 12 Muffins

1 cup buttermilk

1 cup old-fashioned oats

½ cup packed brown sugar

⅓ cup vegetable oil

1 egg

½ cup whole wheat flour

½ cup all-purpose flour

1 teaspoon baking soda

1 teaspoon ground cinnamon

¼ teaspoon salt

1 cup fresh or frozen (thawed and drained) blueberries

1 Heat oven to 400°F. Place paper baking cup in each of 12 regular-size muffin cups, or grease bottoms only with shortening or cooking spray.

2 In small bowl, pour buttermilk over oats; set aside. In large bowl, mix brown sugar, oil and egg with spoon. Stir in flours, baking soda, cinnamon and salt just until flours are moistened. Stir in oat mixture. Fold in blueberries. Divide batter evenly among muffin cups.

3 Bake 15 to 20 minutes or until golden brown. Cool 5 minutes. Remove muffins from pan to cooling rack. Serve warm.

1 Muffin: Calories 180; Total Fat 8g (Saturated Fat 1g, Trans Fat 0g); Cholesterol 20mg; Sodium 180mg; Total Carbohydrate 24g (Dietary Fiber 2g); Protein 4g **% Daily Value:** Vitamin A 0%; Vitamin C 0%; Calcium 4%; Iron 6% **Exchanges:** 1 Starch, ½ Other Carbohydrate, 1½ Fat **Carbohydrate Choices:** 1½

sweet potato, kale and feta muffins

prep time: 25 Minutes ✳ **start to finish:** 1 Hour 15 Minutes ✳ 12 Muffins

2 medium sweet potatoes, peeled, cut into ½-inch cubes (2½ cups)

1 tablespoon olive oil

2 eggs

⅓ cup butter, melted

½ cup milk

1½ cups all-purpose flour

2 tablespoons packed brown sugar

2 teaspoons baking powder

⅛ teaspoon salt

⅛ teaspoon freshly ground pepper

1½ cups baby kale or baby spinach, coarsely chopped

¾ cup crumbled feta cheese (3 oz)

½ cup shredded Gruyère cheese (2 oz)

1 Heat oven to 400°F. In medium bowl, toss sweet potatoes with oil. Place in single layer in ungreased 15x10x1-inch pan. Bake 20 to 25 minutes or until tender, stirring after 10 minutes. Cool completely, about 20 minutes.

2 Spray 12 regular-size muffin cups with cooking spray. In large bowl, beat eggs, melted butter and milk with whisk until well blended. Add flour, brown sugar, baking powder, salt and pepper; stir with spoon just until dry ingredients are moistened.

3 Stir sweet potatoes, kale and cheeses into batter. Divide evenly among muffin cups, filling each about three-fourths full.

4 Bake 18 to 22 minutes or until toothpick inserted in center comes out clean. Remove muffins from pan to cooling rack. Cool 5 minutes. Serve warm.

1 Muffin: Calories 210; Total Fat 11g (Saturated Fat 6g, Trans Fat 0g); Cholesterol 60mg; Sodium 300mg; Total Carbohydrate 21g (Dietary Fiber 1g); Protein 6g **% Daily Value:** Vitamin A 90%; Vitamin C 8%; Calcium 20%; Iron 8% **Exchanges:** 1 Starch, ½ Other Carbohydrate, ½ Medium-Fat Meat, 1½ Fat **Carbohydrate Choices:** 1½

Start Happy Tips

Look for baby kale in the salad section of the produce department.

Sweet potatoes pack a powerful vitamin A punch. What a delicious way to get your vitamins!

citrus-mango muffins

prep time: 10 Minutes ✳ **start to finish:** 45 Minutes ✳ 6 Jumbo Muffins

Muffins

- 1 egg
- 2 cups all-purpose flour
- ⅓ cup granulated sugar
- 1 tablespoon grated lime peel
- 2 teaspoons baking powder
- ½ teaspoon salt
- 1 cup milk
- ¼ cup vegetable oil
- 1 ripe medium mango, seed removed, peeled and diced (1 cup)

Glaze

- ½ cup powdered sugar
- 3 to 4 teaspoons lime juice

1 Heat oven to 375°F. Grease bottoms only of 6 jumbo or 12 regular-size muffin cups with shortening or cooking spray, or line with paper baking cups.

2 In medium bowl, beat egg slightly. Stir in remaining muffin ingredients except mango just until moistened. Stir in mango. Divide batter evenly among muffin cups.

3 Bake 25 to 35 minutes or until golden brown.

4 Meanwhile, in small bowl, mix glaze ingredients until smooth and thin enough to drizzle.

5 Immediately remove muffins from pan to cooling rack. Drizzle glaze over muffins. Serve warm or cool.

1 Jumbo Muffin: Calories 380; Total Fat 11g (Saturated Fat 2.5g, Trans Fat 0g); Cholesterol 40mg; Sodium 390mg; Total Carbohydrate 61g (Dietary Fiber 2g); Protein 7g **% Daily Value:** Vitamin A 8%; Vitamin C 10%; Calcium 15%; Iron 15% **Exchanges:** 2 Starch, 2 Other Carbohydrate, 2 Fat **Carbohydrate Choices:** 4

Start Happy Tip

Substitute 1 cup diced peaches or nectarines for the mango.

slow cooker bourbon-banana bread

prep time: 20 Minutes ❋ **start to finish:** 3 Hours 5 Minutes ❋ 16 Servings

Bread

2⅔ cups Original Bisquick mix

1½ cups mashed very ripe bananas

¾ cup granulated sugar

⅓ cup butter, melted

2 tablespoons bourbon

1 teaspoon vanilla

3 eggs

1 teaspoon ground cinnamon

¾ cup semisweet chocolate chips

¾ cup chopped pecans, toasted*

Glaze

2 tablespoons butter, melted

1 cup powdered sugar

1 tablespoon bourbon

1 teaspoon hot water

1 Grease bottom only of 3½- to 4-quart round slow cooker with shortening or cooking spray. Sprinkle lightly with 2 teaspoons of the Bisquick mix.

2 In large bowl, stir bananas, granulated sugar, ⅓ cup melted butter, 2 tablespoons bourbon, the vanilla and eggs until well blended. Stir in remaining Bisquick mix, the cinnamon, chocolate chips and ½ cup of the pecans until well blended. Pour into slow cooker.

3 Cover; cook on High heat setting 1 hour 30 minutes to 2 hours or until toothpick inserted in center of loaf comes out clean.

4 Turn off slow cooker; uncover and remove ceramic base from cooker to cooling rack. Cool 15 minutes.

5 Loosen edge of bread with thin metal spatula. Remove bread from slow cooker to cooling rack. Cool 1 hour.

6 In small bowl, mix glaze ingredients until smooth and consistency of thick syrup. Drizzle over top of bread. Sprinkle evenly with remaining ¼ cup pecans.

1 Serving: Calories 320; Total Fat 15g (Saturated Fat 6g, Trans Fat 0.5g); Cholesterol 50mg; Sodium 300mg; Total Carbohydrate 41g (Dietary Fiber 2g); Protein 3g **% Daily Value:** Vitamin A 4%; Vitamin C 0%; Calcium 4%; Iron 6% **Exchanges:** 1 Starch, ½ Other Carbohydrate, 3 Fat **Carbohydrate Choices:** 3

Start Happy Tip

Slow cookers vary. Keep an eye on your bread while it's baking so it does not get overdone. Use a slow cooker with a white ceramic base for best results.

*To toast pecans, sprinkle in ungreased skillet. Cook over medium heat 5 to 7 minutes, stirring frequently until pecans begin to brown, then stirring constantly until pecans are light brown.

easy walnut bread

prep time: 10 Minutes ✳ **start to finish:** 2 Hours 20 Minutes ✳ 1 Loaf; 16 Slices

2¾ cups Original Bisquick mix

½ cup sugar

1 cup milk

2 tablespoons butter, melted

1 teaspoon vanilla

3 eggs

1½ cups finely chopped walnuts

1 Heat oven to 350°F. Spray 9x5-inch loaf pan with cooking spray.

2 In large bowl, beat all ingredients except walnuts with electric mixer on low speed 30 seconds, scraping bowl frequently. Beat on medium speed 3 minutes, scraping bowl occasionally. Stir in walnuts. Spread batter in pan.

3 Bake 50 to 60 minutes or until toothpick inserted in center comes out clean. Cool 10 minutes. Run knife or metal spatula around sides of pan to loosen bread; remove from pan to cooling rack. Cool completely, about 1 hour. To store, wrap bread tightly in plastic wrap or foil.

1 Slice: Calories 220; Total Fat 12g (Saturated Fat 3g, Trans Fat 1g); Cholesterol 45mg; Sodium 280mg; Total Carbohydrate 22g (Dietary Fiber 1g); Protein 5g **% Daily Value:** Vitamin A 2%; Vitamin C 0%; Calcium 6%; Iron 6% **Exchanges:** 1½ Starch, 2 Fat **Carbohydrate Choices:** 1½

Start Happy Tip

For a nuttier flavor, bake walnuts uncovered in ungreased shallow pan at 350°F 6 to 10 minutes, stirring occasionally, until light brown.

gluten-free zucchini-apple bread

prep time: 10 Minutes ❖ **start to finish:** 3 Hours 15 Minutes ❖ 1 Loaf; 12 Slices

- 2 cups Bisquick Gluten Free mix
- 1 cup shredded zucchini (about 1 medium)
- 1 small unpeeled apple, shredded (½ cup)
- ¾ cup sugar
- ⅓ cup vegetable oil
- 2 teaspoons ground cinnamon
- ½ teaspoon ground nutmeg
- 1 teaspoon gluten-free vanilla
- 3 eggs

1 Heat oven to 350°F. Grease bottom only of 9x5-inch loaf pan with shortening or cooking spray.

2 In large bowl, beat all ingredients with electric mixer on low speed 30 seconds, scraping bowl occasionally. Beat on medium speed 1 minute, scraping bowl occasionally. Pour batter into pan.

3 Bake 50 to 55 minutes or until toothpick inserted in center comes out clean. Cool 10 minutes. Run knife or metal spatula around sides of pan to loosen bread; remove from pan to cooling rack. Cool completely, about 2 hours. To store, wrap bread tightly in plastic wrap or foil.

1 Slice: Calories 210; Total Fat 8g (Saturated Fat 1.5g, Trans Fat 0g); Cholesterol 45mg; Sodium 240mg; Total Carbohydrate 31g (Dietary Fiber 1g); Protein 2g **% Daily Value:** Vitamin A 0%; Vitamin C 0%; Calcium 4%; Iron 0% **Exchanges:** ½ Starch, 1½ Other Carbohydrate, 1½ Fat **Carbohydrate Choices:** 2

Start Happy Tip

If you are cooking gluten free, always read labels to make sure each recipe ingredient is gluten free. Products and ingredient sources can change.

cranberry–sweet potato bread

prep time: 20 Minutes ✻ **start to finish:** 3 Hours 45 Minutes ✻ 2 Loaves; 12 Slices Each

2	cups mashed cooked dark-orange sweet potatoes (about 1¼ lb)
2⅓	cups sugar
⅔	cup vegetable oil
⅔	cup water
1	teaspoon vanilla
4	eggs
3⅓	cups all-purpose flour
2	teaspoons baking soda
1½	teaspoons salt
1	teaspoon ground cinnamon
½	teaspoon baking powder
½	teaspoon ground nutmeg
1	cup sweetened dried cranberries
1	cup chopped pecans, if desired

1 Heat oven to 350°F. Grease 2 (8x4-inch) loaf pans or 1 (9x5-inch) loaf pan with shortening; lightly flour.

2 In large bowl, mix sweet potatoes, sugar, oil, water, vanilla and eggs until well blended. In medium bowl, mix flour, baking soda, salt, cinnamon, baking powder and nutmeg. Add to sweet potato mixture; stir just until dry ingredients are moistened. Stir in cranberries and pecans. Divide batter evenly between 8-inch pans or spoon into 9-inch pan.

3 Bake 1 hour to 1 hour 10 minutes or until toothpick inserted in center comes out clean. Cool 15 minutes in pans on cooling rack.

4 Run knife or spatula around sides of pans to loosen bread; remove from pans to cooling rack. Cool completely, about 2 hours, before slicing. Wrap breads tightly in plastic wrap or foil and store at room temperature up to 4 days, or refrigerate up to 1 week.

1 Slice: Calories 240; Total Fat 7g (Saturated Fat 1.5g, Trans Fat 0g); Cholesterol 35mg; Sodium 280mg; Total Carbohydrate 41g (Dietary Fiber 1g); Protein 3g **% Daily Value:** Vitamin A 80%; Vitamin C 4%; Calcium 2%; Iron 6% **Exchanges:** 1 Starch, 1½ Other Carbohydrate, 1½ Fat **Carbohydrate Choices:** 3

Start Happy Tip
1 can (23 ounces) sweet potatoes in syrup, drained and mashed can be substituted for the fresh sweet potatoes.

orange-rhubarb bread with almond topping

prep time: 20 Minutes ※ start to finish: 3 Hours 25 Minutes ※ 2 Loaves; 12 Slices Each

1 cup sugar
½ cup vegetable oil
½ cup milk
2 teaspoons grated orange peel
2 eggs
2¼ cups all-purpose flour
2½ teaspoons baking powder
1 teaspoon salt
1½ cups finely chopped fresh rhubarb
½ cup sliced almonds
2 tablespoons sugar

1 Heat oven to 350°F . Grease bottoms only of 2 (8x4-inch) loaf pans with shortening or spray with cooking spray.

2 In large bowl, beat 1 cup sugar, the oil, milk, orange peel and eggs with whisk. Stir in flour, baking powder and salt just until flour is moistened. Stir in rhubarb.

3 Divide batter evenly between pans. Sprinkle each pan with ¼ cup almonds; lightly press almonds into batter. Sprinkle each with 1 tablespoon sugar.

4 Bake 45 to 55 minutes or until toothpick inserted in center comes out clean. Cool 10 minutes. Run knife or metal spatula around sides of pan to loosen bread; remove from pan to cooling rack. Cool completely, about 2 hours. To store, wrap bread tightly in plastic wrap or foil.

1 Slice: Calories 140; Total Fat 6g (Saturated Fat 1g, Trans Fat 0g); Cholesterol 20mg; Sodium 160mg; Total Carbohydrate 20g (Dietary Fiber 0g); Protein 2g **% Daily Value:** Vitamin A 0%; Vitamin C 0%; Calcium 4%; Iron 4% **Exchanges:** ½ Starch, 1 Other Carbohydrate, 1 Fat **Carbohydrate Choices:** 1

Start Happy Tips

When buying rhubarb at the grocery store or farmers' market, look for crisp red stalks with blemish-free green leaves. Cut the rhubarb as you would celery; if the stalks are large, cut them in half lengthwise before chopping. Rhubarb leaves can be toxic, so be sure to only use the stalks of the plant.

Before starting a baking recipe, check the expiration date on your baking powder to make sure it's fresh.

lemon-currant-cream scones

prep time: 20 Minutes ❋ **start to finish:** 50 Minutes ❋ 15 Scones

2 cups all-purpose flour

¼ cup granulated sugar

3 teaspoons baking powder

½ teaspoon salt

½ cup dried currants

1 teaspoon grated lemon peel

1⅓ cups whipping cream

1 cup powdered sugar

2 to 3 tablespoons lemon juice

Additional grated lemon peel, if desired

1 Heat oven to 400°F. Lightly grease cookie sheet with shortening or cooking spray.

2 In large bowl, mix flour, granulated sugar, baking powder and salt with fork. Stir in currants and 1 teaspoon lemon peel. Add whipping cream all at once; stir just until dry ingredients are moistened.

3 On floured surface, gently knead dough 6 or 7 times or until smooth. Pat dough until ¾ inch thick. Cut with 2-inch round cutter; place 2 inches apart on cookie sheet.

4 Bake 12 to 15 minutes or until light golden brown. Remove scones from cookie sheet to cooling rack. Cool 15 minutes.

5 Meanwhile, in small bowl, stir powdered sugar and enough lemon juice until smooth and thin enough to drizzle.

6 Drizzle icing over scones. Top with additional lemon peel. Serve warm.

1 Scone: Calories 180; Total Fat 7g (Saturated Fat 4g, Trans Fat 0g); Cholesterol 25mg; Sodium 180mg; Total Carbohydrate 29g (Dietary Fiber 0g); Protein 2g **% Daily Value:** Vitamin A 4%; Vitamin C 0%; Calcium 8%; Iron 6% **Exchanges:** 1 Starch, 1 Other Carbohydrate, 1 Fat **Carbohydrate Choices:** 2

Start Happy Tips

Feel free to mix the dry ingredients ahead of time and store in a resealable food-storage plastic bag.

If your family isn't big on currants, leave them out and stir in ½ cup dried blueberries instead.

gluten-free bacon-gruyère scones

prep time: 15 Minutes ❋ **start to finish:** 40 Minutes ❋ 12 Scones

2 cups Bisquick Gluten Free mix

4 oz gluten-free Gruyère cheese, shredded (1 cup)

6 slices gluten-free bacon, crisply cooked, crumbled

1½ cups whipping cream

2 tablespoons butter, melted

1 Heat oven to 400°F. In large bowl, stir together Bisquick mix, cheese and bacon. Stir in whipping cream until dough forms.

2 Divide dough in half. On surface sprinkled with Bisquick mix, pat each half into 6-inch round. Cut each round into 6 wedges. On ungreased cookie sheet, place wedges 2 inches apart. Brush with melted butter.

3 Bake 18 to 22 minutes or until golden brown. Immediately remove scones from cookie sheet to cooling rack. Serve warm.

1 Scone: Calories 260; Total Fat 18g (Saturated Fat 10g, Trans Fat 0.5g); Cholesterol 60mg; Sodium 380mg; Total Carbohydrate 18g (Dietary Fiber 0g); Protein 6g **% Daily Value:** Vitamin A 10%; Vitamin C 0%; Calcium 15%; Iron 0% **Exchanges:** 1 Other Carbohydrate, 1 High-Fat Meat, 2 Fat **Carbohydrate Choices:** 1

Start Happy Tip

If you are cooking gluten free, always read labels to make sure each recipe ingredient is gluten free. Products and ingredient sources can change.

blueberry scones

prep time: 15 Minutes ☀ **start to finish:** 35 Minutes ☀ 12 Scones

2¾ cups Original Bisquick mix

1 cup dried blueberries

½ cup granulated sugar

⅓ cup cold butter

1 container (6 oz) French vanilla low-fat yogurt

1 teaspoon almond extract

1 teaspoon vanilla

1 egg, beaten

1 tablespoon whipping cream

1 tablespoon coarse sugar or turbinado sugar (raw sugar)

1 Heat oven to 425°F. Line cookie sheet with cooking parchment paper.

2 In large bowl, stir Bisquick mix, blueberries and granulated sugar. Using pastry blender or fork, cut in butter until mixture looks like coarse crumbs. In small bowl, mix yogurt, almond extract, vanilla and egg until blended. Stir into crumb mixture with fork just until dough forms.

3 Divide dough in half. With hands sprinkled with additional Bisquick mix, shape dough into 2 (6-inch) rounds about 3 inches apart on cookie sheet. Brush with whipping cream; sprinkle with coarse sugar. Using knife sprayed with cooking spray, cut each round into 6 wedges, but do not separate.

4 Bake 13 to 15 minutes or until golden brown. Carefully separate wedges with knife; remove from cookie sheet to cooling rack. Cool 2 minutes. Serve warm.

1 Scone: Calories 270; Total Fat 10g (Saturated Fat 5g, Trans Fat 1g); Cholesterol 30mg; Sodium 400mg; Total Carbohydrate 42g (Dietary Fiber 2g); Protein 3g **% Daily Value:** Vitamin A 6%; Vitamin C 0%; Calcium 6%; Iron 4% **Exchanges:** ½ Starch, 2½ Other Carbohydrate, 2 Fat **Carbohydrate Choices:** 3

rosemary-lemon-cream scones

prep time: 25 Minutes ✳ **start to finish:** 50 Minutes ✳ 8 Scones

Scones

2½ cups Original Bisquick mix

⅓ cup granulated sugar

2 tablespoons cold butter

1 egg, beaten

1 container (6 oz) lemon burst low-fat yogurt

¼ cup whipping cream

1 tablespoon grated lemon peel

1 tablespoon finely chopped fresh rosemary leaves

1 tablespoon whipping cream

1 tablespoon granulated sugar

Glaze

½ cup powdered sugar

1 tablespoon lemon juice

1 Heat oven to 400°F. Generously spray cookie sheet with cooking spray.

2 In large bowl, mix Bisquick mix and ⅓ cup granulated sugar. Using pastry blender or fork, cut in butter until mixture looks like coarse crumbs. In small bowl, mix egg, yogurt and ¼ cup whipping cream. Stir into crumb mixture just until combined. Stir in lemon peel and rosemary. Place dough on cookie sheet.

3 With greased hands, pat dough into 8-inch round. Brush dough with 1 tablespoon whipping cream; sprinkle with 1 tablespoon granulated sugar. Using sharp knife dipped in additional Bisquick mix, cut into 8 wedges, but do not separate.

4 Bake 15 to 20 minutes or until light golden brown. Carefully separate wedges with knife; immediately remove from cookie sheet to cooling rack. Cool 5 minutes. In small bowl, mix glaze ingredients; drizzle over scones. Serve warm.

1 Scone: Calories 310; Total Fat 11g (Saturated Fat 5g, Trans Fat 1.5g); Cholesterol 45mg; Sodium 500mg; Total Carbohydrate 47g (Dietary Fiber 1g); Protein 4g **% Daily Value:** Vitamin A 6%; Vitamin C 0%; Calcium 8%; Iron 6% **Exchanges:** 1½ Starch, 1½ Other Carbohydrate, 2 Fat **Carbohydrate Choices:** 3

dark chocolate chunk 'n cherry scones

prep time: 15 Minutes ❋ **start to finish:** 45 Minutes ❋ 8 Scones

2½ cups all-purpose flour

2 teaspoons baking powder

⅓ cup sugar

½ teaspoon salt

5 tablespoons cold butter

2 eggs

1 cup whipping cream

1 teaspoon vanilla

½ cup dark chocolate chunks

½ cup dried cherries

1 teaspoon water

1 Heat oven to 400°F. Grease cookie sheet with shortening or spray with cooking spray.

2 In large bowl, mix flour, baking powder, sugar and salt. Using pastry blender or fork, cut in butter until mixture looks like coarse crumbs. In medium bowl, beat 1 of the eggs with fork. Stir in whipping cream and vanilla. Stir in chocolate chunks and cherries until combined. Pour over crumb mixture; stir just until dry ingredients are moistened (do not overmix).

3 On lightly floured surface, knead dough lightly 4 times. Pat dough into 7-inch round about 1 inch thick. Transfer to cookie sheet. In small bowl, beat remaining egg; stir in water. Brush egg mixture lightly over top of dough; discard any remaining egg mixture. Cut into 8 wedges; separate slightly so wedges are not touching.

4 Bake 15 to 20 minutes or until toothpick inserted in center comes out clean. Remove scones from cookie sheet to cooling rack. Cool 10 minutes. Serve warm.

Start Happy Tip
These scones are delicious served with butter or whipped cream cheese.

1 Scone: Calories 440; Total Fat 21g (Saturated Fat 13g, Trans Fat 0.5g); Cholesterol 105mg; Sodium 350mg; Total Carbohydrate 54g (Dietary Fiber 2g); Protein 7g **% Daily Value:** Vitamin A 15%; Vitamin C 0%; Calcium 10%; Iron 15% **Exchanges:** 2 Starch, 1½ Other Carbohydrate, 4 Fat **Carbohydrate Choices:** 3½

Chocolate Chunk 'n Cranberry Scones: Substitute semisweet chocolate chunks for the dark chocolate and dried cranberries for the cherries.

herbed pan biscuits

prep time: 15 Minutes ❈ **start to finish:** 30 Minutes ❈ 20 Biscuits

2 cups Original Bisquick mix

½ cup sour cream

6 tablespoons lemon-lime carbonated beverage

2 tablespoons chopped fresh Italian (flat-leaf) parsley

1 tablespoon chopped fresh basil leaves

¼ teaspoon coarse ground black pepper

3 tablespoons butter, melted

1 Heat oven to 425°F. Spray 8-inch round cake pan with cooking spray.

2 In medium bowl, stir Bisquick mix, sour cream, carbonated beverage, parsley, basil and pepper with fork until soft dough forms.

3 With floured hands, divide dough into 20 equal portions. Shape each into a ball. Place in pan with sides touching. Brush evenly with half of the melted butter.

4 Bake 15 minutes or until golden brown. Brush biscuits evenly with remaining melted butter. Serve immediately.

1 Biscuit: Calories 80; Total Fat 4.5g (Saturated Fat 2g, Trans Fat 0g); Cholesterol 10mg; Sodium 170mg; Total Carbohydrate 8g (Dietary Fiber 0g); Protein 1g **% Daily Value:** Vitamin A 2%; Vitamin C 0%; Calcium 0%; Iron 2% **Exchanges:** ½ Starch, 1 Fat **Carbohydrate Choices:** ½

Start Happy Tip

Use your favorite herbs in this biscuit recipe. Or, for plain biscuits, omit the herbs altogether.

apple-cheddar biscuits

prep time: 15 Minutes ✳ **start to finish:** 45 Minutes ✳ 9 Biscuits

2 small apples, peeled, sliced

2 cups Original Bisquick mix

⅔ cup buttermilk

¼ teaspoon salt

¼ teaspoon freshly ground pepper

1 cup shredded sharp Cheddar cheese (4 oz)

1 Heat oven to 450°F. Line cookie sheet with foil or cooking parchment paper. Place apple slices in single layer on cookie sheet. Bake 8 to 10 minutes or until lightly browned and slightly dry to the touch. Cool; chop apples.

2 In medium bowl, stir Bisquick mix, buttermilk, salt and pepper until soft dough forms. Reserve 2 tablespoons of the cheese. Add remaining cheese and the chopped apples to dough; stir until blended.

3 On work surface sprinkled with additional Bisquick mix, knead dough 10 times. Roll dough into ½-inch-thick square. Cut into 9 biscuits. Sprinkle with reserved cheese. Place about 1 inch apart on cookie sheet.

4 Bake 8 to 10 minutes or until golden brown. Remove biscuits from cookie sheet. Serve immediately.

1 Biscuit: Calories 190; Total Fat 9g (Saturated Fat 4g, Trans Fat 1g); Cholesterol 15mg; Sodium 490mg; Total Carbohydrate 22g (Dietary Fiber 1g); Protein 6g **% Daily Value:** Vitamin A 2%; Vitamin C 0%; Calcium 10%; Iron 4% **Exchanges:** 1 Starch, ½ Other Carbohydrate, ½ High-Fat Meat, 1 Fat **Carbohydrate Choices:** 1½

Start Happy Tips

Pears can also be used in these biscuits instead of the apples.

Substitute Colby, pepper Jack or your favorite cheese for the Cheddar.

spicy sweet potato biscuits

prep time: 10 Minutes ❄ **start to finish:** 25 Minutes ❄ 12 Biscuits

2¾ cups Original Bisquick mix

½ teaspoon ground red pepper (cayenne)

⅓ cup cold butter

1 cup mashed cooked sweet potatoes

½ cup milk

2 tablespoons butter, melted

Additional melted butter, if desired

1 Heat oven to 450°F. Spray cookie sheet with cooking spray.

2 In medium bowl, stir Bisquick mix and red pepper. Using pastry blender or fork, cut in ⅓ cup butter until mixture looks like coarse crumbs. In small bowl, mix sweet potatoes and milk until blended; add to butter mixture, stirring with fork until dough leaves side of bowl.

3 Place dough on well-floured surface; gently roll dough in flour to coat. Knead lightly 6 to 8 times. Roll or pat dough until 1 inch thick. Cut with floured 2-inch biscuit cutter; place about 1 inch apart on cookie sheet.

4 Bake 12 to 15 minutes or until light golden brown. Brush biscuits with melted butter. Serve immediately.

1 Biscuit: Calories 210; Total Fat 11g (Saturated Fat 6g, Trans Fat 1g); Cholesterol 20mg; Sodium 410mg; Total Carbohydrate 23g (Dietary Fiber 1g); Protein 3g **% Daily Value:** Vitamin A 90%; Vitamin C 4%; Calcium 4%; Iron 4% **Exchanges:** 1 Starch, ½ Other Carbohydrate, 2 Fat **Carbohydrate Choices:** 1½

cheddar and onion biscuit poppers

prep time: 5 Minutes ❄ **start to finish:** 15 Minutes ❄ 40 Biscuit Poppers

2 cups Original Bisquick mix

⅔ cup milk

½ cup shredded Cheddar cheese (2 oz)

4 medium green onions, sliced (¼ cup)

2 tablespoons butter, melted

Chunky-style salsa, if desired

1 Heat oven to 450°F. Spray large cookie sheet with cooking spray.

2 In medium bowl, stir Bisquick mix, milk, cheese and onions until soft dough forms. Drop dough by rounded teaspoonfuls about 2 inches apart onto cookie sheet.

3 Bake 7 to 9 minutes or until golden brown. Brush biscuits with melted butter. Serve immediately with salsa.

1 Biscuit Popper: Calories 45; Total Fat 2g (Saturated Fat 1g, Trans Fat 0g); Cholesterol 0mg; Sodium 100mg; Total Carbohydrate 5g (Dietary Fiber 0g); Protein 1g **% Daily Value:** Vitamin A 0%; Vitamin C 0%; Calcium 2%; Iron 0% **Exchanges:** ½ Starch, ½ Fat **Carbohydrate Choices:** ½

Start Happy Tip

If you have any leftover poppers, store them tightly wrapped in the freezer. Reheat 3 or 4 poppers at a time in the microwave on High for 20 to 30 seconds.

gluten-free cinnamon rolls

prep time: 15 Minutes ❋ **start to finish:** 45 Minutes ❋ 8 Rolls

Rolls

- ½ cup packed brown sugar
- 2 teaspoons ground cinnamon
- 3 cups Bisquick Gluten Free mix
- ¼ cup granulated sugar
- 1¼ cups milk
- 1 egg
- ¼ cup butter, melted

Glaze

- 1 cup powdered sugar
- ¼ cup whipping cream

1. Heat oven to 425°F. Spray 9-inch round cake pan with cooking spray.

2. In small bowl, mix brown sugar and cinnamon; set aside. In large bowl, stir Bisquick mix, granulated sugar, milk and egg until dough forms.

3. On surface sprinkled with additional Bisquick mix, knead dough 5 times. Roll dough into 16x12-inch rectangle. Brush with 2 tablespoons of the melted butter; sprinkle evenly with brown sugar mixture. Starting at short side, roll up dough tightly; pinch edge to seal well. Cut into 1½-inch slices. Place slices cut side down in pan. Brush with remaining 2 tablespoons melted butter.

4. Bake 20 to 25 minutes or until golden brown. Cool 5 minutes. Remove from pan to cooling rack or serving plate.

5. In small bowl, mix glaze ingredients until smooth. Spread over rolls. Serve warm.

1 Roll: Calories 410; Total Fat 10g (Saturated Fat 6g, Trans Fat 0g); Cholesterol 50mg; Sodium 590mg; Total Carbohydrate 76g (Dietary Fiber 1g); Protein 4g **% Daily Value:** Vitamin A 8%; Vitamin C 0%; Calcium 15%; Iron 0% **Exchanges:** 1½ Starch, 3½ Other Carbohydrate, 2 Fat **Carbohydrate Choices:** 5

Start Happy Tip

If you are cooking gluten free, always read labels to make sure each recipe ingredient is gluten free. Products and ingredient sources can change.

cinnamon-sugar pinwheels

prep time: 20 Minutes ❊ **start to finish:** 40 Minutes ❊ 12 Pinwheels

Pinwheels
- 2¼ cups Original Bisquick mix
- ½ cup milk
- 1 tablespoon butter, softened
- ¼ cup granulated sugar
- 1 teaspoon ground cinnamon
- ½ cup finely chopped walnuts
- ½ cup dried currants
- 1 tablespoon butter, melted

Glaze
- ¾ cup powdered sugar
- ¼ teaspoon vanilla
- 3 teaspoons milk

1 Heat oven to 400°F. Line cookie sheet with cooking parchment paper.

2 In medium bowl, stir Bisquick mix and ½ cup milk until soft dough forms. Place dough on surface generously sprinkled with Bisquick mix; roll in Bisquick mix to coat. Knead 5 times.

3 Press or roll dough into 11x8-inch rectangle. Spread with 1 tablespoon softened butter. In small bowl, mix granulated sugar, cinnamon, walnuts and currants; sprinkle over dough, pressing in slightly. Starting with long side, roll up dough tightly; seal edge. Cut into ¾-inch slices. Place slices about 1 inch apart on cookie sheet. Brush with melted butter.

4 Bake 8 to 10 minutes or until golden brown. Remove from cookie sheet to cooling rack. Cool 10 minutes.

5 Meanwhile, in small bowl, mix powdered sugar, vanilla and 3 teaspoons milk, 1 teaspoon at a time, until glaze is thin enough to drizzle.

6 Drizzle glaze over pinwheels. Serve warm.

1 Pinwheel: Calories 210; Total Fat 8g (Saturated Fat 2.5g, Trans Fat 1g); Cholesterol 5mg; Sodium 290mg; Total Carbohydrate 32g (Dietary Fiber 1g); Protein 3g **% Daily Value:** Vitamin A 0%; Vitamin C 0%; Calcium 4%; Iron 6% **Exchanges:** 1 Starch, 1 Other Carbohydrate, 1½ Fat **Carbohydrate Choices:** 2

metric conversion guide

VOLUME

U.S. Units	Canadian Metric	Australian Metric
¼ teaspoon	1 mL	1 ml
½ teaspoon	2 mL	2 ml
1 teaspoon	5 mL	5 ml
1 tablespoon	15 mL	20 ml
¼ cup	50 mL	60 ml
⅓ cup	75 mL	80 ml
½ cup	125 mL	125 ml
⅔ cup	150 mL	170 ml
¾ cup	175 mL	190 ml
1 cup	250 mL	250 ml
1 quart	1 liter	1 liter
1½ quarts	1.5 liters	1.5 liters
2 quarts	2 liters	2 liters
2½ quarts	2.5 liters	2.5 liters
3 quarts	3 liters	3 liters
4 quarts	4 liters	4 liters

WEIGHT

U.S. Units	Canadian Metric	Australian Metric
1 ounce	30 grams	30 grams
2 ounces	55 grams	60 grams
3 ounces	85 grams	90 grams
4 ounces (¼ pound)	115 grams	125 grams
8 ounces (½ pound)	225 grams	225 grams
16 ounces (1 pound)	455 grams	500 grams
1 pound	455 grams	0.5 kilogram

MEASUREMENTS

Inches	Centimeters
1	2.5
2	5.0
3	7.5
4	10.0
5	12.5
6	15.0
7	17.5
8	20.5
9	23.0
10	25.5
11	28.0
12	30.5
13	33.0

TEMPERATURES

Fahrenheit	Celsius
32°	0°
212°	100°
250°	120°
275°	140°
300°	150°
325°	160°
350°	180°
375°	190°
400°	200°
425°	220°
450°	230°
475°	240°
500°	260°

Note: The recipes in this cookbook have not been developed or tested using metric measures. When converting recipes to metric, some variations in quality may be noted.

index

Page numbers in *italics* indicate illustrations

Recipe Testing and Calculating Nutrition Information

Recipe Testing:

- Large eggs and 2% milk were used unless otherwise indicated.

- Fat-free, low-fat, low-sodium or lite products were not used unless indicated.

- No nonstick cookware and bakeware were used unless otherwise indicated. No dark-colored, black or insulated bakeware was used.

- When a pan is specified, a metal pan was used; a baking dish or pie plate means ovenproof glass was used.

- An electric hand mixer was used for mixing only when mixer speeds are specified.

Calculating Nutrition:

- The first ingredient was used wherever a choice is given, such as ⅓ cup sour cream or plain yogurt.

- The first amount was used wherever a range is given, such as 3- to 3 ½-pound whole chicken.

- The first serving number was used wherever a range is given, such as 4 to 6 servings.

- "If desired" ingredients were not included.

- Only the amount of a marinade or frying oil that is absorbed was included.